JOHN SAXE, LOYALIST

Other Books by George J. Hill

Leprosy in Five Young Men

Outpatient Surgery

*Cancer Chemotherapy:
Therapy of Solid Tumors in Adults*

Clinical Oncology

*Edison's Environment:
Invention and Pollution in the Career of Thomas Edison*

*Intimate Relationships:
Church and State in the U.S. and Liberia, 1917-1947*

*High and Dry:
Adventures of a U.S. Navy Officer on the Indian-Afghan Border
in November-December 1943*

*Ranch Hand:
Two Dot, Montana, in the Summer of 1954*

Edited Work

*A Lesson in Reality:
Poems and Essays, 1991-2000
By David Hedgcock Hill*

John Saxe, Loyalist (1732–1808)

And

His Descendants for Five Generations

Compiled by
George J. Hill, M.D., D.Litt.

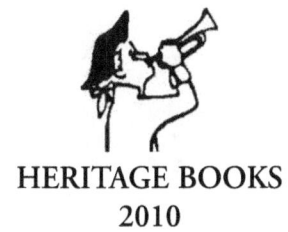

HERITAGE BOOKS
2010

HERITAGE BOOKS
AN IMPRINT OF HERITAGE BOOKS, INC.

Books, CDs, and more—Worldwide

For our listing of thousands of titles see our website
at
www.HeritageBooks.com

Published 2010 by
HERITAGE BOOKS, INC.
Publishing Division
100 Railroad Ave. #104
Westminster, Maryland 21157

Copyright © 2010 George J. Hill, M.D., D.Litt.

*Cover photograph of the home of John Saxe, Saxe's Mills, Highgate, Vermont
by George J. Hill, 2008*

All rights reserved. No part of this book may be reproduced or transmitted in any form or by any means, electronic or mechanical, including photocopying, recording or by any information storage and retrieval system without written permission from the author, except for the inclusion of brief quotations in a review.

International Standard Book Numbers
Paperbound: 978-0-7884-5176-8
Clothbound: 978-0-7884-8380-6

For Georgia and Rosalie

Abbreviations

abt	about
aka	also known as
b. or B	birth
b.c.	birth certificate
b.r.	birth record
bp.	baptism
c. or ca.	*circa*, about
d. or D	death
dau.	daughter
d.c.	death certificate
d.r.	death record
d.s.p.	died *sine* (without) progeny
e.g.	*exempli gratia*, for example
obit.	obituary
m. or M	marriage/married
n.d.	no date
n.p.	no place, no publisher
q.v.	*quod vide*, which see
v.r.	vital record(s)

Contents

Contents	vii
List of Illustrations	ix
Preface	xi
Acknowledgements	xii
Epigraphs	xiv
1 First Generation — John Saxe – His Ancestors, and His Life	1
2 Second Generation — John Saxe's Children	15
3 Third Generation — John Saxe's Grandsons and Granddaughters	35
4 Fourth Generation — John Saxe's Great-Grandchildren	51
5 Fifth Generation — John Saxe's Great-Great-Grandchildren	65
Index of Saxe Family — Five Generations of Descendants and Spouses	73
Annotated Bibliography	87
Notes	97
Appendices	119
General Index	167

List of Illustrations

	Page
St. Peter's Lutheran Church ("Stone Church"), Rhinebeck, N.Y.	4
Map of Rhinebeck, N.Y., prior to 1812	4
Account book of Robert Livingston – detail – entries in 1766-1779	5
Missisquoi Bay, Lake Champlain, Province of Quebec, Canada	8
Saxe's Mills, Highgate, Vermont – historical marker sign	9
Valley of Saxe's Brook, Highgate, Franklin County, Vermont	10
Rock River, near Lake Champlain, Highgate, Vermont	10
Old Protestant Cemetery, Philipsburg, Province of Quebec, Canada	12
The Saxe Homestead, Saxe's Mills, on Saxe's Brook, Highgate, Vermont	26
Soldiers' monument, and detail showing Capt. Conrad Saxe, Highgate, Vermont	31
Gravestone of Anna (Saxe) Stockwell, Clinton Co., N.Y. – drawing	39
Hon. John Godfrey Saxe, LL.D.	42
Baptismal record of Benajah Flavel Stockwell, Stanbridge, Quebec	53
Stockwell graves, Graceland Cemetery, Rowan, Wright Co., Iowa	55
George J. Hill and Jessie Fidelia (Stockwell) Hill	67
George and Jessie Hill and their seven surviving children	68

Preface

This book is a revision and updating of the *Genealogy of the Saxe Family*, which was compiled by "J.G.S." and published in 1930. J.G.S.'s *Genealogy* and this book both begin with a biography of John Saxe, who was born in the Kingdom of Hanover and came to America in about 1750. Both books trace his known descendants for five or more generations. John Saxe was a Loyalist in Dutchess County, N.Y., in the Revolutionary War, and he was one of several Loyalists in Dutchess County who moved after the war with their families to the northeastern tip of Lake Champlain. "J.G.S.," who compiled *Genealogy of the Saxe Family* in 1930, was actually John Godfrey Saxe II, LL.D. He was the grandson and namesake of John Saxe's most famous descendant, John Godfrey Saxe, LL.D., a well-known nineteenth century American poet. The first John Godfrey Saxe was a grandson of John Saxe, by his son Peter. John Saxe the Loyalist, his son Peter, and his grandson John Godfrey Saxe lived in a house that the elder Saxe built in what is now Highgate, Vermont. This house is still standing. A picture of the Saxe farmhouse is on the cover of this book and its history is described briefly on a Vermont historical marker that is on the road beside it at Saxe's Mills, near the border with Quebec.

    I have added as much additional material about John Saxe and his family as I have been able to locate through research in Dutchess County, N.Y., in Vermont, and elsewhere. I have given special attention to the descendants of his son Godfrey Saxe, who is my ancestor. I will thank those who have helped with this research in the Acknowledements, and I will list my Sources in the Notes, the Annotated Bibliography, and the Appendices.

Acknowledgements

I am grateful for the help and encouragement that I have received from many people, over many years, as I assembled the information for this story of John Saxe and his descendants

I particularly appreciate the pioneering genealogical work that was done by Foster Paul Stockwell, from whom I first learned of our ancestor, the Loyalist, John Saxe. Foster and I are both great-grandsons of Benajah Flavel Stockwell – who was a great-grandson of John Saxe – and of Benajah's first wife, Emily Lodiweska Hyde. Additional information about the Saxe, Hyde, and Stockwell families in Highgate, Vermont, was located and very kindly sent to me by Cora Baker, when she was Town Clerk of Highgate. The Town Office of Highgate has continued to be helpful in providing suggestions and information, as has been the Franklin County Probate Office in St. Albans, Vermont, where I was able to find records of many of the descendants of John Saxe. I was also welcomed cheerfully and given good directions by several residents of Philipsburg, Mississquoi County, Quebec.

John Saxe's descendant, Andrew F. Saxe of Boston, Massachusetts, has offered many suggestions and provided much information that I would never have located without his help. Both of us have consulted with Nancy Kelley of Kinship, Rhinebeck, New York, who located many original records and documents that mention John Saxe, his wife Catherine Weaver, their children, and other members of the Weaver family. I am also grateful for research done by Addie Shields, Historian of Clinton County, New York, and for copies of documents and pages from books that she sent to me.

The descendants of Jessie (Stockwell) Hill in Iowa have done much to preserve the history of Hill and Stockwell families in Wright County, and to ensure that their graves, farms, and records are well cared for. Jessie's daughter Ruby (Hill) Woodin kept the Hill Family Bible, in which there is a page recording Stockwell births, deaths and marriages, until she died, at which time the Bible went to her nephew, Myron Hill, Jr. The principal genealogist of the Hill family in Clarion, Iowa, for many decades was a sister-in-law of Myron Hill, Jr., the late Avis (Mrs. Dale) Hill, whose thoughtful suggestions guided much of my research. Avis and my mother, Essie Mae (Thompson) Hill, corresponded frequently until my mother died in 1994, and many of the records that I cite came from one or the other of them. Much new information about the ancestors of Jessie Stockwell's husband, George J. Hill (1857-1952), has been discovered by another of Jessie's descendants – her great-granddaughter Jeanine (Humbert) Johnson – and I am grateful to Jeanine for sharing this information with me.

I also appreciate the help and suggestions given by many others, including Charles Nye, Highgate Town Historian; A. J. Macdonald, Director of the St. Albans Historical Museum; Michel Racicot, UE, Genealogist of the Sir John Johnson Centennial Branch, United Empire Loyalist Association of Canada; Douglas Grant, UE; the late Jean Darrah McCaw, UE; and John Mauk Hilliard.

He took the oath of allegiance to King George of England
– J.G.S., *Genealogy of the Saxe Family* (1930)
Referring to John Saxe upon his arrival in
America in 1750

John Saxe was jailed in the Revolutionary War as a British Loyalist.
His fifth son, Godfrey Saxe, died August 16, 1807. His daughter,
Anne Saxe, married Joseph H. Stockwell on July 8, 1823.
– Foster P. Stockwell (1960)[*]

Of the many children of John Saxe, Godfrey remains a mystery
– Andrew Saxe (2008)[†]

Anna was a Saxe . . . buried in Mooers in the Woodley Lot.
– Addie L. Shields (2008)
Historian, Clinton County, New York

What a story the Saxe family have!
– Michel Racicot (2009)
Registrar, Sir John Johnson Centennial Branch,
United Empire Loyalist Association of Canada

---

[*] Foster Paul[7] Stockwell is manager of the web site for the Stockwell Family Association (Stockwellfamilysite.com) and one of their designated genealogists. He is a descendant of *Francis Olin[6], Eugene Sanford[5], Benajah Flavel[4] Stockwell, Anna Maria[3], Godfrey[2], John[1] Saxe*.

[†] Andrew F.[7] Saxe drafted the plaque at Saxe's Mills. He is a descendant of *John Brooke[6], John Burtis[5], John Walter[4], Charles Jewett[3], Peter[2], John[1] Saxe*

1

First Generation

John Saxe had "great physical strength and endurance and indomitable courage"
---J.G.S., *Genealogy of the Saxe Family*

JOHN SAXE,[*] son of Godfrey Saxe, was born at Langensalza, Kingdom of Hanover, (now Germany), 10 November 1732; died at his home, Saxe's Mills, in Highgate, Franklin Co., Vermont, 12 March 1808. He was buried in the town cemetery at Philipsburg, Missisquoi Co., Quebec, Canada. His name has been spelled many ways. His given name has also been spelled Johan, Johann, and Johannes, and his surname as Sachs, and Sachse, and Sax. His descendants have usually spelled their surname as either Saxe or Sax, although Saxe is now the most commonly used spelling.[1]

John Saxe was the youngest of several children of a prosperous man who owned eight acres of land near Saxe-Gothe, which is about 19 miles northwest of the cities known as Erfurt and Bad Langensalza. John's father Godfrey Saxe is said to have been "a man of influence," who was a "stern man of great strength and courage." John Saxe's grandson, Oliver Perry Scovell, said that his mother, Hannah (Saxe) Scovell, told him that her Saxe ancestors "belonged to the Royal Family of Saxe-Gotha."[2]

The area of German-speaking central Europe in which John Saxe was born has been called Thuringia since ancient times. The city now known as Bad Langensalza first

---

[*] John Saxe (1732-1808) is Person #1 in this genealogy of the Saxe Family. His descendants for five generations who were known to me as of 31 May 2009 were entered into computer software of Sierra "Family Tree" and printed as a Register Report, concluding with #328. Captain Robert Jameson Scovell.

appeared in history in 932, when it was a village named "Salzaha." The village was named Langensalza in about 1578 and it was renamed Bad Langensalza ("long salt bath") in 1956. In 2006 it had a population of about 18,500. In 1075 the Emperor Henry IV defeated the rebelling Saxons and Thuringians at the First Battle of Langensalza. The town was badly damaged by fire during the Thirty Years' War in 1632. Additional fires occurred in the eighteenth century, most notably during the Seven Years War (which was called the French and Indian War in America) of 1756-63. In 1815, Langensalza became part of the Prussian Province of Saxony. The Second Battle of Langensalza occurred in 1866 in the war between Prussia and Hanover. American troops briefly occupied the city in 1945, after which it was part of East Germany (the Deutsche Democratishe Republic, D.D.R.) until the reunification of Germany in 1990. Bad Langensalza is now in the County of Unstruct-Hainich, State of Thuringia, Germany. This area is popular with tourists, because of its sulfur baths, hiking trails, and medieval ruins. Bad Langensalza is the gateway to the Hainich National Park.[3]

John Saxe was ten when his father died. He left school at thirteen to begin to work and earn his own living. At age fourteen, entrusted with the family Bible, Saxe left home and began to travel in Europe with a companion who was two years his senior in age. Three years later the two young men arrived in Amsterdam, where they remained for six months. His companion then decided to go to America, and John, then eighteen, agreed to go with him. In about 1750, after a voyage of some fifteen weeks, the ship bearing John Saxe arrived in Philadelphia. Saxe and his companion immediately took the oath of allegiance to King George II of England, who was, of course, also the hereditary ruler of Saxe's home state of Hanover. Saxe had not enough money to pay for his trip, so as was the custom, the ship's captain bound him for three years of service in America to repay the cost of the passage. Saxe was fortunate to find a place as an apprentice to a miller who paid off his debt to the captain. During the next three years, Saxe learned the trade of milling and he also learned to read, write, and speak English. In about 1753, at the age of twenty-one, John Saxe was prepared to begin his life as a free man. Saxe was now an experienced traveler, with the *wanderlust* that is typical of many Americans, and he would move several more times during the rest of his long life.[4]

After John Saxe finished his apprenticeship, he remained for a while in Pennsylvania and he rose to become superintendent of a flouring mill at Valley Forge. He then moved on to New York City. While living in New York City, Saxe rode north from time to time to Rhinebeck, in Dutchess County, to court a young German woman who had moved there from Philadelphia with her parents and other members of her family. In 1771, in Rhinebeck, shortly after his 39th birthday, Saxe married his 27-year old Philadelphia-born sweetheart, Catherine Weaver. John is said to have been nearly six feet tall, with broad shoulders, small feet, light brown hair, blue eyes, an aquiline nose, and a firm mouth and chin. He was a champion athlete, with "great physical strength and endurance and indomitable courage," a man who had "strength of character" and "temperate habits." His wife was described as a beautiful woman, somewhat below medium height, with a fair complexion, black eyes, and dark curling hair – and "an excellent housekeeper, a faithful wife and mother."[5]

Saxe was born in a Protestant area of Germany, and he was brought up as a Lutheran. The marriage record of John and Catherine does not show the church or denomination in which the marriage took place, and the baptisms of the Saxe children appear in records of both Lutheran and Reformed Churches. Many Weaver graves from this period are in the Reformed Church Cemetery in Rhinebeck. The newlywed Saxes lived in Rhinebeck for the next thirteen years, during which time the first eight of their nine children were born. The records of baptism of six of the Saxe children have been found – in five different churches – some of whom were baptized by Lutheran and some by Reformed Church pastors. Catherine Weaver had a sister, Elizabeth, who married Conrad Barr (of whom more, below), and another sister who married a man named George Fellows. The baptism of of John and Catherine's first child, John, was witnessed in 1772 by John Merkle and Margaret Weaver, who was probably another sister of Catherine, and the name William Weaver – perhaps the father or a brother or uncle of Catherine – appears next to her name in an account book in Dutchess County in 1781.[6]

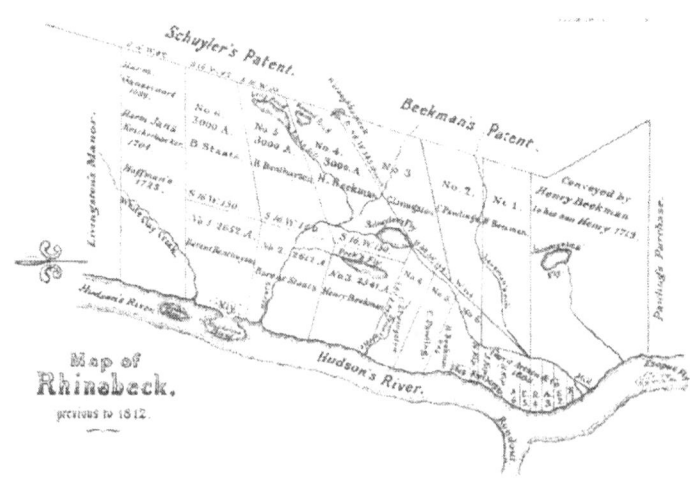

St. Peter's Lutheran Church, Rhinebeck, N.Y. ("Stone Church"). Records of this church show the baptism of John Saxe's son George in 1773.

The property of Robert Livingston is in the center of this map of Rhinebeck

John Saxe, Loyalist

John Saxe continued his trade as miller after he moved to Rhinebeck. He is believed to have been the manager of the mill of Robert Livingston, who was one of the most powerful and wealthy men in that part of the Hudson Valley. Livingston's property was located in the center of Rhinebeck, on Mill Street, and on one side it abutted the Reformed Church and its graveyard. It is likely that the Saxes lived there, on or near Mill Street, when their next two children were born: George (1773) and William (1774).

The account book of Robert Livingston shows records of transactions of a William Weaver ("W^m. Weaver") in 1766 and John Saxe ("John Sax") in 1779 (below); and of Catherine Saxe in 1781-83.[7]

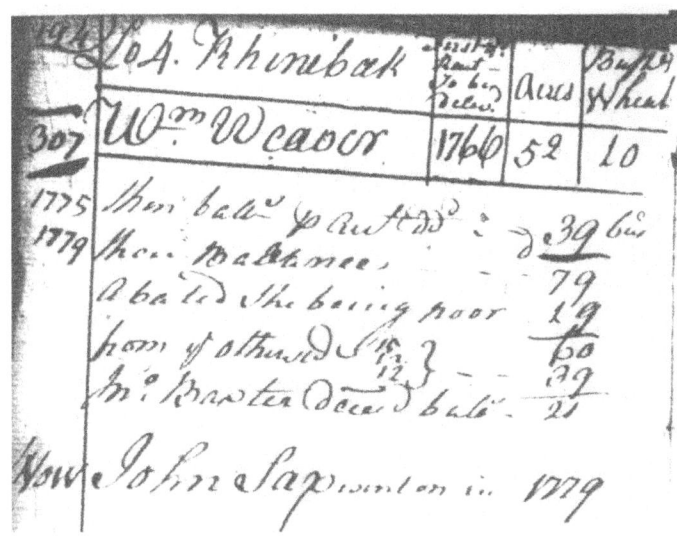

Account book of Robert Livingston

The towns in New York State that figure in the history of John Saxe and his family at this time are in what is now called the Mid-Hudson Valley. They are Esopus/Kingston, and Rhinebeck. Esopus/Kingston is on the west side of the Hudson River in Ulster County, downstream from Saxe's home town of Rhinebeck, which is just north of Poughkeepsie in Dutchess County. Rhinebeck Precinct was formed in 1737. It was named for the Rhine River in Germany, from which many of its first settlers had come. The land on which Rhinebeck stands was purchased from Esopus Indians in 1686, and its early Dutch settlers included the Beekman, Kip, and Schuyler families. Margaret Beekman, a descendant of the founder, William Beekman, married Robert Livingston. Their children included Janet (wife of Major General Richard Montgomery, who was killed in the attempt to capture Quebec City on 31 December 1775), and Robert and John Livingston. Janet, Robert, and John Livingston were long regarded as brave and exemplary patriots, but research has revealed a more complex history of the Revolutionary War in the mid-Hudson Valley. It is now clear that, like other gentry in Rhinebeck, the Livingston brothers were deeply engaged in money-making trade with the British and Loyalists in New York and Philadelphia, and that their sister Janet Montgomery was also involved in some of their schemes. They were, however, principally associated with the winning side, whereas others such as John Saxe were on the losing side. Life went on during the early years of the war, however, and the Saxes had two more sons in Rhinebeck: Matthew (1776) and Godfrey (1778), although John Saxe was known to be a Loyalist. [8]

At the onset of the Revolutionary War, Saxe declared himself a Loyalist, having given an oath to the King upon his arrival in America. There are many references that attest to his having been a Loyalist, and that for this reason he and his family left Rhinebeck for Canada after the Revolutionary War was over. "John Sax" appears on a list published in 1785 of "suspected persons" in New York State whose property was "sold, or converted to the use of the State ... in 1781 and 1782 ... on account of their Attachments to the Enemy." The *Genealogy of the Saxe Family* says that Saxe aided the British army in New York, and that he was arrested and thrown into prison in Esopus, New York, after which he "was set at liberty or escaped." The *Genealogy* cites a manuscript written in 1824 by his son William, in which John is said to have assisted a Major Cautine of the British Army "to penetrate through the lines of American troops."[9]

John Saxe's descendant Andrew Saxe believes the evidence is sufficient to conclude that John was arrested as a Loyalist in 1779, after which he escaped and then joined the Ansbach Jaegers (probably as a scout) – a Hessian regiment that was active in the Hudson River valley and in Connecticut in 1779. John Saxe's son Peter was probably conceived in February-March 1779, for Peter Saxe was born early in December 1779. This suggests that John was arrested in the spring of 1779, that he spent a few months in prison at Esopus, and that he joined the Ansbach Jaegers in the summer of 1779. That regiment was transferred to South Carolina in December 1779, so Andrew suggests that John Saxe was probably discharged at about that time. This is consistent with the entry for November 1779 that shows "John Sax" in the Robert G. Livingston Rent Ledger.[10]

John and Catherine Saxe lived in Rhinebeck for the rest of the war and perhaps even for a year or more after the war ended. Some if not all of Saxe's property was confiscated in 1781 or 1782 but the family did not immediately depart for Canada. Catherine Saxe is shown as paying rent to Mrs. Livingston in 1781 and 1783. Four years after Peter was born, Catherine Saxe had two more children in New York: Jacob (1783) and Conrad (1784). Accounts vary, but it appears that John Saxe and his family and their in-laws, the Conrad Barrs, did not move to Canada until after Conrad Saxe was born in 1784, or perhaps even until June 1786. The Saxes and a man servant, whose name is unknown, journeyed up the Hudson River to Glens Falls or Fort Edward. They portaged across the narrow height of land to Lake George and then went down Lake Champlain in an open boat to Missisquoi Bay, where they established the settlement that is now

Philipsburg, Quebec. Philipsburg is now the western part of the town of Saint-Armand, which is the southernmost town in Missisquoi County, Province of Quebec.[11]

Missisquoi Bay on Lake Champlain, Philipsburg (St. Armand-West), Quebec, Canada
View to the southwest from the landing site of John Saxe and other Loyalists from New York

The Loyalists who came from the mid-Hudson Valley were among the nearly ten thousand who were displaced to Canada after the Revolutionary War. About three thousand Loyalists settled around Missisquoi Bay on the northeastern shore of Lake Champlain. The Proclamation Act of 1792 made it possible for these settlers to receive full title to the land on which they had settled. The Eastern Townships of Lower Canada were established in 1792 and this region, which included what is now Missisquoi County, was surveyed into townships. The name Eastern Townships appears as early as 1806 in the Quebec Almanac. Lower Canada was called Canada East after the Union Act of 1841, and on 1 July 1867 Canada East became the Province of Quebec. The Eastern

John Saxe, Loyalist

Townships area includes twelve counties, including Missisquoi County. The Missisquoi Historical Society and Museum is located in Stanbridge East.[12]

John Saxe appears on a list of nineteen men who were the first permanent settlers in St. Armand West (Philipsburg), Missisquoi Co., Quebec, in the autumn of 1784. Whether or not Saxe had moved his family there by 1784 is unknown, but we know that two years later John Saxe was living in Vermont, for his last child and only daughter was born in Highgate in 1786. By one account, after two years in Quebec, Saxe settled near Highgate, Vermont, where he built the first grist mill at a place that became known as Saxe's Mill. In another version of this story, it is said that "he settled at Phillipsburg, P.Q., Canada, and built a grist mill on Rock Mill, cleared the land, and settled down as a Canadian. However, when the government resurveyed the boundary line, he found that his mill was in Highgate, Vermont." It appears that "Rock Mill" in this version of the story would be what is now known as Rock River, for John Saxe's farm house near Highgate Village is on Saxe's Brook, a tributary of Rock River.[13]

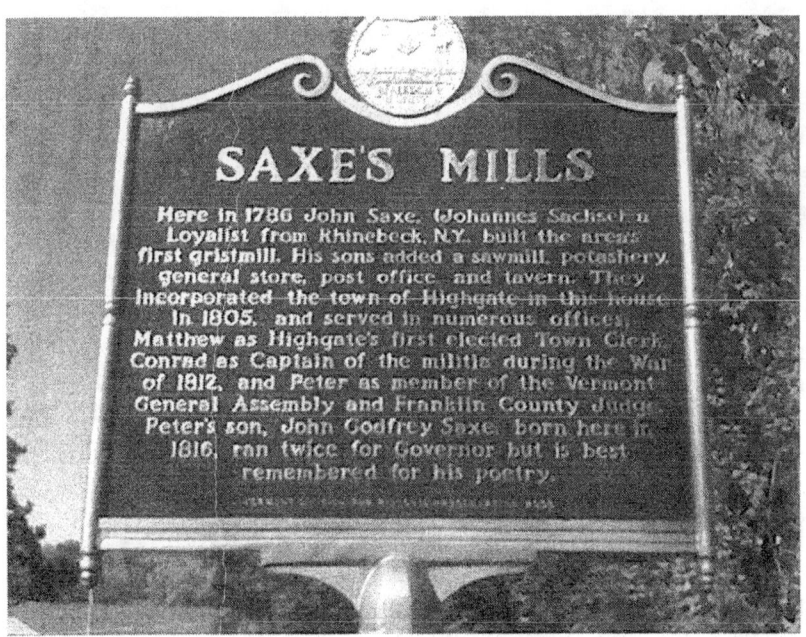

The text on the Vermont historical sign on the road beside John Saxe's house was composed by Andrew F. Saxe. It was approved by the Highgate Town Historian, Charles Nye.

John Saxe, Loyalist

Life on the frontier was surely challenging. The Saxe *Genealogy* says that the next years "were times of severe trials to the strong man." According to the *Genealogy*, John Saxe struggled in this "new country and severe climate … harassed by Indians, and wild beasts," and he "was at one time obliged to swim the river, breaking the ice with his hands." His wife Catherine died in 1791 – hers being the first recorded death in Highgate. Their eldest son, John, died two years later, and another son, Godfrey, died in 1807. The other seven children, however, outlived their parents and were each successful in their own ways. John Saxe Sr. was a prominent figure in the early years of Highgate. The first Post Office was located at his farm house, and the first town meeting was held there. Utilizing a run of stone beside his log grist mill, he soon added a carding mill and a potashery. At that time there were no other mills closer than Burlington, thirty-five miles to the south. And there were no settlers between Highgate and Burlington when John Saxe made the trip to Burlington alone in 1786, with only a compass for his guide.[14]

Valley of Saxe's Brook, Highgate Vt., view to west   Rock River, near entry of Saxe's Brook

The cluster of mills and other works at the Saxe farm in northern Highgate soon became the center of a growing population of migrants to this community. Conrad Barr and his wife Elizabeth – Catherine Saxe's sister – lived nearby, and in 1791 the first school in Highgate was taught by a man named Simeon Foster in a house on the Barr farm. Ira Allen, brother of the famed Ethan – leader of the Green Mountain Boys – sold John Saxe a piece of property on Lot 45 in Highgate on 31 July 1792. By 1796 there were 23 voters residing in Highgate, and in the following year Andrew Potter built the first saw mill at Highgate Falls. A brother of Andrew Potter later married a descendant of John Saxe. In 1799, Conrad Barr built one of the first framed barns in Highgate, and in 1801, Peter Saxe (who later spelled his name Sax) was a partner in the first store and tavern in Highgate. One of the first framed houses in town was built in 1802 by Conrad Barr, near Saxe's Mills. The first Highgate proprietor's meeting was held in John Saxe's house in January 1804 and in 1805 Matthew Saxe was elected as the first town clerk when the town was organized. Heman Allen, brother of Ethan and Ira, purchased Andrew Potter's mill when Potter moved across Lake Champlain to settle in New York State. Potter's house was bought the following year by Ebenezer Stockwell, who became the "principal agent, or foreman" for Heman Allen. Indeed, the list of "principal actors" in the history of Highgate between 1793 and 1803 includes not only John Saxe, but many of his sons and several others who later become members of his extended family. These names include Matthew and Peter Saxe, Andrew and Noel Potter, and Conrad Barr.[15]

John Saxe was a Lutheran, and he lived by the Scriptures, which were read aloud by him and his children from the German Bible that he brought when he left home in Saxony. After his death, Saxe's Bible passed to his son Peter, and thence to Peter's descendants. Saxe made his will on 28 March 1807, naming each of the seven children who survived him: Matthew, Peter, and Jacob received his property in Highgate, and George, William, Conrad, and Hannah received his property in Canada. He also named his grandson John Saxe, son of his son George, as an heir of his property in Canada.

Matthew and two others who were not related to him were named as executors. John Saxe died on 12 March 1808 at his home in Highgate and he was buried beside his wife in the town cemetery in Philipsburg, Quebec.[16]

Old Protestant Cemetery, Philipsburg, Missisquoi County, Quebec. John Saxe, his wife Catherine, and his son Godfrey are said to be buried here.

John Saxe's second son, George, became a hunter and drover. His next son, William, returned to Canada and was a noted surveyor. Matthew became a wheelwright, and later was a successful businessman, landowner, and elected official in New York State on the west side of Lake Champlain. Peter stayed on the Saxe homestead and was a successful farmer, merchant, and public official in Vermont. Jacob became a merchant, and the youngest son, Conrad, was a much-admired farmer and captain of the local militia in the War of 1812. The youngest child, Hannah, married a prominent man from New York State who was a colonel in the War of 1812. She moved with him to Cambria, Niagara County, N.Y.[17]

John Saxe married, 18 November 1771, at Rhinebeck, Dutchess Co., New York, Catherine Weaver (probably originally Weber), one of three or more children of German parents, born at Philadelphia in 1744; died at Highgate, Franklin Co., Vermont, 10 January 1791. She was buried in the town cemetery in Philipsburg, Quebec. John and

Catherine (Weaver) Saxe had nine children, eight sons and one daughter: John (1772-1793), George (1773-1853), William (1774-1840), Matthew (1776-1836), Godfrey (1778-1807), Peter (1779-1880), Jacob (1783-1866), Conrad (1784-1871), and Hannah (1786-1859). Most sources say that the eight sons were born at Rhinebeck, N.Y., although one source says that their sixth child was born at Woodstock, N.Y., and that their next child was born in Vermont. Their youngest son was born at Rhinebeck and their ninth and youngest child, a daughter, was born at either Highgate, Vt., or at Missisquoi Bay, Quebec, Canada.[18]

The children of John and Catherine Saxe married members of the Leroy, Trembly, Holt, Lockwood, Graves, Jewett, Keith, Dunning, and Scovell families. Although "most of his sons and grandsons became Vermonters," John Saxe's great-granddaughter Mary Sollace Saxe (1868-1942), who was born in St. Albans, Vt., became a naturalized Canadian citizen and later was a well-known author, playwright and librarian in Montreal and Westmount, Quebec. John Saxe's most famous descendant is a grandson, the American humorist and poet John Godfrey Saxe (1816-1887), who was the son of John's son Peter. John Godfrey Saxe, who was born in St. Albans and died in Albany, N.Y., was profiled in Scribner's *Concise Dictionary of American Biography* (1964), and more than one-half page of his poetry is reproduced in *Bartlett's Familiar Quotations* (1955).[19]

John Saxe's fifth son, Godfrey Saxe (1778-1807), had a daughter by a wife whose name is unknown (perhaps Anna). Godfrey Saxe's daughter, Anna Maria Saxe, was born in Vermont, 10 February 1804; died at Mooers, N.Y., 4 February 1890, and was buried there. She married Joseph H. Stockwell, son of Ebenezer and Abi (Holbrook) Stockwell, born at Bennington, Vt., 5 May 1802; he died at Burlington, 22 September 1870, and he is believed to have been buried there. Joseph and Anna (Saxe) Stockwell are my great-great grandparents.[20]

John and Catherine (Weaver) Saxe had the following children[21]:
2	i.	John (1772-1793)
3	ii.	George (1773-1853)
4	iii.	William (1774-1840)
5	iv.	Matthew (1776-1836)
6	v.	Godfrey (1778-1807)
7	vi.	Peter (1779-1839)
8	vii.	Jacob (1783-1866)
9	viii.	Conrad (1784-1871)
10	ix.	Hannah (1786-1859)

2

Second Generation

A family of 8 sons and 1 daughter -- namely John, George, William, Matthew, Godfrey, Peter, Jacob, Conrad and Hannah
-- Robinson and Skeels, *History of Highgate* (1871)

2. John SAXE, Jr., eldest child of John and Catherine (Weaver) Saxe, was born at Rhinebeck, Dutchess County, N.Y., 17 April 1772; died without progeny at Saxe's Mills, Highgate, Vermont, 22 August 1793. He was baptized as the son of John Saxe and Catherine Weaver at the Kaatsban Reformed Church in Dutchess County on 23 June 1772. The sponsors of his baptism were John Merkle and Margaret Weaver. Although nothing else is known about this Margaret Weaver, this record suggests that she may have been a sister of his mother. Nothing more is known about John Saxe, Jr., who was the namesake of his father and who died less than a decade after his parents and their children moved from Dutchess County, N.Y., to Quebec and then settled in Highgate, Vermont.[22]

3. George SAXE, second son and second child of John and Catherine (Weaver) Saxe, was born in Rhinebeck, Dutchess County, N.Y., 31 August 1773; died at Stanbridge, Quebec, Canada on 18 September 1853. He was baptized as the son of John Saxe and Catherine Weaver at the Stone Church in Rhinebeck on 30 August 1773. Either the date of his birth or the date of his baptism must have been misread by a previous transcriber, but we can nevertheless presume that he was born in August 1773 and that he was baptized in the same month. The sponsors of his baptism were George Ring and Catherine Tremper. Little else is known about George Saxe, other than that he lived to a ripe old age in Canada, where he died at the age of 80, and that he was named in his father's will as one of the inheritors of his father's property in Canada. He married Rachel Leroy, probably in the 1790s, since their sixth child was born in 1801. George and Rachel (Leroy) Saxe had nine children, many of whom also had descendants.[23]

They had the following children:
- 11   i.   Catherine
- 12   ii.   Simon
- 13   iii. Charlotte (-1886)
- 14   iv.   John
- 15   v.   Matthew
- 16   vi.   Peter (1801-1848)
- 17   vii. Cecile
- 18   viii. Anna
- 19   ix.   George J.

4. William SAXE, third son and third child of John and Catherine (Weaver) Saxe, was born at Rhinebeck, Dutchess County, N.Y., 16 December 1774; died in Quebec, Canada, 13 January 1840. He was baptized as the son of John Saxe and Catherine Weaver at the Kingston, N.Y., Reformed Church on 23 March 1775, with sponsors named as Philip Hotaling and his wife Janet Elting. He assisted in the survey of three million acres in Quebec between 1792 and 1824. One of his three children was a priest who founded the parish of Sainte Romauld near Quebec City. William Saxe was named as a recipient of property and other goods in the will of his father, which was written in 1807.[24]

William Saxe wrote[25] that he left home in 1788 at the age of fourteen and joined M. S. Z. Watson, land surveyor, to learn his profession and science. Saxe said that he lived with Watson for seven years,

> during which we surveyed a number of seigniorys and townships.... In the year 1792, after the division of the Province of Quebec into the two provinces of Lower and Upper Canada, the first considerable surveys were ordered by the government of Lower Canada, which were actual surveys to be made by a number of Provincial Land Surveyors, accordingly, in the month of March of that year, the River Sorel or Richelieu

from its mouth to the Province line at Latitude 45. Accordingly, we set out from Quebec on the 12th of June 1792 in three batteaux, with provisions and necessaries, each surveyor having received an advance of currency from the Government. In twelve days we arrived at the Basin of Chambly (having seen before our departure and during our journey two elections for members of Parliament). From Chambly we had our batteaux taken to St. Johns and thence, passing the Isle-aux-noix and rounding the tongue of Alburgh, we entered and ascended the Missisquoi River to the first falls, where, leaving our batteaux, we proceeded in birch canoes, which we had procured at St. Francois (as also an Indian for each party) to nearly the head of Missisquoi River by making many portages, where the surveyors parted company.

Our party continued on eastward, the Indian carrying the birch canoe on his head to Lake Memphramagog and we -- our provisions on our backs -- ascending and descending many mountains and ledges till we finally arrived at the Lake Memphramagog which was about the middle of July. We ferried ourselves across the Lake, about two miles wide, making three trips to cross the whole of the party and baggage and provision, with which we all landed safely on the Eastern shore, where we left the canoe covered by branches, and our party nine in number, continued our route Eastward on the Province line, measuring as we went the extent of the Townships of Stansledd, Barnston, Barford and Hereford to the Western bank of Connecticut River and then proceeded to run the outlines of Barford, Hereford, Cliffton, Ayckland and part of Barnston, Newport, Eaton and Compton. Our party was divided into two surveying parties one under Mr. Watson and the other under my immediate direction. I surveyed that part or branch of Connecticut River called Indian Stream, wading in the water at times up to our necks and suffering all the hardships it was possible for human nature to sustain or bear up against.

Also, having scaled the south shore of a small lake called Laachl in the Township of Hereford, which the Province line intersects, in fording the mouth of a brook which falls into the Lake, the party having crossed and being before me, I suddenly sank to the bottom, with the Theodolite in my hand, and would perhaps never have risen alive again, had not fortunately one of the party, seeing me go down, hastened to the spot and, putting the flag and staff he held in his hand down, I laid hold thereof and was drawn out of the water by him, having been under water upwards of three minutes and had taken in much water. Besides this disaster, I underwent all the fatigue it is possible to be conceived in this extensive wilderness of nature where no settlements of any kind were yet made or roads or paths even opened. The canopy of heaven being our only covering during the whole of this survey which terminated late in October, when, being fatigued and exhausted much for the want of provisions which we had scarcely any left, we set out on our return on foot carrying on our backs what little baggage remained. Arrived after eight days' march through the wilderness at the banks of Lake Memphramagog, found our canoe, and in the night crossed three different trips to the west shore, thence continued on our march westward to the settlement of Missisquoi Bay, where we all arrived the latter end of October, having travelled about ninety miles westward carrying our baggage all the way on our backs; it would have been impossible from our exhausted state to have gone any farther without some repose. Thence we went to our winter quarters on the Isle-aux-noix."

The *Genealogy of the Saxe Family* adds that "before leaving on this trip, William saw on the fourth of the month on parade the Regiment of Prince Edward reviewed by himself – 'a grand sight.' From 1792 until 1824, in a lapse of about thirty-two years, Saxe had assisted in the survey of about three million acres, in townships, laid out in the field which now contains a population of about 30,000 and in 1792 was a wilderness."

William Saxe became a Roman Catholic and married in, say, 1812, Mary Osiette Trembly; she died after 1827. William and Mary Osiette (Trembly) Saxe had three children.[26]

They had the following children:
    20   i.   William (1813-1834)
    21   ii.   Pierre (Peter) Telesphore (1822-1881)
    22   iii.   George (1827-1900)

5. Matthew SAXE, fourth son and fourth child of John and Catherine (Weaver) Saxe, was born at Rhinebeck, Dutchess County, N.Y., 16 March 1776; died at Chazy, Clinton County, N.Y., 2 August 1836. Matthew Saxe, son of John Saxe and Catherine Weaver, was baptized at the Kingston, N.Y., Reformed Church on 21 April 1776, sponsored by Matthew Smith and his wife Catherine Wagner.[27]

    According to *Genealogy of the Saxe Family*, Matthew and his younger brother Jacob

> were brought up in Highgate, where they learned the iron business, there having been a deposit of iron ore in the town in the locality still known as "Furnace Lot." Later, they moved to Chazy, and engaged in the iron business there. For some years, they were prosperous, but a freshet swept away their dam and ruined their plant. Jacob returned to Vermont and settled at Sheldon, where he died. Matthew and his family remained, and descendants of his are still living at Saxe's Landing, near Chazy, on Lake Champlain.

Indeed, the *Genealogy* traces Matthew Saxe's descendants for four more generations, including his great-great grandson, First Lieutenant Lawrence Colt Lovell, born 11 April 1894; killed in France where he was a member of the Aviation Section, Signal Reserve Corps, A.E.F., 29 July 1917.[28]

Census records show that a boy of Matthew Saxe's age was living in the household of John Saxe in Highgate in 1790, and that a man of his age was in John Saxe's household in 1800. Matthew Saxe appears as the head of his own family in Chazy, N.Y., in 1810, and his name then disappears from the census records.[29]

Matthew Saxe appears as one of 37 petitioners in 1804 for a ferry that was proposed to be established between Highgate, Vermont, and Alburgh, N.Y. Other signers included his cousin Conrad Barr and his brother Godfrey Saxe. In 1805, Matthew was a Justice of the Peace and his brother Peter was a Selectman in Alburgh, Vt. And in 1808, Peter and Matthew advertised for the sale of a "plaining and jointing machine" in Highgate, Swanton, and Milton, Vermont. It is clear from these bits of information that Matthew was in business on both sides of Lake Champlain in the first decade of the nineteenth century. Records show that Matthew did business with the innkeeper at Isle La Motte in 1835.[30]

Matthew Saxe married three times.

On 4 Feb 1805 when Matthew was 28, he first married Charlotte HOLT; born 8 January 1787; died 25 December 1811, age 24.

They had the following children:

23	i.	William Holt (1809-1880)
24	ii.	Maria Ann (1807-1891)
25	iii.	Charlotte Holt (1810-1811)

Matthew second married Maria LOCKWOOD. She died without progeny (d.s.p.)

Matthew third married Betty GRAVES.

They had the following children:

26	i.	George W. (1818-1854)
27	ii.	Henry G. (1819-1897)
28	iii.	Elizabeth Catherine (1828-)
29	iv.	Julia Frances (1830-1914)
30	v.	Matthew Conrad (1832-)
31	vi.	Mary Helen (1834-1913)

6. Godfrey SAXE, fifth son and fifth child of John and Catherine (Weaver) Saxe, was born in Rhinebeck, Dutchess County, N.Y., 28 January 1778; died 16 August 1807, perhaps at Philipsburg, Missisquoi County, Quebec. He may have been buried in the Old Philipsburg Cemetery.[31]

Only a few facts are known about Godfrey Saxe, who died of unknown causes at the age of 29. He was born during the Revolutionary War when the community that his parents lived in was torn apart by strife between supporters of the Revolution, who called themselves Patriots, and those who supported the King, who were called Tories or Loyalists. His father was imprisoned as a Loyalist at about the time that he was born, and his mother had to support the family in some way, by herself or with the help of other members of her family. In November 1779, when Godfrey was a little less than two years old, his father's name appears on Livingston Rent Book, so the family was probably reunited by that time. However, a record of his baptism has not been found. He is listed in many secondary sources as being one of the children who accompanied John and Catherine Saxe and their other children and other Loyalists on their long journey up the Hudson River, across the height of land at Fort Edward and down Lake George and Lake Champlain to Missisquoi Bay, where they settled in about 1784. Their settlement at the southern part of Philipsburg, Quebec, was later found to be within Vermont, and the Saxe family thereby became some of the earliest settlers of Highgate, Vermont.

A boy of the right age to be Godfrey Saxe was present in the household of John Saxe in Highgate, Chittenden County, Vermont, in 1790, and a young man of the right age to be Godfrey was in John Saxe's household in 1800, when Highgate was in Franklin County. None of the members of the family are named in these censuses, other than the head of the family. The *History of Highgate* says Matthew, Godfrey, and Peter Saxe kept the first store and tavern in Highgate in 1801. A contemporaneous record that mentions Godfrey is a petition signed by 37 men on 12 August 1804, in which "Godfrey Sax" and the other petitioners proposed "a ferry across Missisquoi Bay from 'Hog Island' in Highgate to Alburgh in Franklin Co. [N.Y.] it being the most direct route from this part of Vermont to Montreal." The petition was "Passed by the General Assembly, 1 Nov 1804 (Ms. Vt. State Papers, Vol. 44, pg. 150.) (Laws of Vt., 1804, pg. 56.)." Among the other signers of this petition were Godfrey's brother Matthew Saxe and his cousin Conrad Barr. Godfrey's daughter was six months old when he signed this petition.[32]

Godfrey Saxe may have been married by about January 1803, given that his daughter was born in February 1804. His wife's name and the record of their marriage has not been found, but her name may be Anna, inasmuch as a woman named Anna Saxe appears as one of the founders of the Congregational Church of Highgate in 1811. By that time, Godfrey Saxe had been dead for four years and his daughter Anna Saxe was only seven years old. There are no other married or single adult women named Anna Saxe in 1815 the *Genealogy of the Saxe Family*, so we may conclude by exclusion that this Anna Saxe was probably Godfrey's widow. Four other founders of the Highgate

Congregational Church were related to Godfrey Saxe: Conrad Barr, John Barr, Martha Barr, and Sarah Drury. Conrad, John, and Martha Barr were children of Conrad Barr and Elizabeth Weaver – a sister of Catherine (Weaver) Saxe. They were therefore first cousins of Godfrey Saxe. Sarah (Keith) Drury was the mother-in-law of Col. Peter Saxe, son of Godfrey's brother Peter Sax.[33]

Godfrey Saxe and a woman whose name is unknown but may be Anna _____, had a daughter, Anna Maria (a k a Anne) Saxe, whose middle initial has been variably given as either M. or W.; born in Vermont, 10 February 1804. Godfrey's daughter Anne /Anna died at Mooers, Clinton County, N.Y., 4 February 1890 and she was buried there in the Old Mooers Village Cemetery. Anna Saxe married Joseph H. Stockwell, son of Ebenezer and Abi (Holbrook) Stockwell, who lived for a time in Highgate.[34]

Godfrey Saxe had the following child:

32   i.   Anna Maria (1804-1890)

I believe we can speculate about Godfrey Saxe as follows:

Godfrey was probably a bit odd, and he was not well-liked by his father, John Saxe – the crusty old Loyalist. Godfrey's two oldest surviving brothers, William and George, lived in Canada, whereas Godfrey stayed with the younger brothers in Vermont. His brothers were all rather successful, but Godfrey just barely got by. He did, however, succeed in becoming the partner of two of his brothers when the three brothers opened a store and tavern in Highgate in 1801. And he joined two of them in signing a petition to establish a ferry on Lake Champlain in August 1804, six months after a girl was born in Highgate, of whom Godfrey was said to be the father. There is nothing in any record to prove that Godfrey was married to the child's mother. However, Godfrey and the mother probably lived together, and this was accepted by the Saxe brothers and the rest of the community – if not by their father. The child was named Anna Maria – a German name – so the mother may have been from a German family.
    The name Anna Maria was, however, not unusual in the early years of the Saxe family of Vermont. Various forms of this name were given to five women in the next three generations. This name was given to John Saxe's daughter, Hannah, who was called Anna by her brother Peter; to three of John Saxe's granddaughters; and to one of his great-granddaughters: Anna Maria Saxe (b. 1804, daughter of Godfrey); Maria Ann Saxe (b. 1807, daughter of Matthew); and Maria Saxe (b. 1826, daughter of Jacob Saxe). John Saxe's great-granddaughter, Maria Ann See (b. about 1814), was the daughter of George Saxe's daughter Catherine Saxe and her husband David See.

Godfrey Saxe died in 1807 and was probably buried near his mother, Catherine (Weaver) Saxe, in the town cemetery in Philipsburg, Quebec, just across the international border from the Saxe farm in Highgate. Godfrey's father did not mention him when he wrote his will in March 1807, although Godfrey was still alive – Godfrey died in August 1807. I believe the omission was more likely deliberate than accidental, because John Saxe also paid no attention to Godfrey's daughter, although he named another grandchild in his will. We do not know the cause of Godfrey's death, but it was probably an accident. Trauma was the most common cause of death of young men in those days, and Godfrey was only 29 years old. It could have been drowning, an accident with firearms, a falling tree, a runaway horse, a rambunctious bull, or any one of the many ways that cause the death of unlucky and careless young men. It was not a spectacular event, nor was it a homicide – for both of those causes of death were later memorialized in the history of Highgate. It could have been suicide, because that would not be mentioned, but that, too, is unlikely, if he was buried in hallowed ground. It could have been tuberculosis, which was beginning to be a major cause of death in America.

Godfrey's widow probably continued to live in Highgate and she brought up her daughter as a single mother. Whether or not she was married to Godfrey, I think she took the surname Saxe. I think she could be the Anna Saxe who was one of the founding members of the Congregational Church in Highgate in 1811. Three of the other founding members of this church were children of John Barr and Elizabeth Weaver – Elizabeth Barr was a sister of Catherine Saxe – and they were therefore first cousins of Godfrey Saxe. There was at least one other child in that family – a daughter Elizabeth Barr. If Anna Saxe was, say, 18 when her daughter was born, she would have been born in about 1786. It would thus be plausible to imagine that this Anna Saxe was a Barr – a sister of John (born in 1775), Conrad (b. 1777), Martha (b. 1792), and Elizabeth (b. 1794) Barr.

Hannah Saxe, the youngest child of John and Catherine (Weaver) Saxe, was known as Anna Saxe at the time of her marriage in 1813, and Robinson's *History of Highgate* says that she became a Congregationalist after she was married. If the history is wrong, and she was already a member of the Congregational Church when she was married, this would suggest that John Saxe's daughter was the "Anna Saxe" who was a founder of the Highgate Congregational Church. Unfortunately, the Highgate Congregational Church's records were not kept in Highgate after the church went out of existence in 1956, and it is unknown if they were preserved anywhere. They are not in the national archives of the Congregational Church, nor are they in the files of the Highgate Town Historian, Charles Nye. Mr. Nye says that the church building was purchased and owned for a while by the town but the building was cleaned out and not even the stove – which was made in a foundry in Highgate – was preserved. Copies of the Highgate Congregational Church papers are not in the microfilm files of the Family History Center of the Latter Day Saints, nor are any of those records in the St. Albans Historical Museum.

Anna Maria Saxe may have lived with the Barr family after the death of her father, Godfrey Saxe. Whether or not she was their biological sister, in the language of the church, Anna Maria Saxe was a "sister" to John, Conrad, and Martha Barr. We can suppose that Anna Maria Saxe was still living in Highgate when she married Joseph H. Stockwell in 1823 because the genealogy of the Saxe family, based on Highgate records that have since vanished, show that Anna Saxe married Joseph Stockville [sic]. This transcription error in the spelling of Stockwell could only have occurred when someone misread the handwritten record of the marriage many years later.

In summary, I speculate that Godfrey Saxe had a daughter, perhaps out of wedlock, by a woman whose name may have been Anna, perhaps Anna Barr, who would have been his first cousin. The Highgate community must have known who Anna Maria Saxe's mother was, but her mother's name was never inscribed in the town records. I speculate that whatever her maiden name was, Anna Maria Saxe's mother then became known as Anna Saxe and brought up her daughter, Anna Maria Saxe, in Highgate. In 1823, Anna Maria Saxe married, in Highgate, Joseph H. Stockwell, son of Ebenezer Stockwell, who had first come to Highgate Falls in about 1798. Ebenezer moved about from time to time and Joseph was born in Bennington, but Ebenezer came back to Highgate and died there in 1828. When he lived in Highgate, Ebenezer Stockwell lived near the Barrs and, like the Saxes and the Barrs, he was a miller. It is thus easy to see how Ebenezer Stockwell's son Joseph became acquainted with Anna Maria Saxe. Joseph Stockwell and Anna Maria Sace were probably not concerned about whether Anna Maria's mother was married to Godfrey Saxe, for that was a long time ago. Godfrey Saxe had been dead for sixteen years when Anna Maria Saxe and Joseph H. Stockwell were married in 1823.

7. Hon. Peter SAX (a k a SAXE), sixth son and sixth child of John and Catherine (Weaver) Saxe, was born in either Rhinebeck or Woodstock, N.Y., in or prior to September 1779; his baptism was recorded at St. Paul's Lutheran Church, West Camp, N.Y. on 3 September 1779. He died on 27 May 1839 in Cambria, Niagara County, N.Y. He was buried in the Scovell family plot of the Cambria Centre Cemetery, where his sister, Hannah (Saxe) Scovell and many members of her husband's family are buried. His will was written on 13 May 1839 when he was of Cambridge, Lamoille County, Vt., and it was entered into probate in Franklin County, where it was filed in the county probate record office in St. Albans.[35]

In the *Genealogy of the Saxe Family* (1930) it is stated that "60. Peter Saxe, B. Dec. 15, 1779, at Woodstock, N. Y., D. May 27, 1839, at Cambria, N. Y." It is impossible to say with certainty when and where Peter Saxe (later shortened to Sax) was born, although most other accounts – none of them primary sources – say that all of the sons of John Saxe were born in or near Rhinebeck, N.Y. The children were baptized either in different locations near Rhinebeck or in Rhinebeck by ministers of different churches. It is also impossible to say which of those possibilities is true. Peter Saxe's baptism is recorded at the West Camp Church, near Rhinebeck, on 3 September 1779.

He is shown in the baptismal record as the son of John Saxe and Catherine Weaver, and his sponsors were "John Kraft & wife." The discrepancy between the alleged date of his birth in December and the record of his baptism three months earlier cannot be reconciled, but inasmuch as the baptismal record is a primary source and the birth date is from an unknown source, it seems reasonable to state that he must have been born in or before September 1779.[36]

Genealogy of the Saxe Family continues,

Peter Saxe was one of Vermont's early statesmen ... His wife was a woman of great strength of character and fine intellect. She attained the age of ninety years, with her faculties wholly unimpaired. The Montreal Saxes have a very beautiful portrait of her. It is recorded that when she was a girl of eighteen she rode on horseback from her home in Weybridge to Troy, N. Y., with four servants as an escort, travelling the whole distance through a dense forest, inhabited by Indians, and accomplished the trip of one hundred miles in forty eight hours, and carrying with her a valuable consignment of silver coin.[37]

The entry for Peter Saxe in the *Genealogy of the Saxe Family* extends over some 22 pages, due largely to the long entry for his second son, John Godfrey Saxe, and a shorter but still extensive entry for the twin sons of his eldest son, Charles Jewett Saxe.[38]

A boy whose age is consistent with that of Peter Saxe appears in the census records in the family of John Saxe of Highgate, Vt., in 1790, when Peter was 11; and again in 1800, as a young man when Peter was 21. There are no Saxe or Sax families in Highgate in 1810, but Peter Saxe was the head of a family in Highgate in 1820 and 1830.

Information from the *History of Highgate* adds more to what we know about Peter Saxe: In 1801, Matthew, Godfrey and Peter Saxe opened the first store and tavern in Highgate. Peter is said to have been one of the "principal actors" in the early years of the town, from 1793-1803. He was a Representative to the Vermont Legislature in 1806, 1818, and 1827. He was the Town Clerk in 1810, 1811, 1828, and 1829. Amos Skeels then summarized his life as follows, as edited by Robinson: "Peter remained on the old homestead, a farmer and merchant, a man of business: he several times represented the town; the poorer class always voted for him, for, said they, we all owe Peter. He is the father of the famous John G. SAXE, the poet." The Saxe homestead still stands near Saxe's Brook where it flows into Rock River, in the northern part of Highgate.

The Saxe Homestead, on Saxe's Brook, Highgate, Vermont

On 17 December 1838, his wife Elizabeth was named as his guardian by the Franklin County Court in St. Albans. He was, however, still considered competent to make his will, which he executed on 13 May 1839. For reasons that are unknown to us, but which often happen as older men and women need to move in with their children and in-laws, Peter (now spelling his last name as Sax) moved away from Highgate and was living in Cambridge, Lamoille County, Vt., when he died less than three months later, on 3 September 1839. Cambridge, Vt., is on the western edge of Lamoille County, just across the county line from Franklin County, where Peter Sax had lived for most of his life.[39]

On 17 May 1813 when Peter Sax was 33, he married, in Highgate, Franklin Co., Vt., Elizabeth Jewett, daughter of Samuel and Lucy (Hungerford) Jewett; born on 8 Jan 1790 in Weybridge, Vt.; died in St. Albans, Franklin Co., Vt., 18 April 1880. The Jewett family was connected to the Saxe family through at least two other marriages. Charles Jewett, a brother of Peter Sax's wife, married Charlotte Catherine Scovell, daughter of Col. Josiah Scovell and Hannah Saxe, who was Peter's sister. Elizabeth's brother, whose name is unknown, had a daughter Elizabeth who married the Hon. Oliver Perry Scovell, son of Col. Josiah and Hannah (Saxe) Scovell.

Elizabeth (Jewett) Saxe died on 19 Apr 1880, she was 90. Peter and Elizabeth (Jewett) Saxe had the following children:

33	i.	Charles Jewett (1814-1867)
34	ii.	John Godfrey (1816-1887)
35	iii.	Peter (1819-1891)
36	iv.	James (1823-1884)

8. Jacob SAXE, seventh son and seventh child of John and Catherine (Weaver) Saxe, was born at Rhinebeck, Dutchess County, N.Y., 2 August 1783; died in Sheldon, Vermont, 12 November 1866. A record of his baptism has not been found.[40]

In about 1784 or 1785, Jacob Saxe traveled up the Hudson River and across Lake Champlain to Canada with his parents, his brothers, and other families who were associated with Loyalists of the mid-Hudson Valley. At the time of this forced migration, Jacob was only a year or two old. His parents and the others who came with them settled along Missisquoi Bay and once the line between Quebec and Vermont was surveyed, their land straddled the border. Jacob was raised on his father's farm at Saxe's Mills, in Highgate, Vt. He was named in his father's will, in which he and his brothers Matthew and Peter shared equally in the ownership of John Saxe's property in Highgate.[41]

Local history states that Jacob and his brother Matthew learned the iron business in Highgate, there having been a deposit of iron ore in the town in the locality that was known as "Furnace Lot." Later, they moved to Chazy, N.Y., and engaged in the iron business there. For some years, they were prosperous, but a freshet swept away their dam and ruined their plant. Jacob returned to Vermont and settled at Sheldon, where he died. Another source elaborates on this story, stating that Jacob was first engaged in business in Sheldon and then moved to West Chazy, where he was in business with his brothers Matthew and Peter. According to this source, at the beginning of the War of 1812, Jacob removed his merchandise to the storehouse at Chazy Landing, and on the approach of a large force of British, took the same on batteaux to Orwell, Vt., where the only sister of the Saxe brothers cared for them. After the war over, he spent a short time in Chazy before he removed to the mouth of the Salmon River (Port Gilliland) where he built a blast furnace, sawmill, dams, charcoal kilns, etc., employing forty men. The freshet of 1830 swept all these buildings and dams into the lake, but the stone dwelling which he built still stands. He spent the closing years of his life in Sheldon to which his wife had gone during the British invasion and where she plainly heard the booming of cannon during the battle of Plattsburgh."[42]

The census records for Highgate, Vt., in 1790 and 1800 show John Sax as the head of a family. No other Saxe or Saxe names are in those censuses for Highgate, and there is no one named Saxe in the 1810 census. In 1790, Highgate was in Chittenden Co. There were then 17 families in Highgate. John Sax then was head of a family of 11: 3 free white males over age 16, 6 free white males under 16, and 2 free white females. This accounts for the entire family. John 58, John Jr 18, George 17, William 16,

Matthew 14, Godfrey 12, Peter 11, Jacob 7, and Conrad 6. The ages of the women were not recorded in the census; Catherine was 46 and Hannah was 4.

In 1800, Highgate was (as it still is) in Franklin Co. There were then 77 families. John Sax was head of a family of 7: Free white males - 5 aged 16-25 (who would be Matthew 24, Godfrey 22, Peter 21, Jacob 17, and Conrad 16), 1 age 45+ (John Sr.), and one free white female age 10-15 (Hannah 14). By this census, we can see that oldest three sons were not recorded in this census. They were John Jr., who died in 1793, and two who had moved to Quebec, George 27 and William 26. Their mother, Catherine, had died in 1791, so she is not in this census.

Jacob Sax (or Saxe) cannot be found in any U.S. Census except possibly in 1810 when a Jacob Sax was in Greenfield, Saratoga Co., N.Y.

On 23 Dec 1812 when Jacob was 29, he married Rowena Keith.[43]

Jacob and Rowena (Keith) Saxe had the following children:

37	i.	Alfred (1814-1846)
38	ii.	Robert Jenkins (1816-1894)
39	iii.	Edward (1818-1862)
40	iv.	Arthur Wellesley (1820-1891)
41	v.	George Godfrey (1822-1896)
42	vi.	Frederic (~1823-<1824)
43	vii.	Rowena (~1824-<1825)
44	viii.	Maria (1826-1854)
45	ix.	Jacob William (1830-1883)
46	x.	Caroline (1832-1851)
47	xi.	Hannah (1834-1916)
48	xii.	Heman Allen (1836-1915)
49	xiii.	Rowena Keith (1839-1915)

9. Conrad SAXE, eighth son and eighth child of John and Catherine (Weaver) Saxe, was born in or near Rhinebeck, Dutchess County, N.Y., 18 October 1784; died at Highgate, Franklin County, Vt., 5 July 1871. Of his place of birth, only the following information is available: "John and Catherine lived in Rhinebeck and vicinity for nineteen years and had eight sons born to them there." His baptism on 28 November 1784 was sponsored by Conrad Bahr and his wife Elizabeth Weaver, who was his mother's sister. The baptism was recorded at St. Paul's Lutheran Church in Red Hook, Dutchess County, N.Y., although it is not known if his parents were living there at that time, or even if he was baptized there. Red Hook is about five miles north of Rhinebeck.[44]

Conrad Saxe was just a babe in arms when his parents traveled with several other Loyalist families up the Hudson River and then north across Lake Champlain to settle in Canada. The area that they came to east of Missisquoi Bay was later found to straddle the border between Canada and Vermont, and the Saxe farmhouse thus was one of the earliest buildings to be erected in what became Highgate, Vermont. Conrad appears in the census records of 1790 and 1800 as the youngest son in the family of John Saxe, and he eventually outlived all of his brothers. Conrad Saxe was not in the census of 1810 but he was probably missed by the census taker, for he was in a Highgate military unit in the War of 1812, and he was back in Highgate in the Census of 1830 and 1840.

In the *Genealogy of the Saxe Family*, Conrad Saxe was described as follows[45]:

Conrad Saxe was the last survivor of his family. He lived to be over eighty. He was about 5 feet 7 inches in height – straight and finely built – remarkably strong and active. His head was not large, but symmetrical – and showed decided moral and intellectual development. He had brown, curly hair, regular features, and a very expressive black eye, commonly loving and humorous. In the early days of rough, muscular sports and combats, he was a champion; and a terror to much larger men who gave him just cause of offense. He had besides great muscular power, strong nerves and a steady eye, could, when necessary, endure or witness physical suffering without a quiver. He was for sometime Custom House officer in perilous times and his power over the rough and unscrupulous smugglers was said to have been marvelous. He would go quietly among them alone and in the night, and in spite of their threats and curses seize their contraband property and hold it – no one could tell how – but he did it, talking in a low firm tone of his duty and their peril in their unlawful deeds. He carried the charm of real bravery about him. He was eminently social in his nature, warm in his attachment, generous and hospitable. He was interesting in conversation and an inimitable story teller.

He is said to have lived a careless, irreligious life till about thirty-five years of age, when he came deliberately to the conclusion that he ought to be a Christian. From that time on, to the close of life, he was an active and efficient official member of the church. His remarks in public were original and appropriate, and always interesting. He was free from formality. His nephews remember that in their boyhood, his reading of the Scriptures at family prayers always arrested their attention, by its naturalness and simplicity. A minister of our Church to whom he was much attached, becoming unsettled in his theological views, withdrew from the Church and joined the Unitarians. The first opportunity that occurred, Uncle Conrad sent him a kindly greeting, as usual, but added: "Ye have taken away my Lord and I know not where ye have laid him." It was a touching reproof, skillfully administered, and may have been among the influences that afterwards brought the man back to the Church of his early choice.

He was beautiful in old age. When one of his nephews alluded to his infirmities after a long journey, he humorously replied: "Yes, I am pretty lame, but when I get aboard the cars I can travel as fast as anybody." A nephew writes: "The last time I saw him was not long before his death. He could not rise from his seat except with assistance. He could barely walk by the use of two canes, yet he exhibited the same cheerful, sunny spirit. Taking him for all in all, he was the best example of "Christian perfection" I have ever known."

Conrad was one of two Captains of Companies raised in Highgate for the War of 1812:

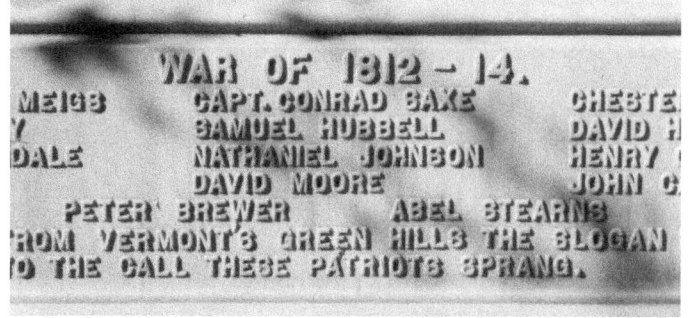

Capt. Conrad Saxe on Soldiers' Monument, Highgate, Vermont (above)

Soldiers' Monument, Highate, Vermont (left)

Captain Conrad Saxe, at the time of the battle of Plattsburgh, raised a company of volunteers, principally from Highgate, and started for the battle ground, and succeeded in reaching Grand Isle, but failed to get passage in season to participate in that memorable .

.. battle. Frequent rumors of approaching squads of Indians were circulated among the inhabitants, and families were congregated together, every moment expecting the tomahawk and scalping-knife. On these occasions the older members of the families would relate the anecdotes of Indian massacres during the Revolutionary war that would raise the hair upon the beads of us urchins, as the quills of a porcupine. However the Indians never came during the war. The victory on Lake Champlain and the skedadling of the British land forces back to Canada gave the frontier settlers quiet again.[46]

The early records of Highgate show that Conrad Saxe bought a blacksmith shop there for $100 sometime before 1820, and that he was a Selectman in 1821. Shortly before he died, the Highgate historian wrote that "Conrad Saxe, blacksmith and farmer, is still living. He has long been an esteemed member of the M. E. church, and for near 40 years a class-leader. He is now aged and infirm, waiting quietly on the banks of the dark river for the last summons, 'Come this side'."[47]

Conrad died in Highgate in 1871 and his widow Clarissa died in Highgate in 1875. His sons Horace Jacob (d. 1847) and Edwin (d. 1899) apparently did not marry and although they do not appear in census records we may presume that they lived somewhere in Highgate. If so, Edwin Saxe would be the last with the surname Saxe to live in Highgate.

On 5 Feb 1816 when Conrad Saxe was 31, he married Clarissa Duuning; born 19 August 1792; died at Highgate, Vt., 18 December 1875.[48] Conrad and Clarissa (Dunning) Saxe had six children. Their fifth child, Hannah, kept the town records for her husband, Zephaniah Keith Drury, who was the Town Clerk of Highgate for many years. Hannah (Saxe) Drury's "well-rounded, painstaking hand-writing fills many a page of the old records" that John Godfrey Saxe II cited in his *Genealogy of the Saxe Family*. These records have subsequently disappeared.

They had the following children:

50	i.	Loan D. (1816-1851)
51	ii.	Horace Jacob (1818-1874)
52	iii.	Edwin A. (1819-1899)
53	iv.	Clarissa Eliza (1824-1870)
54	v.	Hannah (1827-1909)
55	vi.	Harriet T. (1830-1833)

10. Hannah SAXE, only daughter and ninth child of John and Catherine (Weaver) Saxe. She was born at Highgate, Franklin County, Vt., 5 November 1786; died at Cambria, Niagara County, N.Y., 20 March 1859. She was sometimes called "Anna."[49]

The *Genealogy of the Saxe Family* provides this information about the life of Hannah Saxe, her marriage, and her descendants:

Hannah Saxe was … only four years of age when her mother died . ... She early became the hausfrau in her father's home and continued as such until his death on March 13, 1808, being his comfort and his closest confidant during his declining years. She was married at Highgate on March 5, 1813, to Josiah Boardman Scovell of Orwell, Vermont, who was an officer in the Vermont Militia during the War of 1812 and had met her while conducting military operations along the Canadian border in northern Vermont.

Her brother, Peter Saxe (60), in a post-script to his letter to Elizabeth Jewett, proposing their marriage, wrote: "Sister Hannah has just joined heart and hand with Colonel Scovell of Orwell; I guess it is a pretty good match." They had seven children, all born in Orwell, and all of their sons were named after naval heroes of the War of 1812. Her husband was the son of Thomas Scovell, Jr. who was a member of 1st Lieut. Samuel Nichols' Company in Colonel Benjamin Bellows Regiment. That Company marched from Lempster and Newport on the Alarm of June 29, 1777, to reinforce the garrison at Fort Ticonderoga. Her husband was a farmer at Orwell and in 1836 moved with his family to Cambria, Niagara County, New York, where he owned several farms and where he died December 17, 1855. He was buried in the Cambria Centre Cemetery, where, in the family lot, are also buried his mother, Rachael Boardman Scovell, his wife, Hannah Saxe Scovell, his daughter, Fidelia Scovell McCollum, and his brother-in-law, Peter Saxe. Her son, Thomas Scovell, inherited the farms in Cambria, and she resided with him in Cambria until her death there on March 20, 1859.

She was brought up a Lutheran and after her marriage, united with the Congregational Church. All of her children were brought up as Congregationalists. Her daughter, Fidelia, married Hiram McCollum of Lockport, who later became a Roman Catholic; and all of his descendants, so far as learned, have been reared in the Roman Catholic faith. Her other descendants, so far as learned, have been protestants and many of them have held important spiritual and temporal offices, especially in churches of the Presbyterian and Congregational denominations. Her education was the best that the times and circumstances permitted. She spoke, read and wrote in German as fluently as in English. All of her children were educated at Lewiston Academy, where her nephew,

John Godfrey Saxe (602) was one time principal; and her husband founded a family scholarship at Oberlin College where four of their grandchildren were educated. Her husband was a Whig in politics, but advised each of his sons as they attained majority to identify themselves with the Abolitionist Party. She was a loving, sensible and efficient mother, though a strict disciplinarian in her family. Her daughter, Juliette, frequently told of being punished by her for picking up a pear to eat on the Sabbath, which had fallen from a tree near the kitchen door, the rule being that only such pears as had been picked up before the Sabbath might be eaten on that day.

In 1861, her son, Oliver Perry Scovell (906), and her nephew, Charles Jewett Saxe (601), were both members of Assembly; and in the sketch of the former in "Biographical Sketches of the State Officers and Members of the Legislature of the State of New York in 1861," published that year, it is stated that "His paternal ancestors were genuine Yankees, and his maternal German, the latter having belonged to the Royal Family of Saxe-Gotha, Germany, from which Prince Albert of England and all the Saxes of this country-including John G. Saxe, the famous poet-are descended." This statement was based on what his mother had related to her children.

In the one hundred seventeen years since the marriage of Josiah Boardman Scovell and Hannah Saxe, they have had over one hundred eighty direct descendants, but the bearers of the Scovell name have not multiplied in that family line, for only three of their male descendants are now living who bear the Scovell surname, one each in the fourth, fifth and sixth generations of the Saxe Family in America, namely, Josiah Boardman Scovell of Lewiston, and Robert Jameson Scovell, and his son, Rolf Scovell, both of Antwerp, Belgium.[50]

Hannah Saxe married, on 5 March 1813, Col. Josiah Boardman Scovell of the Vermont Militia, son of Thomas Scovell Jr. and his wife Rachel (Boardman) Scovell; born 6 November 1786; died at Cambria, Niagara County, N.Y., 17 December 1855. Col. Scovell was an officer in the Vermont Militia during the War of 1812, and he lived in Orwell, Vt., before relocating to Cambria, N.Y., in 1836.

Josiah Boardman and Hannah (Saxe) Scovell had seven children:

56	i.	Charlotte Catherine (1814-1883)
57	ii.	Rowena (1815-1815)
58	iii.	Juliette (1816-1890)
59	iv.	Fidelia (1817-1853)
60	v.	Stephen Decatur (1819-1850)
61	vi.	Oliver Perry (1820-1912)
62	vii.	Thomas McDonough (1823-1898)

3

Third Generation[51]

> Beneath the hill, you may see the mill
> With wasting wood and crumbling stone;
> The wheel is dripping, clattering still,
> But Jerry, the miller, is dead and gone.
> -- John Godfrey Saxe, "Little Jerry, the Miller"

11. Catherine SAXE.[*] Occupation: Married twice; mother of 9 by her first husband. Catherine first married David SEE. David died after March 1827.
They had the following children:

63	i.	David (1812-1869)
64	ii.	Maria Ann Saxe
65	iii.	Charles
66	iv.	William
67	v.	Caroline (1828-1882)

After 1828 Catherine second married John WIGHT, in Port Hope, Ontario.

12. Simon SAXE. Simon married Anna CARTER. Occupation: Mother of 11.
They had the following children:

68	i.	William H. (1834-)
69	ii.	Charlotte (1836-)
70	iii.	Agnes (1838-)
71	iv.	Lucy (1840-)
72	v.	George (1842-1863)
73	vi.	Cecile (1846-1859)
74	vii.	John Matthew (1848-)
75	viii.	Simon Peter (1850-)
76	ix.	Mary (1854-)
77	x.	Ira Charles (1857-)
78	xi.	Harriett Jane (1862-)

13. Charlotte SAXE. Charlotte died in 1886. Charlotte married Ira CARTER.

14. John SAXE. John first married Katy RYCARD. Katy died before Mar 1849.
They had the following children:

---

[*] The somewhat awkward text for most of John Saxe's descendants in Generations Three to Five was composed by the software of Sierra "Family Tree." I have edited it slightly in some places to adjust the line lengths.

79	i.	Jane
80	ii.	Olivia
81	iii.	Cecile
82	iv.	John

Before 28 Mar 1849, John second married Emily PHILLIPS. Emily died after Apr 1857. They had the following children:

83	i.	Emily (1849-1908)
84	ii.	Mary R. (1856-)
85	iii.	Nettie (1857-)

15. Matthew SAXE. Matthew married Delia HADLEY.

16. Peter SAXE. Born on 20 Mar 1801. Peter died on 8 Sep 1848, he was 47.
Peter married Anna WILSON.
They had the following children:

86	i.	George (1833-1844)
87	ii.	Helen (1836-)
88	iii.	Cecile (1843-1868)

17. Cecile SAXE. Cecile married Luther SARTELL.
They had one child:

| 89 | i. | William |

18. Anna SAXE. Anna married John GIBBS.
They had one child:

| 90 | i. | Caroline |

19. George J. SAXE. Never married.

20. William SAXE. Born in Sep 1813. William died in Apr 1834, he was 20.

21. The Rev. Pierre (Peter) Telesphore SAXE. Born on 11 Nov 1822. Pierre (Peter) Telesphore died in Dec 1881, he was 59.

"Father Saxe was a Roman Catholic priest, founder of a quaint little French parish, known as Sainte Romauld, on the south bank of the St. Lawrence, near Quebec. His mother was French, a native of Lacadie in Quebec Province. She is described by Abbe d'Emirs in La Parvisse de St. Romauld as 'an extraordinary woman, full of virtue and merit, of whom Quebec has not yet lost the memory.' Young Pierre studied at the Quebec seminary with his brother William, who died at twenty-one. He was a talented young man, and by reason of his intelligence, excellent memory, and a profound taste for reading serious and instructive works, gave much promise for the future. On October 1, 1846, he was ordained priest, and served for a time as Vicar at the Quebec Cathedral. In 1847, a scourge visited Quebec, a sort of ships' fever; thousands died; many children were orphaned. Some of them were placed in St. Bridget's Asylum in Father Saxe's charge and he … contracted the terrible fever which endangered his life for many days.

"In September, 1850, he was designated to represent his diocese at Rome at the consecration of Grand Vicar C. F. Bailargeon as Bishop of Quebec. In October, 1854, he was named by the Bishop as priest of Sainte Romauld, and it is there, according to Abbe d'Emirs, 'that Providence decreed that all the qualities of his fine intelligence and of his truly broad and judicial spirit, should flourish.' Emirs continues: 'From the first words that he addressed to his parishioners on October 8th, in an improvised chapel in which they found themselves tightly packed, he asked of them three things – courage, generosity and good will; courage to build a rectory and a church commensurate with the present and future needs of the new parish; – generosity, to face the very considerable expenses that were required from the small resources at hand, and, above all, good will was required, to overcome difficulties, to preserve harmony among all, and to direct every effort toward a common end. On coming from the chapel, after the first sermon, which the priest had delivered both in French and English with equal facility, a venerable old gentleman pronounced the ... prophetic words, 'We have just the priest that we need.'

"Father Saxe built his church. The Canadian Government assisted his parishioners by contributing $20,000, and he himself contributed most of his own inheritance from his father and mother. Later, on one of several missions on which his Bishop sent him to Rome, he brought back with him a celebrated Munich artist, named Lamprich, who resided with him for three years and decorated the interior of the church. Both the church and its beautiful decorations, including a portrait of Father Saxe, still remain, a shrine frequently visited by tourists.

"Pierre Saxe, follower after Pierre Marquette, is held in the affectionate memory of Canadians and of his family, who associate with his name the romanticism of all our early pioneers. Simple and courageous, he realized his great ambition, though it did not transcend a parish, and his work lives after him."

22. George SAXE. Born in Sep 1827. George died in 1900, he was 72.[*]

23. William Holt SAXE. Born on 10 May 1809. William Holt died on 26 Aug 1880, he was 71. Buried in 1880 in Chazy, Clinton Co., N.Y. Father of one by the second of his three wives.

    About 1840 when William Holt was 30, he first married Eliza J. BURROUGHS. Born on 25 Feb 1823. Eliza J. died in 1859, she was 35.

    About 1860 when William Holt was 50, he second married Sarah E. BURROUGHS. Born on 17 Sep 1843. Sarah E. died on 25 Oct 1865, she was 22. Occupation: Mother of 1; 3 grandchildren.
They had one child:
    91   i.   William Holt (1861-1917)

    About 1867 when William Holt was 57, he third married Louisa J. HALL, daughter of Hiram HALL & Susan HALL. Born on 19 Jun 1840 in Isle La Motte, Grand Isle, Vt. Louisa J. died on 13 Jan 1817 in Isle La Motte, Grand Isle, Vt. Buried in 1817 in Chazy, N.Y. Her middle initial is given as M. in *Genealogy of the Saxe Family*, but it is J. in Stratton's *Isle La Motte*, p. 294.

---

[*] One error in the Sierra "Family Tree" software should be noted: The age of individuals is sometimes computed incorrectly unless both the exact date of birth and death are known. For example, in the case of 22. George Saxe, it would have more accurate to say, "he was 72, or in his 72d year."

24. Maria Ann SAXE. Born on 10 Nov 1807. Maria Ann died in Lockport, N.Y. on 27 Sep 1891, she was 83. Occupation: Mother of 3 by her second husband.
On 31 Dec 1825 when Maria Ann was 18, she first married Edmund RICHARDSON, in Montreal, Quebec, Canada.
Maria Ann second married Hezekiah Wilcox SCOVELL, in Lockport, N.Y.

25. Charlotte Holt SAXE. Born in Dec 1810. Charlotte Holt died in Dec 1811, age 1.

26. George W. SAXE. Born on 17 Jan 1818. George died on 28 Aug 1854, age 36.

27. Henry G. SAXE. Born on 12 Jul 1819. Henry G. died on 27 Nov 1897, he was 78.
On 10 Oct 1848 when Henry G. was 29, he married Elizabeth DOUGLASS; born in 1823. Elizabeth died in 1903, she was 80. Occupation: Mother of 5.

28. Elizabeth Catherine SAXE. Born on 7 Apr 1828. Occupation: Mother of 4.
Elizabeth Catherine married Andrew FERGUSON, M.D.

29. Julia Frances SAXE. Born on 17 Jun 1830. Julia died on 13 Feb 1914, age 83.
Julia Frances married Rev. Derwin SHARTS.

30. Mathew Conrad SAXE. Born on 15 Aug 1832. Mathew Conrad died in Fresno, Calif. Unmarried.

31. Mary Helen SAXE. Born on 28 Oct 1834. Mary Helen died on 4 Nov 1913, she was 79. Resided at Suspension Bridge, N.Y.
On 7 May 1856 when Mary Helen was 21, she married Leander COLT.
They had one child:
    92   i.   Julia Maria

32. Anna Maria SAXE,[52] daughter and only child of Godfrey Saxe, was born in Vermont, 13 February 1804; died at Mooers, Clinton County, N.Y., 4 February 1890 and was buried there in the Old Mooers Village Cemetery. Her given name has also been spelled as Anne W., and her surname as Sachs. The name of her mother is not known, but it may be Anna. She married, 8 July 1823, Joseph H. Stockwell, son of Ebenezer and Abi (Holbrook) Stockwell; born at Bennington, Vermont [or possibly New Hampshire], in April or May 1802; died at Bennington, 22 September 1870. Joseph and Anna (Saxe) Stockwell had 12 children, of whom the seventh, Benajah – who was born at Stanbridge, Quebec – was the father of Jessie F. Stockwell. A younger son, Samuel S. Stockwell, who was perhaps their eleventh child, married Susan Woodley of Mooers, N.Y.

    The Woodleys and the Stockwells were connected through the marriage of Samuel S. Stockwell to Susan Woodley. Samuel probably cared for his widowed mother, Anna (Saxe) Stockwell, until she died in 1890. He died sometime thereafter, survived by his wife, Susan (Woodley) Stockwell. Susan arranged for her mother-in-law to be buried in the Woodley family plot or section of the Old Mooers Cemetery.

Many members of the Woodley family were buried in the Old Mooers Cemetery, and Woodley burials continued there until well into the twentieth century. A tall gravestone in this cemetery is inscribed "WOODLEY" on the base. On one side is inscribed "Anna M. Saxe / Wife of Jos. Stockwell / Died Feb. 4, 1890 / AE. 86 Ys." On another side is inscribed "Wilbur K. / 1872-19   / Jennie L. / His Wife / 1872-1939 /." In this plot, there are also headstones for Wilbur / Jennie. Wilbur K. Woodley is the nephew of Anna's daughter-in-law, Mrs. Samuel S. (Susan Woodley) Stockwell. It is not clear why she was interred in this plot, for she died in 1890 when Wilbur and his wife Jennie were only 18 years old. Indeed, it is not known if Wilbur and Jennie were even married by 1890.[53]

The tall stone on which Anna's name is inscribed was probably erected in the twentieth century, but her name and that of her late husband are recorded clearly. Her age on the tombstone is not quite correct, in that she died six days before her 86th birthday. Susan (Woodley) Stockwell died in 1921 at age 77 in Nashua, N.H., and although her burial site is unknown, it seems likely that she may also be buried in the Woodley plot in the Old Mooers Cemetery.

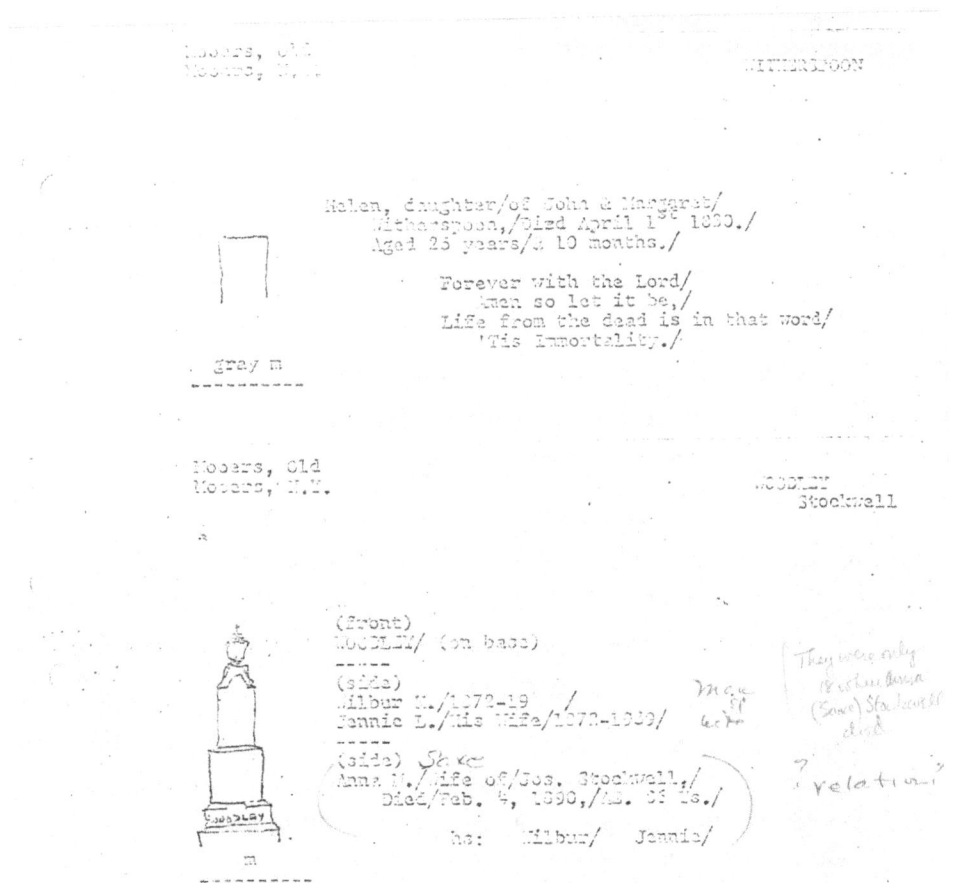

Gravestone of Anna (Saxe) Stockwell, Woodley lot, Old Mooers Cemetery, Clinton Co., N.Y.

In a letter to George Hill on 12/21/05, Addie L. Shields, Historian, Clinton County, N.Y., suggests a reason that Anna (Saxe) Stockwell was buried in the Woodley lot in the Old Mooers Cemetery: "I believe that she may have been living with her sister [actually, not her sister, but her daughter-in-law, Susan (Woodley) Stockwell] . ... Note that she died in February in the year of 1890 ... and the Woodley Family were respectful of her and placed her name on the stone as Stockwell's widow. Where ever and when ever he died there may not have been money for a stone [actually, he was buried in Bennington]. As a widow lady she endeared herself to this family ... and there is no stone for Joseph. Widows had a difficult time in that time frame. This was a wilderness for a long time."[54]

A page of Stockwell births that is laid into the Hill Family Bible (which was in the possession of Myron Hill, Jr., of Clarion, Iowa, in 2005) shows "Joseph H. Stockwell was born May 5th, 1802 ... Anna M. Saxe was born February 10th, 1804 ... Joseph Stockwell was married to Anna M. Saxe July 8th, 1823." The births of eleven children are given, ending with Samuel S., and two lines which appear to be deaths of children.

Anna Saxe married, on 8 July 1823 (or possibly 1825), Joseph H. Stockwell, elder son and third of the seven children of Ebenezer and Abi (Holbrook) Stockwell; born in Bennington, Vermont, 5 May (or possibly April) 1802; died in Bennington, 22 September 1870, and was buried there.[55]

There is some doubt about Joseph Stockwell's birthplace. On the census of 1860, his birthplace is given as New Hampshire. However, there are no other references to New Hampshire in the migrations of his family, so Bennington, Vt., is likely to have been his birthplace. His mother was the widow of Joseph Lee of Dedham, Massachusetts, with two children by her first marriage. His parents moved several times during their married life. They first lived in Highgate Falls, Vermont, for about two years. In about 1800 they were located in Swanzey, a town that does not appear on the 1993 map of Vermont. They returned to Bennington for a short time, and finally went back to Highgate Falls, where his father died in 1828 and his mother died in 1846. Joseph Stockwell apparently did not have a middle name, but his middle initial was doubtless intended to recognize his mother's maiden name, Holbrook.

Joseph Stockwell and Anne Saxe were both living in the vicinity of Highgate, Vermont, when they were married. They lived in Highgate for about ten years and then moved to Stanbridge, Missisquoi County, Quebec, Canada, where they remained for about two decades. Stanbridge is only a few miles north of Lake Champlain and the Quebec-Vermont border. Joseph and Anna Stockwell had eleven or twelve children, who were born between 1824 and 1851. Their sixth child (Joseph Matthew) is said to have been born in Highgate, Vermont, in 1834, and their seventh (Benajah) in Stanbridge, Quebec, in 1836. At least two more of their children were born in Stanbridge, so we can assume that the family lived in Stanbridge from about 1835 until they moved back to the United States. Sometime after the adult baptism of some of their children in 1856, Joseph and Anna moved to New York State and lived just west of Lake Champlain at Mooers, Clinton County, N.Y. In 1860, at the age of 58, Joseph was living on a farm at Mooers, N.Y., with his 56-year old wife and their three youngest children – daughters aged 18 and 20 and a son aged 16 – and a 9-year old boy of unknown parentage. In this census, their son Joseph Matthew was then living in Highgate, Vt., at age 20; he was said to have been born in Vermont. Joseph H. Stockwell eventually returned to his birthplace, Bennington, Vermont, and died there. His son Godfrey E. Stockwell was named for his grandfather Godfrey Saxe, who was named for his grandfather Godfrey Saxe of Saxony. The name Godfrey also continued in the Saxe family for additional generations.[56]

Joseph and Anna (Saxe) Stockwell had eleven or twelve children, probably seven sons and five daughters, born at Stanbridge, Quebec: Mary (1824/26-ca. 1898); Godfrey (1827-1878); Abi (b.1828); David (1830-1912); Harriet (b.1832); Joseph (1834-1901); Benajah (1836-1919); Hermit or Kermit (b.1838); Lucy (b.1840); Malona (b.1842), Samuel (b.1844); and perhaps Joseph A. (b. 1851). Their fourth son and seventh child, Benajah Flavel, is the father of Jessie F. Stockwell. Marriages were recorded for all five daughters and five of the sons. The five married sons all had issue, although nothing more is known of the families of the daughters. The daughters married members of the Seagel, Safford, Bickford, Dunham, and Woodley families. The sons married members of the Dill, Tye, Hogaboom, Hyde, and Woodley families.

They had the following children:
93	i.	Mary A. [174131] (1824-<1898)
94	ii.	Godfrey E. [174132] (1827-1878)
95	iii.	Abi R. [174133] (1828-)
96	iv.	David [174134] (1830-1912)
97	v.	Harriet S. [174135] (1832-)
98	vi.	Joseph Matthew [174136] (1834-1901)
99	vii.	Benajah Flavel [174137] (1836-1919)
100	viii.	Hermit (Kermit) [174138] (1838-<1898)
101	ix.	Lucy Ann [174139] (1840-)
102	x.	Malona Marcia [1-7-4-1-3-10] (1842-)
103	xi.	Samuel S. [1-7-4-1-3-11] (1844-<1921)
104	xii.	Joseph A. (1851-)

33. Hon. Charles Jewett SAXE. Born on 25 Mar 1814 in Highgate, Franklin Co., Vt. Charles Jewett died in Troy, N.Y. on 1 Oct 1867, he was 53. Occupation: Member of the N.Y. Assembly. He is #601, p. 24 in *Genealogy of the Saxe Family*, which on p. 64 quotes from "Biographical Sketches of the State Officers and Members of the Legislature of the State of New York in 1861" regarding his ancestors, who he was told by this aunt Hannah (Saxe) Scovell were of the Royal Family of Saxe-Gotha.[57]

On 22 Feb 1844 when Charles Jewett was 29, he first married Susan Maria BAKER. Born on 4 Dec 1822. Susan Maria died on 5 Nov 1847, she was 24. Occupation: Mother of 2.

They had the following children:
105	i.	Amelia Elizabeth (1844-1845)
106	ii.	Charles Hammon (1846-1847)

Charles Jewett second married Ellen GRIGGS. Born on 5 May 1824. Ellen died in Brookline, Mass. on 27 Mar 1904, she was 79. Occupation: Mother of 6, all of whom were born at Troy, N.Y.

They had the following children:
107	i.	Charles Griggs (1855-1862)
108	ii.	William Arthur (1857-1917)
109	iii.	Edward Thomas (1860-1924)
110	iv.	James Alfred (1863->1930)

| 111 | v. | John Walter (1863-1929) |
| 112 | vi. | Mary Ellen (1865-1903) |

34. Hon. John Godfrey SAXE L.L.D.[58] Born on 2 Jun 1816 in Highgate, Franklin Co., Vt. John Godfrey Saxe died in Albany, Albany Co., N.Y., on 31 Mar 1887, he was 70. Occupation: lawyer, humorist, and "a noted American poet" who wrote "The Blind Men and the Elephant." Education: Middlebury College, B.A. (1839), LL.D. (1866).

He was Attorney General of Vermont in 1856 and twice ran unsuccessfully for Governor of Vermont. The *Concise Dictionary of American Biography* (1964) says that he was the author, among other books, of *Progress: A Satirical Poem* (1846), *The Money-King and Other Poems* (1860), and *Leisure-Day Rhymes* (1875). *Bartlett's Familiar Quotations* (1955) quotes from his poems "My Castle in Spain," "The Gifts of the Gods," "Wishing," "I'm Growing Old," "My Familiar," "The Game of Life," "The Blind Men and the Elephant," "The Library," and "Echo." He is profiled on several websites that appear in a search via Google, such as "Strangers to Us All: Lawyers and Poetry" with a copy of pages from Evert A. and George L. Duyckinck, *The Cyclopedia of American Literature* (1880), which shows his autograph and a drawing of his face and shoulders in profile at age 32, and other illustrations and citations. From <http://www.edu/~lawfac/jelkins/lp-2001/saxe.html> accessed 7/31/2005.

His biography appears in *The Poetical Works of John Godfrey Saxe* (Boston: Houghton, Mifflin, 1892 [orig. 1859]), v-vi. Although the introduction to this work says, "Of his ancestry and of his early life little has been recorded," the biographical sketch states that he was born in Highgate, Vt., 2 June 1816, and entered Wesleyan University at age 19 but left and then entered Middlebury College, from which he received the bachelor's degree in 1839. Middlebury awarded him the LL.D. in 1866. He suffered a "shock" in a railway accident in Virginia in 1874, from which he "never wholly recovered," and was in "almost absolute" seclusion after a series of bereavements in which over a brief period of time he lost his wife, three daughters, and his eldest son. He then left Brooklyn to live with a son in Albany, and he died there on 31 March 1887.

Several citations on the website of the *New England Historical and Genealogical Register* state that John G. Saxe, L.L.D., was a descendant of Samuel Slafter, first treasurer of the proprietors of New Hampshire (and thus of Vermont). It is said that "John Slaughter . . . came from Great Britain to Lynn about 1680, and to Connecticut about 1716. A son Samuel, one of the original proprietors and first treasurer of Norwich, Vermont, had twelve children; among them were Eunice Slafter of Norwich, grandfather [?] of John G. Saxe the poet, and . . ." It therefore appears that John G. Saxe's mother, Elizabeth Jewett, was the granddaughter of Eunice Slafter. See *NEHGR* 23:70 (1869) and 24:97 (1870).

A man named John Godfrey Saxe is said to be the author known as J.G.S. who wrote *Genealogy of the Saxe Family* ([n.p.], 1930), 88 pp. This work is listed in "Recent

Publications" in *NEHGR* 84:240 (1930). J.G.S. says that he was a grandson of the poet, and I have therefore referred to him as John Godfrey Saxe II.

On 9 Sep 1841 when John Godfrey was 25, he married Sophia Newell SOLLACE, daughter of Judge Calvin SOLLACE & Sophia BASCOME. Occupation: Mother of 6.
    "In September, 1841, the young poet was married to Sophia Newell Sollace, a daughter of Judge Calvin Sollace. There were three intermarriages between the Saxes and the Sollaces. Calvin Sollace married Sophia Bascome, daughter of Susannah Stetson Bascome; Calvin's sister, Hepsibeth, married Nathaniel Bosworth; Calvin's daughters Sophia Newell Saxe and Sarah S. Saxe married John Godfrey Saxe and James Saxe, respectively; Nathaniel Bosworth's son, Justice Joseph Sollace Bosworth, married Frances Pumpelly. John and Sophia's son, John Theodore, married Justice Bosworth's daughter, Mary Bosworth."

They had the following children:
- **113**   i.   John Theodore (1843-1881)
- **114**   ii.   George Brown (1846-1847)
- **115**   iii.   Charles Gordon (1848-1893)
- **116**   iv.   Sarah Elizabeth (1850-1879)
- **117**   v.   Harriet Sollace (1853-1881)
- **118**   vi.   Laura Sophia (1856-1874)

35. Col. Peter SAXE. Born on 27 Jul 1819 in Highgate, Franklin Co., Vt. Peter died in San Francisco, Calif. on 7 Nov 1891, he was 72.
"603.[*] PETER SAXE, M. Sarah Keith Drury, Sept. 14, 1839, who was born March 24, 1818 at Highgate, D. May 28,1896, at San Francisco, Cal. Colonel Peter Saxe left Highgate while a young man and moved to Western New York, and later to Troy and then to Battle Creek, Michigan, where he was engaged in business for many years. In 1870, he went to live in San Francisco, where he died. He was over six feet in height, with a commanding presence. He was famed as a wit and was generally admired and beloved."
On 14 Sep 1839 when Peter was 20, he married Sarah Keith DRURY, daughter of Abel DRURY & Sarah KEITH. Born on 24 Mar 1818 in Highgate, Vt. Sarah Keith died in San Francisco, Calif. on 28 May 1896, she was 78.
They had the following children:
- **119**   i.   Rollin Peter (1840-1903)
- **120**   ii.   Minerva Drury (1842-1851)
- **121**   iii.   Homer Polk (1844-1921)
- **122**   iv.   Howard Martin (1847-1863)

36. James SAXE. Born on 9 Nov 1823 in Highgate, Franklin Co., Vt. James died in St. Albans, Franklin Co., Vt. on 15 Jun 1884, he was 60.
"604. JAMES SAXE, M. Sarah Storrs Sollace …
  B. Dec. 9, 1828, D. May 20, 1921 at Montreal, Canada. James Saxe lived at St. Albans, Vermont, and his family was born there. His residence was one of the outstanding places

---
[*] Numbers such as this (603) are in the original document by J.G.S., *Genealogy of the Saxe Family*.

in the community and a picture of it was carried at one time on the official maps. He was a fine type of old country gentleman, distinguished in appearance, six feet, two inches in height, always dignified and courteous. When he died, Mrs. Saxe moved to Montreal, Canada, with her family, which included John Godfrey Saxe, then an orphan. She bought a residence on St. Luke Street, where, in 1929, her three daughters, Lillian, Fanny and Mary (Mollie), and her son Charles still reside. She lived to be ninety-three years of age, and was very sweet and beautiful, both in youth and middle age, and as an old lady. James married Sarah Storrs SOLLACE, daughter of Judge Calvin SOLLACE of Vermont & Sophia BASCOME. Born on 9 Dec 1828. Sarah Storrs died in Montreal, Quebec, Canada on 20 May 1921, she was 92.

They had the following children:

123	i.	Elizabeth Lillian "Lillie" Sophia (1852-)
124	ii.	Franklin James (1854-)
125	iii.	William Henry (1856-1903)
126	iv.	Ellen Sollace (1858-1862)
127	v.	Fanny Maria (1860-)
128	vi.	Mary Sollace "Mollie" (1865-1942)
129	vii.	Charles Jewett (1870-)

37. Rev. Alfred SAXE. Born on 5 Sep 1814. Alfred died on 8 Oct 1846.
701. REV. ALFRED SAXE, M. Elizabeth Chase.

Rev. Alfred Saxe was a graduate of Wesleyan University, 1838. At fifteen, he matured his purpose to preach and worked industriously so as to get through school and college before he became of age. It was said of him that "from the moment he resolved upon the ministry, almost to the hour of his death, his energies were devoted to his work. Every hour was employed to its full extent to the accomplishment of some high purpose." Judged by his contemporaries, "he was a man of vigorous and active intellect, characterized by quickness of apprehension and soundness of judgment. Energy and perseverance were also striking traits of character." He bequeathed unto several of his descendants the noble aspirations of preacher and missionary.

Alfred married Elizabeth CHASE.

They had the following children:

130	i.	Alfred Henry (1839-1881)
131	ii.	Walter
132	iii.	William F. (1842-1884)
133	iv.	Ellen B.

38. Robert Jenkins SAXE. Born on 23 Jun 1816. Robert Jenkins died on 11 May 1894, he was 77. On 25 Dec 1843 when Robert Jenkins was 27, he married Rebecca Munson WEAD. Born on 20 Jun 1819. Rebecca Munson died in Omaha, Neb. on 1 Apr 1887, she was 67. Occupation: Mother of 7, all born at Sheldon, Vt.

They had the following children:

134	i.	Alfred Jenkins (1846-1847)
135	ii.	Frances Maria (1847-1847)
136	iii.	Elizabeth Wead (1848-1877)
137	iv.	Alfred (1852-1871)

138	v.	Arthur Wellesley (1857-1919)
139	vi.	DeForest Wead (1858-1924)
140	vii.	Robert Jenkins (1861-1876)

39. Edward SAXE. Born on 19 Nov 1818. Edward died in Corinth, Miss. on 6 Apr 1862, he was 43. Mrs. George Fuller Tuttle, *Three Centuries in Champlain Valley* (Plattsburgh, N.Y.: Saranac Chapter, D.A.R., 1909), 99: "April 6 1862 Was killed in battle Capt. Edward Saxe, grandson of the pioneer John Saxe and son of Jacob who first engaged in business in Sheldon, Vt., and afterwards with his brothers Matthew and Peter at West Chazy."[59] This was the battle known thereafter as the Battle of Shiloh. Edward married Kate C. VOSBURGH. Mother of 4, the youngest b. 14 Jan 1861.
They had the following children:

141	i.	Rowena
142	ii.	Louise Maria
143	iii.	Edward Jacob
144	iv.	Alfred Jenkins (1861-)

40. Dr. Arthur Wellesley SAXE. Born on 30 Oct 1820. Arthur Wellesley died in Santa Clara, Calif. on 26 May 1891, he was 70. In Dec 1844 when Arthur Wellesley was 24, he married Mary E. JUDSON. Born on 11 Jan 1821. Mary E. died in California on 14 Jan 1894, she was 73. Occupation: Mother of 4.
They had the following children:

145	i.	Frederick Judson
146	ii.	Mary Elizabeth
147	iii.	Arthur William
148	iv.	Frank K.

41. Rev. George Godfrey SAXE. Born on 11 Aug 1822. George Godfrey died on 22 Dec 1896, he was 74.
705. REV. GEORGE GODFREY SAXE, M. May 23, 1849, Huldah K. Merwin,
George Godfrey Saxe was born at Plattsburg, N. Y. In 1848 he entered the ministry and became Pastor of the Methodist Church at Fairhaven, Vermont. In 1856, his health becoming impaired, he was constrained to retire from the active ministry. Later, he accepted a professorship in the Troy Conference Academy at Poultney, Vermont. In 1862, he came to New York City and entered business, forming partnerships of Saxe & Robertson and, later, Estey & Saxe. He was an active member of the latter firm at the time of his death. During the last thirteen years of his life, he and his family resided at Madison, N. J., he taking an active part in the First Methodist Episcopal Church, occasionally occupying its pulpit.
On 23 May 1849 when George Godfrey was 26, he married Huldah K. MERWIN. Occupation: Mother of 8.
They had the following children:

149	i.	Ellen Merwin (1850-1889)
150	ii.	Edward C. (1851-1854)
151	iii.	Arthur M. (1853-1855)
152	iv.	Carrie A. (1857-1858)

153	v.	George G. (1864-1900)
154	vi.	Herbert Kimball (1868-)
155	vii.	Theodore James (1869-1870)
156	viii.	Marion Freer (1871-)

42. Frederic SAXE. Born abt 1823. Frederic died bef 1824, he was 1.

43. Rowena SAXE. Born abt 1824. Rowena died bef 1825, she was 1.

44. Maria SAXE. Born on 23 Jul 1826. Maria died on 30 Dec 1854, she was 28.
Occupation: Mother of 1, with 4 grandchildren.
In 1848 when Maria was 21, she married George Byron HYDE.
They had one child:
157	i.	Alice Rowena

45. Jacob William SAXE. Born on 2 Mar 1830. Jacob William died on 13 Dec 1883, he was 53. Occupation: Father of 9 by 2 wives.
Jacob William first married Grace B. DRURY. Occupation: Mother of 7.
They had the following children:
158	i.	Frances Caroline (1856-1888)
159	ii.	Mabel Wead (1858-1925)
160	iii.	Luther Drury (1861-1861)
161	iv.	Ralph Jacob (1862-1908)
162	v.	Grace Maria (1865-1914)
163	vi.	Charles Philip (1867-1909)
164	vii.	William Jenkins (1871-1908)

Jacob William second married Abagail DREW. Occupation: Mother of 2.
They had the following children:
165	i.	Katherine (1882-)
166	ii.	Alfred Keith

46. Caroline SAXE. Born on 18 Apr 1832. Caroline died on 4 Nov 1851, age 19.

47. Hannah SAXE. Born on 18 Mar 1834. Hannah died on 31 May 1916, she was 82.

48. Heman Allen SAXE. Born on 27 Feb 1836. Heman died on 30 Mar 1915, he was 79.
On 6 Sep 1865 when Heman Allen was 29, he married Flora Jane DANIELS.
Occupation: Mother of 4.
They had the following children:
167	i.	John D. (1868-)
168	ii.	Alfred W. (1870-)
169	iii.	Emma Rowena (1873-)
170	iv.	Robert Edward (1883-)

49. Rowena Keith SAXE. Born on 21 Apr 1839. Rowena Keith died on 29 Mar 1915, she was 75. Occupation: Mother of 4.

John Saxe, Loyalist

On 9 Jun 1863 when Rowena Keith was 24, she married Emerson Willard KEYES. Occupation: Editor of *Keyes' N.Y. Court of Appeals Reports*.
They had the following children:
- 171 i. Arthur (1864-1878)
- 172 ii. Conrad Saxe (1874-)
- 173 iii. Homer Eaton (1875-)
- 174 iv. Rowena Keith (1880-)

50. Loan D. SAXE. Born on 20 Nov 1816. Loan D. died on 25 Sep 1851, age 34.

51. Horace Jacob SAXE. Born on 21 Mar 1818. He died on 14 Feb 1874, age 55.

52. Edwin A. SAXE. Born on 13 Nov 1819. Edwin A. died on 19 Feb 1899, age 79.

53. Clarissa Eliza SAXE. Born on 15 Jun 1824. Clarissa Eliza died on 19 Nov 1870, she was 46. Occupation: Mother of 6.
On 1 Jan 1845 when Clarissa Eliza was 20, she married James P. PLACE.
They had the following children:
- 175 i. Lizzie Landis (1846-1851)
- 176 ii. Harriet Saxe (1848-)
- 177 iii. Sarah Griffin (1850-1929)
- 178 iv. William Aubrey (1852-1907)
- 179 v. James Conrad (1854-)
- 180 vi. Charles Henry (1856-1907)

54. Hannah SAXE. Born on 16 Jan 1827. Hannah died in Swanton, Vt. on 28 Nov 1909, she was 82. Occupation: Mother of 3. She was the principal source of the Highgate, Vt., Town Records that J.G.S. used to prepare *Genealogy of the Saxe Family*.
805. HANNAH SAXE, M. Zephaniah Keith Drury, Oct. 31, 1849.[60]

"Hannah Saxe Drury was born at Saxe's Mills, Highgate, Vermont. Throughout her long life, the members of the Saxe family rallied around her. She knew all of her relatives, even to the more remote ones. To the home which she and Zephaniah Drury established at the very edge of the States, a mile north of Saxe's Mills, came Saxes and Drurys from all points of the compass, from Quebec; Toronto; Montreal; Alton, Illinois; Lockport, New York, Boston and San Francisco. She corresponded with them all. Family records compiled by her have been extensively used in this Genealogy. With a district school beginning, she educated herself by much reading of books and periodicals. Few women read newspapers as she did. From the visitors to her hospitable home she learned constantly, for she preferred to talk of the more important affairs rather than the trivial. She traveled, too. As a little girl, with her father, she took a boat on the Erie Canal to visit her aunt, Mrs. Scovell, at Lockport. She went twice to St. Louis, the second time continuing her trip to Arizona and California. New York, Boston and Quebec she visited many times. Following her own schooling, she taught school for a number of terms. After her marriage, she kept the town records of the Town of Highgate for her husband, who was Town Clerk. Her well-rounded, painstaking hand-writing fills many a page of the old records. On one occasion, several people voted for her for Town

Clerk, although at that time, it was an almost unheard of thing for a woman to be considered for public office. During the last seventeen years of her life, she lived with her daughter, Mrs. Clarence E. Allen, at Swanton, Vermont, and to the end, in her eighty-second year, her keen interest in the Saxe family continued."

Before May 1851, when Hannah was 24, she married Zephanaih Keith DRURY, son of Abel DRURY & Sarah KEITH. Zephanaih Keith died about 1892. Occupation: Town Clerk of Highgate, Vt., assisted by his wife, who survived him. He was a brother of Sarah Keith Drury, wife of Col. Peter Saxe.

They had the following children:
- **181**   i.   Horace S. (1852-1871)
- **182**   ii.   Sarah C. (1857-)
- **183**   iii.   Minerva Saxe (1866-)

55. Harriet T. SAXE. Born on 19 Feb 1830. Harriet died on 7 Jan 1833, age 2.

56. Charlotte Catherine SCOVELL. Born on 15 Mar 1814 in Orwell, Vt. Charlotte Catherine died in Niles, Mich. on 15 May 1883, she was 69.

On 11 Jun 1836 when Charlotte Catherine was 22, she married Hon. Charles JEWETT, son of _____ JEWETT, in Orwell, Vt. Occupation: Lawyer and judge of Weybridge, Vt., and later of Niles, Mich. Education: Middlebury College, A.M., 1834.

They had the following children:
- **184**   i.   Erwin Scovell (1839-1910)
- **185**   ii.   Edward Saxe (1842-1900)
- **186**   iii.   Ada Anna (1842-1907)
- **187**   iv.   Charles (1849-1850)
- **188**   v.   Charles (1854-1870)

57. Rowena SCOVELL. Born in Jul 1815. Rowena died in Aug 1815.

58. Juliette SCOVELL. Born on 20 Jul 1816 in Orwell, Vt. Juliette died in Lewiston, N.Y. on 15 Jul 1890, she was 73. Occupation: Mother of 1.

On 20 Jul 1841, she married Hetzel COLT, in Cambria, N.Y.

They had one child:
- **189**   i.   Josiah Boardman Scovell (1843-1914)

59. Fidelia SCOVELL. Born on 15 Nov 1817 in Orwell, Vt. Fidelia died in Lockport, N.Y. on 21 Feb 1853, she was 35. Occupation: Mother of 5.

On 1 Jan 1844 when Fidelia was 26, she married Hiram McCOLLUM, in Cambria, N.Y. Religion: He became a Roman Catholic, and all of his descendants were Roman Catholics.

They had the following children:
- **190**   i.   Hiram Thomas (1845-)
- **191**   ii.   Silas Wright (1846-)
- **192**   iii.   Anna Fidelia (1848-1913)
- **193**   iv.   John Timon (1850-1918)
- **194**   v.   Mary Elizabeth (1852-1918)

60. Stephen Decatur SCOVELL. Born on 16 Jan 1819 in Orwell, Vt. Stephen Decatur died in Vermontville, Mich. on 6 Jan 1850, he was 30.

On 17 Jan 1840 when Stephen Decatur was 21, he married Caroline Miranda PARKER, in Cambria, N.Y. Occupation: Mother of 4.
They had the following children:
- **195**   i.   Josiah Thomas (1841-1915)
- **196**   ii.   Augusta (1843-1869)
- **197**   iii.   William Parker (1846-1848)
- **198**   iv.   Alice Louisa (1848-1852)

61. Hon. Oliver Perry SCOVELL. Born on 24 Mar 1820 in Orwell, Vt. Oliver Perry died in Lewiston, N.Y. on 25 Mar 1912, he was 92. Occupation: Member of the N.Y. Assembly in 1861.

On 22 Nov 1846 when Oliver Perry was 26, he first married Elizabeth Eddy SHEPARD, in Lewiston, N.Y. Elizabeth Eddy died before May 1855.
They had the following children:
- **199**   i.   Elizabeth Shepard (1847-1847)
- **200**   ii.   Leonard Shepard (1853-1853)

Before Jun 1857 when Oliver Perry was 37, he second married Elizabeth JEWETT, daughter of _____[Father of Elizabeth2] JEWETT. Elizabeth died after December 1869. Occupation: Mother of 5.
They had the following children:
- **201**   i.   Anna Saxe (1858-1858)
- **202**   ii.   Oliver Perry (1859-1882)
- **203**   iii.   Elizabeth Eddy (1861-1876)
- **204**   iv.   Philo Jewett (1865-1914)
- **205**   v.   Josiah Boardman (1869-)

62. Thomas McDonough SCOVELL. Born on 12 Oct 1823 in Orwell, Vt. Thomas McDonough died in Lockport, N.Y. on 8 Aug 1898, he was 74.

On 18 Aug 1848 when Thomas McDonough was 24, he first married Mary ONDERDONK. Occupation: Mother of 3.
They had the following children:
- **206**   i.   Ella Elizabeth (1849-1851)
- **207**   ii.   Frank Thomas (1852-1874)
- **208**   iii.   Sammons Onderdonk (1866-1867)

On 1 Sep 1880 when Thomas McDonough was 56, he second married Nancy Valina CAMPBELL. Nancy Valina died after 1898. Occupation: d.s.p., residing at Buffalo.

4

Fourth Generation

63. David SEE. Born in 1812. David died in 1869, he was 57.
64. Maria Ann Saxe SEE.
65. Charles SEE.
66. William SEE.
67. Caroline SEE. Born on 12 Jan 1828. Caroline died on 14 Sep 1882, she was 54.
68. William H. SAXE. Born on 18 Mar 1834.
69. Charlotte SAXE. Born on 16 Feb 1836. Charlotte married John BROWN.
70. Agnes SAXE. Born on 14 Feb 1838. Agnes married J. WOODWARD.
71. Lucy SAXE. Born on 23 Mar 1840. Lucy married William N. GRIGGS.
72. George SAXE. Born on 7 May 1842. George died on 3 Mar 1863, he was 20.
73. Cecile SAXE. Born on 24 Mar 1846. Cecile died on 8 May 1859, she was 13.
74. John Matthew SAXE. Born on 29 May 1848.
75. Simon Peter SAXE. Born on 7 Sep 1850.
76. Mary SAXE. Born on 3 Mar 1854.
77. Ira Charles SAXE. Born on 24 Feb 1857.
78. Harriett Jane SAXE. Born on 22 Nov 1862.
79. Jane SAXE.
80. Olivia SAXE.
81. Cecile SAXE.
82. John SAXE.
83. Emily SAXE. Born on 28 Dec 1849. Emily died on 9 Apr 1908, she was 58.
84. Mary R. SAXE. Born on 30 Jan 1856.
85. Nettie SAXE. Born on 20 Apr 1857.
86. George SAXE. Born on 13 Sep 1833. George died on 10 Feb 1844, he was 10.
87. Helen SAXE. Born on 26 Aug 1836.
88. Cecile SAXE. Born on 18 Jul 1843. Cecile died on 27 Apr 1868, she was 24.
    Cecile married David S. HILLIARD.
89. William SARTELL.
90. Caroline GIBBS.
91. William Holt SAXE. Born on 8 Mar 1861. William Holt died in Chazy, Clinton Co., N.Y. on 7 Sep 1917, he was 56. On 7 Jan 1884 when William Holt was 22, he married Cora LADD.
They had the following children:
    209   i.   Sarah Electa
    210   ii.   William Holt (1889-1913)
    211   iii.   Emmerson Ladd
92. Julia Maria COLT. Born on Feb. 10, 1866. Julia married Francis F. LOVELL.

They had one child:
 212 i. Lawrence Colt (1894-1917).

93. Mary A. [174131] STOCKWELL[*] Born on 18 May 1824. Mary A. died before 5 Oct 1898, she was 74. Mary A. [174131] married _____ SEAGEL.

94. Godfrey E. [174132] STOCKWELL. Born on 7 Feb 1827. Godfrey E. [174132] died on 8 Mar 1878, he was 51. In 1848 when Godfrey E. was 20, he married Adelia Sophia DILL.
They had the following children:
 213 i. George J. [1741321]
 214 ii. Albert [1741322]
 215 iii. Charles H. [1741323]

95. Abi R. [174133] STOCKWELL. Born on 23 Dec 1828. Lived in Hannibal, NY, on 5 Oct 1898. Abi R. [174133] married ? SAFFORD.

96. David [174134] STOCKWELL. Born on 13 Nov 1830 in New York State. David [174134] died in St. Albans, VT on 9 Apr 1912, he was 81. He may have been a soldier in the Civil War.[61]
David married Margaret TYE (TIGHS). Born in Ireland. They had the following children:
 216 i. Willard [1741341] (1855-1913)
 217 ii. Margaret [1741342] (1858-1945)
 218 iii. Catharine H. [1741343] (1864-~1888)
 219 iv. Daniel [1741344] (1869-1967)
 220 v. Samuel A. [1741345] (1871-)
 221 vi. David [1741346] (1873-)

97. Harriet S. [174135] STOCKWELL. Born on 18 Dec 1832. Lived at Albert Lea, MN, on 5 Oct 1898. Harriet S. married ? BICKFORD.

98. Joseph Matthew [174136] STOCKWELL.[62] Born on 25 Nov 1834 in Highgate, VT. Joseph Matthew [174136] died in Highgate, VT on 29 Jun 1901, he was 66.
 Occupation: Joseph Stockwell appears as a farm laborer in Highgate, Vt., aged 20, in the census of 1860; b. in Vt. He was a soldier in the Civil War.
On 8 Feb 1861 when Joseph Matthew [174136] was 26, he first married Cordelia HOGABOOM, in Highgate, VT.
On 25 Jan 1867 he second married Eliza Ann HOGABOOM, daughter of Samuel HOGABOOM & Catharine BRYCE. Born on 10 Jul 1833. Eliza Ann died in St. Albans, VT on 25 Apr 1906, she was 72.
They had the following children:
 222 i. Annette V. [1741361] (1868-)
 223 ii. Millard Arthur [1741362] (1872-)

99. Benajah Flavel [174137] STOCKWELL,[63] third son and seventh child of Joseph and Anna Maria (Saxe) Stockwell, was born at Stanbridge, Quebec, Canada, 14 August 1836; died at Oklahoma City, Oklahoma, 28 March 1919.

---
[*] Person numbers in brackets are from Kennedy, *Stockwell Genealogy*, for this person and the Stockwells that follow.

Baptismal record of Benajah Flavel Stockwell, son of Joseph H. and Anna Maria Stockwell

He was baptized at the Methodist Church, Clarenceville, Quebec, on 16 November 1856, when he was 20 years old, and he was buried at Graceland Cemetery, Rowan, Iowa. He was a school teacher and a preacher. In 1851 he was living with his parents in Stanbridge, Missisquoi County, Quebec. In 1861 he was living in Mooers, New York, when he married a young woman from Highgate, Vermont, on the other side of Lake Champlain. He soon moved with her to Peoria, Illinois. After two years in Peoria, where their first two children were born, they moved back to Vermont, where they had another child. Benajah then moved to Fryeburg (later known as Rowan), Wright County, Iowa, in about 1870 with his wife and three children. Three more children were born in Iowa, in 1871, 1874, and 1877. His wife died in May 1879 and he remarried in November of the same year. His second wife was a widow with at least one child – a fifteen-year-old son – who was living with her, and probably also a daughter, who may have been married by then and was no longer living with her mother. In 1880, Benajah was living in Murray, Clarke County, Iowa, about 150 miles due south of Rowan, with his six children, who ranged in age from three to sixteen, and his second wife and her son, who was shown as a stepson, aged sixteen. In 1898 and 1900 he lived in Murray, Iowa, with his second wife and two daughters. In about 1912 he moved to Oklahoma, where he lived with a son. His second wife died in Oklahoma City in 1914 and he died there in 1918.[64]

A reunion of the entire Stockwell family took place in August 1909 at the home of B. F. Stockwell's daughter Jessie (Stockwell) Hill in Rowan, Iowa. The six children had not been together in the previous 23 years, and it is unlikely that they ever were all together again. Eugene was then living in Muskogee, Oklahoma, and Ruby was living in Sedgwick, Colorado. Herbert was in Beatrice, Nebraska. Grace and Emma were missionaries in Burma, although both were home on furlough at that time.[65]

His great-grandson, Foster Stockwell, wrote that, "He came with his family to Mooers, N.Y., about 1852. On October 5, 1861, he married Emily Lodiweska Hyde at Highgate, Vt., and shortly after the wedding, they moved to Peoria, Ill., where Benajah taught school and the first two children were born. They then returned to Vermont for three years, where the third child was born, and in the Spring of 1870 the family went to Fryeburg, near Rowan, Wright County, Iowa. There they homesteaded and the other children were born. Emily died on May 28, 1879, and Benajah then married Mrs. Lucy Hannings on Nov. 20, 1879. Benajah had no children by this second marriage, and Lucy died on March 30, 1914. Stockwell was a local preacher in the Methodist church. It is said in the family that he cast his first vote for Lincoln. His son, Eugene, cast his first vote for the Prohibition Party. Benajah died in this son's home in Oklahoma City, Okla., on March 28, 1919, after living with Eugene's family for six or seven years."

His grandson, the Rev. F. Olin Stockwell, wrote that, "He was a man who worked hard to wring a living out of the tough frontier soil. He wore a full white beard and impressed everyone with the joy of his Christian faith. He had an almost fanatical love of the church. He would borrow money at the bank to pay the preacher. He would go to prayer-meeting several miles away, no matter what the difficulty. One winter day, when one of the horses was sick, he put himself beside the other horse and helped draw the sleigh and the family to church."

He married (1), at Highgate, Vermont, 8 April 1861, Emily (or Emma F.) Lodiweska Hyde, fifth of the seven children of Harvey and Fidelia Gadcourt (Potter) Hyde; born 27 November 1840 at Highgate, Vermont; died in Wright County, Iowa, 28 May 1879. She was buried at a rural cemetery near Rowan that is no longer in existence and was later re-interred at the Graceland Cemetery in Rowan.

Benajah and Emily (Hyde) Stockwell had six children: Jessie Fidelia (1863-1940); Eugene Sanford (1865-1921); Ruby Ellen (b. 1868); Emma Caroline (b. about 1871); Herbert Emery (b. 1874); and Grace Lymna (b. 1877). The order of birth of the six children varies in the different references. Five of the children married and at least four had issue. At the time of his death, he was survived by 16 grandchildren and 18 great-grandchildren.

He married (2), in Wright County, Iowa, on 20 November 1879, Mrs. Lucy J. Hannings; born in New York State, 18 October 1833; died at Oklahoma City, Okla., 30 March 1914. Mrs. Hannings' maiden name is unknown. She had by her first husband a son, David A. Hannings (born about 1863), and perhaps also a daughter, Edith Hannings (born about 1853). There was no issue from the second marriage of Benajah Stockwell. Lucy (Hannings) Stockwell is buried in the Graceland Cemetery, Rowan, Iowa.[66]

Emily Lodiweska HYDE,[67] fifth of the seven children of Harvey and Fidelia G. (Potter) Hyde, was born at Highgate, Vermont, 27 November 1840; died at Wright County, Iowa, 28 May 1879. Her name has been variously spelled in different references; it has also been written as Emma F., Emma Lodwisca and Emily F.

After her marriage in 1861 to Benajah Stockwell, a teacher and Methodist preacher, she moved to Peoria, Illinois, where her husband taught school, and their first two children were born. They returned to Vermont for three years in about 1867, and their third child was born there in 1868. In the spring of 1870 they moved again, to Wright County Iowa, where they homesteaded at Fryeburg, near Rowan and the Iowa River. Fryeburg, too, has been spelled in various ways, including Fryburg and Fryeburgh. The three youngest children were born there, in 1871, 1874 and 1877. She died when her youngest child was two years old.

Benajah and Emily (Hyde) Stockwell had the following children:
224	i.	Jessie Fidelia [1741371] (1863-1940)
225	ii.	Eugene Sanford [1741372] (1865-1921)
226	iii.	Ruby Ellen [1741373] (1868-)
227	iv.	Herbert Emory [1741374] (1871-)
228	v.	Emma Caroline [1741375] (1874-)
229	vi.	Grace Lymna [1741376] (1877-)

Stockwell plot, graves of Benajah and Emily (Hyde) Stockwell, Graceland Cemtery, Rowan, Ia.

100. Hermit (Kermit) [174138] STOCKWELL. Born on 10 May 1838. Hermit (Kermit) [174138] died bef 5 Oct 1898, he was 60. Name is spelled Hennet C. Stockwell by Foster P. Stockwell.

101. Lucy Ann [174139] STOCKWELL. Born on 13 Aug 1840 in Stanbridge, CANADA. Was living 5 Oct 1898. On 19 Apr 1862 when Lucy Ann [174139] was 21, she married Martin DUNHAM. She was later of Bennington, VT.

102. Malona Marcia [1-7-4-1-3-10] STOCKWELL. Born on 20 Jun 1842 in Stanbridge, P.Q., CANADA. Was living at Mooers, NY, 5 Oct 1898. Malona Marcia [1-7-4-1-3-10] married ? WOODLEY.

103. Samuel S. [1-7-4-1-3-11] STOCKWELL,[68] sixth son and youngest of the eleven children of Joseph H. and Anna (Saxe) Stockwell, was born at Stanbridge, Quebec, Canada, 28 May 1844; died befor 16 Feb 1921. Samuel Stockwell was living in Mooers, N.Y., at the time of the U.S. census in 1880, and he and his family were living in Murray, Clarke County, Iowa, in October 1898. Samuel Stockwell died sometime before February 1921. His widow returned to New England and died at Nashua, N.H., in 1921.

He married, in about 1879, Susan A. Woodley, daughter and perhaps the fourth child of Samuel and Margaret Woodley; born at Scotia, N.Y., 17 June 1846; died at Nashua, N.H., 16 February 1921.[69]

Samuel and Susan (Woodley) Stockwell had the following children:
230	i.	Elizabeth M. [1-7-4-1-3-11-1] (1880-)
231	ii.	Ulysses S. [1-7-4-1-3-11-2] (1867-1891)
232	iii.	Charlie G. [1-7-4-1-3-11-3] (-1892)

| 233 | iv. | Ida [1-7-4-1-3-11-2] (1867-) |
| 234 | v. | Gertrude {1-7-4-1-3-11-4} (1873-) |

104. Joseph A. STOCKWELL. Born in 1851 in Stanbridge, CANADA.
105. Amelia Elizabeth SAXE. Born on 20 Dec 1844. Amelia died on 10 Apr 1845.
106. Charles Hammon SAXE. Born on 12 Nov 1846. Charles died on 20 Oct 1847.
107. Charles Griggs SAXE. Born on 21 Feb 1855. Charles died on 11 Jul 1862, age 7.
108. William Arthur SAXE. Born on 3 May 1857. William Arthur died in Baltimore, Md. on 28 Nov 1917, he was 60. On 31 Dec 1885 when William Arthur was 28, he first married Gertrude LOWRY.
They had one child:
    235   i.   Charles William
On 20 Oct 1913 when he was 56, he second married Ida May CONNOR.
They had one child:
    236   i.   Arthur Griggs
109. Edward Thomas SAXE. Born on 6 Jul 1860. Edward Thomas died in West Yarmouth, Mass. on 6 Jun 1924, he was 63. On 17 Sep 1891 when Edward Thomas was 31, he married Louise Wheaton CRUMP. Occupation: Mother of 3.
They had the following children:
    237   i.   Charles Edward
    238   ii.   Eugene Crump
    239   iii.   Katherine Louise
110. James Alfred SAXE.[70] Born on 2 Dec 1863. James Alfred died after 1930, he was 66. He was the twin brother of John Walter Saxe; he d.s.p.

"James and John were born in Troy, N. Y. on December 2, 1863. James devoted himself, during his early days at school and college, to athletics; but devoted sufficient time on study to pass all examinations. John devoted himself to his books. Both were musical; James had a good voice and played the violin; John played the flute remarkably well. They matriculated at Wesleyan University in 1881 and graduated in 1885, when twenty-one, each receiving the decree of Bachelor of Arts. James was captain of the baseball and football teams, and John an honor student; both were members of the Xi Chapter of Psi Upsilon. After a year's travel in the West and another year in Europe, they entered the senior year at Harvard College. They graduated with the Harvard Class of 1888, Bachelors of Arts, and, attending also the Commencement at Wesleyan for their triennial, they there received Master's degrees.

"James spent the following year in Germany studying music; John spent the year in a law office in Troy, N. Y. and attended the Albany Law School. The following summer, they spent walking in Switzerland, and then decided to graduate from the Harvard Law School and be admitted to the Massachusetts Bar. James spent the following year at Harvard Law School, while John studied at the Albany Law School, received his Bachelor of Laws degree and was admitted to the New York Bar. The following year, he was admitted to the second year law at the Harvard Law School on examination, and both of them graduated from the Harvard Law School in 1892, Bachelors of Laws, – John an honor man, – and were admitted to the Massachusetts Bar. In 1890, the family moved from Troy, N. Y. to Brookline, Mass. and occupied their grandfather Griggs' homestead. James married immediately after being admitted to the bar, and spent the year in Europe with his wife. On his return, he and John opened their offices in Boston, as Saxe & Saxe.

"A Harvard class-mate who was at the head of the Massachusetts Title Insurance Co. made James its head examiner in the Middlesex Registry and two years later the State sent him to Worcester, Mass. for special work. There he founded the Worcester County Abstract Co. John married at thirty-five and had a charming home and successful office practice. His daughter was graduated from Radcliffe College, an honor student in Art. His son, John, was graduated from Harvard, an honor student in electrical engineering. His son, James, was graduated from the Connecticut Agricultural School, and is now a realtor in Santa Barbara, California. When John's wife died, he moved to Worcester and became attorney for the Worcester County Abstract Company. He lived for a time with James. For the last ten years, John lived at the Worcester Country Club. There, he died on the night of March 24, 1929. He had made his best score at golf that day. He is buried in the family lot at Oakwood Cemetery at Troy, N. Y. He ever 'proved an honor to his brother.' James 'carries on'. He and his wife spend their summers at Worcester, Mass., and their winters at the Isle of Pines, Cuba."

On 23 Jun 1892 when James Alfred was 28, he married Mary Alfred WICK, in Cleveland, Ohio.
They had the following children:
- **239a**   i.   a daughter
- **239b**   ii.   John
- **239c**   iii.   James

111. John Walter SAXE.[71] Born on 2 Dec 1863. John Walter died in Worcester, Mass. on 25 Apr 1929, he was 65. He was the twin brother of James Alfred Saxe. See above for a joint biography of James and John Saxe.
On 11 Apr 1899, at age 35, he married Sara F. BURTIS, in Brooklyn, N.Y.
They had the following children:
- **240**   i.   Eleanor Burtis
- **241**   ii.   John Burtis (1902-)
- **242**   iii.   James Burtis

112. Mary Ellen SAXE. Born 18 Dec 1865; died in Brookline, Mass., 11 May 1903.
113. John Theodore SAXE.[72] Born on 22 Apr 1843; died on 30 Jul 1881, he was 38.
John Theodore married Mary A. BOSWORTH, daughter of Justice Joseph Sollace BOSWORTH & Frances PUMPELLY.
They had one child:
- **243**   i.   John Godfrey (1877-)

114. George Brown SAXE. Born on 1 Feb 1846; died on 18 Nov 1847, he was 1.
115. Charles Gordon SAXE. Born on 7 Jan 1848; died on 16 Mar 1893, he was 45.
Charles Gordon Saxe married Ellen Merwin SAXE (149), daughter of Rev. George Godfrey SAXE (41) & Huldah K. MERWIN. Born on 19 Mar 1850. Ellen Merwin died on 14 Oct 1889, she was 39. Mother of 5, all born at Albany, N.Y.
They had the following children:
- **244**   i.   Laura Huldah
- **245**   ii.   Charles Merwin

246	iii.	Sophia Sollace
247	iv.	Jessie Ellen
248	v.	Ellen Mildred

116. Sarah Elizabeth SAXE. Born on 10 Feb 1850. Sarah died on 3 Oct 1879, age 29.

117. Harriet Sollace SAXE. Born on 14 Aug 1853. Harriet died on 3 Jun 1881, age 27.

118. Laura Sophia SAXE. Born on 13 Nov 1856. Laura died on 2 Jul 1874, she was 17.

119. Rollin Peter SAXE. Born on 22 Aug 1840. Rollin died on 25 May 1903, he was 62. Rollin Peter married Jodelphia Amelia ATWELL. Occupation: Mother of 1.

120. Minerva Drury SAXE. Born on 4 Jul 1842. Minerva died on 7 Nov 1851, age 9.

121. Homer Polk SAXE. Born on 5 Jun 1844. Homer Polk died on 22 Dec 1921, age 77.

122. Howard Martin SAXE. Born 1 Apr 1847; died on 25 Nov 1863, age 16.

123. Elizabeth Lillian "Lillie" Sophia SAXE-HOLMES. Born on 18 Sep 1852 in St. Albans, Franklin Co., Vt. No children. Elizabeth Lillian "Lillie" Sophia married John B. HOLMES.

124. Franklin James SAXE.[73] Born on 2 Jul 1854 in St. Albans, Franklin Co., Vt.

Franklin James married Mary MICKLE, daughter of Andrew H. MICKLE. No children by marriage to Frank Saxe. Her name was Mary (Reynolds) Mickle, so she may have been previously married. Her father was mayor of New York City in 1846.

125. William Henry SAXE. Born on 31 Mar 1856 in St. Albans, Franklin Co., Vt. William Henry died on 8 Aug 1903, he was 47.

126. Ellen Sollace SAXE. Born on 19 Feb 1858 in St. Albans, Franklin Co., Vt. Ellen Sollace died on 1 Feb 1862, she was 3.

127. Fanny Maria SAXE. Born on 6 May 1860 in St. Albans, Franklin Co., Vt.

128. Mary Sollace "Mollie" SAXE.[74] Born on 23 Feb 1865 in St. Albans, Franklin Co., Vt. Mary Sollace "Mollie" died in 1942, she was 76. Occupation: author and playwright of Montreal; libararian of Westmount, Quebec; unmarried.

129. Charles Jewett SAXE. Born on 6 May 1870. Occupation: architect, Montreal, Canada. Charles Jewett Saxe, member Royal Canadian Academy, was an architect of prominence at Montreal, Canada. He designed the new Court House and won many competitions, including the new Club House of the Royal Montreal Golf Club.

130. Rev. Alfred Henry SAXE. Born on 5 Aug 1839. Alfred Henry died in Walden, N.Y. on 11 Nov 1881, he was 42.

On 28 Feb 1866 when Alfred Henry was 26, he married Phoebe WISNER.
They had the following children:

249	i.	Alfred Jacob
250	ii.	Henry Wisner
251	iii.	Rowena Keith
252	iv.	Mary G.
253	v.	Maud Elizabeth
254	vi.	Agnes Esther

131. Walter SAXE.

132. William F. SAXE. Born on 30 Jul 1842. William F. died on 31 Jan 1884, age 41. William F. married Elizabeth SCOTT. Occupation: Mother of 1.
They had one child:

255	i.	Helen Douglas

133. Ellen B. SAXE.

134. Alfred Jenkins SAXE. Born on 30 Dec 1846. Alfred Jenkins died on 7 Nov 1847.
135. Frances Maria SAXE. Born on 30 Sep 1847. Frances Maria died on 24 Oct 1847.
136. Elizabeth Wead SAXE. Born on 31 Dec 1848. Elizabeth Wead died in Danville, N.Y. on 2 Jun 1877, she was 28. In 1870 when Elizabeth Wead was 21, she married Henry BASCOM.
137. Alfred SAXE. Born on 3 May 1852. Alfred died on 26 May 1871, he was 19.
138. Arthur Wellesley SAXE. Born on 29 Jun 1857. Arthur Wellesley died in Pittsburgh, Pa. on 3 May 1919, he was 61. On 25 Jun 1884 when Arthur Wellesley was 26, he married Mary Montgomery TILLOTSON. Occupation: Mother of 3.
They had the following children:
    256   i.   Marguerite
    257   ii.   Theodosia Wead
    258   iii.   Grace Elizabeth
139. DeForest Wead SAXE. Born on 30 Aug 1858. DeForest Wead died in Piedmont, Calif. on 30 Jun 1924, he was 65. DeForest Wead married Jimmie D. STITT. Occupation: Mother of 1.
They had one child:
    259   i.   Mary Franklyn
140. Robert Jenkins SAXE Jr. Born on 15 May 1861; died on 14 Aug 1876, he was 15.
141. Rowena SAXE.
142. Louise Maria SAXE.
143. Edward Jacob SAXE.
144. Alfred Jenkins SAXE. Born on 14 Jan 1861.
145. Frederick Judson SAXE.
146. Mary Elizabeth SAXE.
147. Arthur William SAXE.
148. Frank K. SAXE.
149. Ellen Merwin SAXE. Born on 19 Mar 1850. Ellen Merwin died on 14 Oct 1889, she was 39. Occupation: Mother of 5, all born at Albany, N.Y. Ellen Merwin married Charles Gordon SAXE (115), son of Hon. John Godfrey SAXE, L.L.D. (34) & Sophia Newell SOLLACE. Born on 7 Jan 1848. Charles died on 16 Mar 1893, he was 45.
Charles Gordon and Ellen Merwin (Saxe) Saxe had the following children:
    244   i.   Laura Huldah
    245   ii.   Charles Merwin
    246   iii.   Sophia Sollace
    247   iv.   Jessie Ellen
    248   v.   Ellen Mildred
150. Edward C. SAXE. Born in Jul 1851. Edward C. died on 16 Jan 1854, he was 2.
151. Arthur M. SAXE. Born on 14 Jan 1853. Arthur M. died on 16 Aug 1855, he was 2.
152. Carrie A. SAXE. Born on 6 Feb 1857. Carrie A. died on 1 Oct 1858, she was 1.
153. George G. SAXE. Born on 9 Jul 1864. George G. died on 25 Jun 1900, he was 35. George G. married Frances M. HARPER.
154. Herbert Kimball SAXE. Born on 29 May 1868. Herbert Kimball married Evelyn Foster FISHER. Occupation: Mother of 2.
They had the following children:
    260   i.   Ralph Godfrey

    261   ii.   Elizabeth D.

155. Theodore James SAXE. Born on 29 May 1869; died on 7 May 1870.

156. Marion Freer SAXE. Born on 27 Aug 1871. Occupation: Mother of 5.
On 30 Jun 1897 when Marion Freer was 25, she married Rev. Ralph Brainard URMY.
They had the following children:
    262   i.   Herbert
    263   ii.   Thomas Van Orden
    264   iii.   Ralph Brainard
    265   iv.   Keith Merwin
    266   v.   Marion Mabel

157. Alice Rowena HYDE. On 11 Sep 1871 Alice Rowena married Fayette DURANT.
They had the following children:
    267   i.   Ellen Hannah
    268   ii.   Caroline Maria
    269   iii.   Julia Ella
    270   iv.   Homer Eaton

158. Frances Caroline SAXE. Born on 4 Jul 1856. Frances Caroline died on 18 Mar 1888, she was 31. Occupation: Mother of 3. Frances Caroline married Rev. Edwin Pitman STEVENS.
They had the following children:
    271   i.   Grace Drury
    272   ii.   Elizabeth Frances
    273   iii.   Franklin Rand

159. Mabel Wead SAXE. Born on 3 Oct 1858 in Cambridge, Vt. Mabel Wead died in Swanton, Vt. on 13 Oct 1925, she was 67. Occupation: Mother of 3 by 1st husband.
On 1 Dec 1880 when Mabel Wead was 22, she first married Nahum Edward JENNISON, in Medford, Mass.
They had the following children:
    274   i.   Clark Saxe
    275   ii.   Ralph Drury
    276   iii.   Robert Farrar
Mabel Wead second married James Henry McKECHNIE.

160. Luther Drury SAXE. Born on 9 May 1861. Luther Drury died on 12 Oct 1861.

161. Ralph Jacob SAXE. Born on 21 Oct 1862; died in Tampa, Fl. in Jul 1908, age 45.
Ralph Jacob married Alice May PRESCOTT.

162. Grace Maria SAXE. Born on 1 Apr 1865. Grace Maria died on 16 Jan 1914, she was 48. Occupation: Mother of 3. On 14 Jun 1892 when Grace Maria was 27, she married Charles Lewis SEAVEY.
They had the following children:
    277   i.   Helen Saxe
    278   ii.   Harold V.
    279   iii.   Malcolm deForest

163. Charles Philip SAXE. Born on 12 Dec 1867. Charles Philip died in Wheaton, Ill. on 4 Nov 1909, he was 41. On 14 Oct 1896 when Charles Philip was 28, he married Ellen OFFICER, in LaGrange, Ill. Occupation: Mother of 4.
They had the following children:

280	i.	Frances Drury
281	ii.	Catherine Officer
282	iii.	Mary
283	iv.	Philip

164. William Jenkins SAXE. Born on 3 Sep 1871. William died in Feb 1908, age 36. William Jenkins married Gertrude COYLE.

165. Katherine SAXE. Born on 19 Jan 1882.

166. Alfred Keith SAXE.
Alfred Keith married Emma Marie JOHNSON. Occupation: Mother of 1.
They had one child:

284	i.	John Drew

167. John D. SAXE. Born on 4 Oct 1868. On 18 May 1903 when John D. was 34, he married Alice AGUIRE.

168. Alfred W. SAXE. Born n 22 May 1870. On 31 Dec 1895 when Alfred W. was 25, he married Florence OWEN.

169. Emma Rowena SAXE. Born in Apr 1873.
On 1 Oct 1892 when Emma Rowena was 19, she married Augustin RANKIN.

170. Robert Edward SAXE. Born on 22 May 1883.

171. Arthur KEYES. Born on 6 Aug 1864. Arthur died on 26 Jul 1878, he was 13.

172. Conrad Saxe KEYES. Born on 11 Sep 1874.
On 15 Sep 1903 when Conrad Saxe was 29, he married Grace Merwin BICKFORD.

173. Homer Eaton KEYES. Born on 21 Dec 1875.
On 2 Apr 1903 when Homer Eaton was 27, he married Caroline ABBOTT.
They had one child:

285	i.	Katherine Keith (1903-)

174. Rowena Keith KEYES. Born on 19 Feb 1880.

175. Lizzie Landis PLACE. Born on 3 Apr 1846. Lizzie died on 19 Nov 1851, age 5.

176. Harriet Saxe PLACE. Born on 22 Sep 1848. Occupation: Mother of 2.
On 7 Jan 1868 at age 19, she married George SMITH. Born on 28 May 1846.
They had the following children:

286	i.	Clara Fannie
287	ii.	Nellie Sophia

177. Sarah Griffin PLACE. Born on 23 Oct 1850. Sarah Griffin died in 1929, age 78. Sarah Griffin married Edgar J. CHAMBERLIN. Occupation: President, Grand Trunk Railroad.

178. William Aubrey PLACE. Born on 3 Nov 1852; died on 29 Aug 1907, age 54. William Aubrey married Emily HEFLON.

179. James Conrad PLACE. Born on 14 Aug 1854.
James Conrad married Alice May SEWARD. Occupation: Mother of 6.
They had the following children:

288	i.	James Fay
289	ii.	Olive F.
290	iii.	Clara L.
291	iv.	Ethel G.
292	v.	Ruth Saxe
293	vi.	Carl O.

180. Charles Henry PLACE. Born on 14 Aug 1856; died on 3 Nov 1907, age 51. Charles Henry married Lotta HALL. Born on 15 Nov 1884 in Ohio. Lotta died in Bersen, Calif. in Nov 1927, she was 42. Occupation: Mother of 1.
They had one child:
    294   i.   Graham

181. Horace S. DRURY. Born on 23 Feb 1852. Horace S. died on 8 Nov 1871, age 19.

182. Sarah C. DRURY. Born on 21 May 1857. Occupation: Mother of 4.
On 10 Dec 1878 when Sarah C. was 21, she married Edmond A. BOURETT.
They had the following children:
    295   i.   Hannah Lucile
    296   ii.   Hortense V. S.
    297   iii.   Edmond Calvin
    298   iv.   Frederick Drury

183. Minerva Saxe DRURY. Born on 8 Feb 1866. Occupation: Mother of 3. She provided a home for her mother, Hannah (Saxe) Drury, for the last 17 years of her life.
On 9 Oct 1888 when Minerva Saxe was 22, she married Clarence E. ALLEN M.D. Born on 23 Jan 1856.
They had the following children:
    299   i.   Horace Eugene (1890-)
    300   ii.   Clarence Keith
    301   iii.   Dorcas Irene

184. Capt. Erwin Scovett JEWETT. Born on 29 Apr 1849 in Niles, Mich. Erwin Scovett died in Kansas City, Mo. on 13 Feb 1910, he was 70. Occupation: Republican Councilman for many years in Kansas City, Mo. Capt., 1st Mich. Reg., 1864. Acting Assistant Inspector General for Department of the South; participated in Battles of James Island and Baldwin Field; and Aide to Gen. Potter at Pocolaligo, DeVeaux Neck and Honey Hill.
On 26 Nov 1862 when Erwin Scovett was 23, he married Amelia Virginia COX.
They had the following children:
    302   i.   Charles Cox (1863-)
    303   ii.   Thomas Scovell (1866-)
    304   iii.   Harry Erwin (1871-1901)
    305   iv.   May (1876-)

185. Major Edward Saxe JEWETT. Born on 21 Jul 1842 in Niles, Mich. Edward Saxe died in Kansas City, Mo. on 26 May 1900, he was 57. Entered West Point Military Academy Sept. 1, 1861; discharged Feb. 3, 1863 and later served as Major in Civil War.
On 21 Oct 1867 when Edward Saxe was 25, he first married Sarah Louise KIRSH, in Conneautville, Penn. No children.
On 1 May 1879 when Edward Saxe was 36, he second married Mary Hawley DAVIES, in Emporia, Kan.
They had the following children:
    306   i.   Katherine
    307   ii.   Charles Dean
    308   iii.   Edward Dickinson
    309   iv.   Gid Henry Chipman
    310   v.   Mabel Platte

John Saxe, Loyalist

186. Ada Anna JEWETT. Born on 21 Jul 1842 in Niles, Mich. Ada Anna died in St. Louis, Mo. on 18 Jan 1907, she was 64. On 11 Jan 1871 when Ada Anna was 28, she married William Edward JONES, in Niles, Mich. Occupation: Lawyer; General Claim Agent of Missouri Pacific R.R., St. Louis.
They had the following children:
- 311   i.   Allan Saxe
- 312   ii.   Katherine Scovell
- 313   iii.   George Bayard
- 314   iv.   Roland Jewett
- 315   v.   Walter Boardman

187. Charles JEWETT Jr. Born 1 Apr 1849 in Niles, Mich.; died 7 Sep 1850, age 1.

188. Charles JEWETT II. Born on 21 Jul 1854 in Niles, Mich. Charles died in Aug 1870, he was 16.

189. Josiah Boardman Scovell COLT. Born on 17 Mar 1843 in Lewiston, N.Y. Josiah Boardman Scovell died in Pittsburgh, Pa. on 14 Aug 1914, he was 71. Education: Oberlin. On 15 Jun 1865 when Josiah Boardman Scovell was 22, he married Mary Lydia HEWITT, in Lewiston, N.Y.
They had one child:
- 316   i.   Mary Elizabeth Scovell (1878-)

190. Hiram Thomas McCOLLUM. Born on 10 Sep 1845 in Lockport, N.Y. Occupation: Deputy Collector of Port of Suspension Bridge.
On 3 Feb 1868 when Hiram Thomas was 22, he married Margaret KEENAN, in Waterloo, N.Y. Occupation: Mother of 7.
They had the following children:
- 317   i.   James Bernard (1875-)
- 318   ii.   Francis Xavier (1887-1918)
- 319   iii.   Eugene Lawrence (1879-)

191. Silas Wright McCOLLUM. Born on 23 Dec 1846 in Lockport, N.Y. Occupation: Post Master, Lockport, N.Y. On 27 Nov 1873 when Silas Wright was 26, he married Ella K. ALLEN, in Houston, Texas. Occupation: Mother of 10.
They had the following children:
- 320   i.   Hiram (1878-1905)
- 321   ii.   Ella Kate (1885-)
- 322   iii.   Josephine (1890-)
- 323   iv.   Camille Scovell (1892-)

192. Anna Fidelia McCOLLUM. Born on 28 Dec 1848 in Lockport, N.Y. Anna Fidelia died in St. Catherines, Ontario, Canada on 24 Jan 1913, she was 64. Mother of 5.
Anna Fidelia married Dennis Charles McGUIRE.

193. John Timon McCOLLUM. Born on 8 Oct 1850 in Lockport, N.Y. John Timon died in Brawley, Calif. on 23 Nov 1918, he was 68. Education: Seminary of Our Lady of Angels, now Niagara University.
In Jun 1870 when John Timon was 19, he first married Mary MULLOY, in Newfane, N.Y. Occupation: Mother of 2.
On 26 Jul 1880 when John Timon was 29, he second married Mrs. Martha BALDWIN FLANNERY, in Franklin, La. Occupation: Mother of 1 by McCollom.
On 25 Nov 1913 when John Timon was 63, he third married Martha Jane STEWART, in

Brawley, Calif. No children.

194. Mary Elizabeth McCOLLUM. Born on 12 Sep 1852 in Lockport, N.Y. Mary Elizabeth died in El Paso, Texas on 1 Nov 1918, she was 66. Occupation: Mother of 8. On 30 Dec 1877 when Mary Elizabeth was 25, she married Francis Waters GALLAGHER M.D., in Lockport, N.Y. Occupation: Physician of Lockport, N.Y., St. Mary's, Kansas, and El Paso, Texas.

They had the following children:

324	i.	Paul
325	ii.	Hiram
326	iii.	Leo
327	iv.	Donald Joseph

195. Josiah Thomas SCOVELL.[75] Born on 29 Jul 1841 in Vermontville, Mich. Josiah Thomas died in Terre Haute, Ind. on 8 May 1915, he was 73. Occupation: Professor Sciences at Terre Haute, author, explorer. Education: Oberlin College, A.B. 1866, A.M., 1875; University of Michigan, post-graduate study in medicine.

On 25 Dec 1876 when Josiah Thomas was 35, he married Joanna JAMESON, in LaFayette, Ind. Occupation: Mother of 3.

They had:

328	i.	Robert Jameson (1887-)

196. Augusta SCOVELL. Born on 18 Jul 1843. Augusta died on 18 Jan 1869, she was 25. Occupation: d.s.p.

197. William Parker SCOVELL. Born 1 Jun 1846; died on 16 Feb 1848, he was 1.

198. Alice Louisa SCOVELL. Born on 29 Apr 1848; died on 28 Feb 1852, she was 3.

199. Elizabeth Shepard SCOVELL. Born in Sep 1847. Elizabeth Shepard died in Sep 1847. She died in the month she was born.

200. Leonard Shepard SCOVELL. Born in Jul 1853. Leonard died in Sep 1853.

201. Anna Saxe SCOVELL. Born on 6 Mar 1858. Anna Saxe died on 6 Mar 1858.

202. Oliver Perry SCOVELL. Born on 3 Jun 1859 in Lewiston, N.Y. Oliver Perry died in Lewiston, N.Y. on 22 Sep 1882, he was 23. Oberlin College.

203. Elizabeth Eddy SCOVELL. Born on 12 Oct 1861. Elizabeth Eddy died on 19 Dec 1876, she was 15.

204. Philo Jewett SCOVELL. Born on 17 May 1865 in Lewiston, N.Y. Philo Jewett died in Lewiston, N.Y. on 23 Feb 1914, he was 48. Occupation: Musician. Education: Oberlin Conservatory of Music.

205. Josiah Boardman SCOVELL.[76] Born on 1 Dec 1869 in Lewiston, N.Y. Occupation: Lawyer and publisher. He compiled the Hannah Saxe (9.0) section of *Genealogy of the Saxe Family* (pp. 62-88). Education: Cornell University, LL.B. 1891. On 16 Jun 1909 when Josiah Boardman was 39, he married Rhoda Ann GODFREY, in Lewiston, N.Y. Occupation: Mother of 3.

206. Ella Elizabeth SCOVELL. Born on 11 Jul 1849. Ella died on 9 Aug 1851, age 2.

207. Frank Thomas SCOVELL. Born on 1 Sep 1852 in Cambria, N.Y. Frank Thomas died in Mobile, Alabama on 10 May 1874, he was 21.

208. Sammons Onderdonk SCOVELL. Born on 28 Mar 1866. Sammons Onderdonk died on 20 May 1867, he was 1.

5

Fifth Generation[77]

---

209. Sarah Electa SAXE. Sarah Electa married Warren S. FAIRBANKS.

210. William Holt SAXE. Born on 5 Jan 1889. William Holt died in Medicine Hat, Alberta, Canada in 1913, he was 23.

211. Emmerson Ladd SAXE.

212. 1st Lieut. Lawrence Colt LOVELL, Aviation Section, Signal Reserve Corps, A.E.F. Born on 11 Apr 1894; killed in France on 29 Jul 1917, he was 23.

213. George J. [1741321] STOCKWELL. Foster Paul Stockwell gives his name as George E. Stockwell. On 27 Jul 1898 he married Sarah Grace SMITH, daughter of Moses SMITH & Nancy Helen EDWARDS. Born on 7 Aug 1864 in Utica, NY. Daughter of Moses and Nancy Helen (EDWARDS) SMITH.
They had one child:
      i.   L. Albert [17413211] (1900-)

214. Albert [1741322] STOCKWELL. Occupation: Shirt salesman.

215. Charles H. [1741323] STOCKWELL. Real estate dealer in Hoosick Falls, NY.

216. Willard [1741341] STOCKWELL. Born on 2 Oct 1855 in Rutland, VT. Willard [1741341] died in Swanton, VT on 18 Mar 1913, he was 57.
On 24 Dec 1882 when Willard [1741341] was 27, he first married Maryette FOSTER, in Sheldon, VT. Maryette died about 1900.
They had one child:
      i.   Merrow [17413411] (1893-)

On 12 Dec 1900 when Willard [1741341] was 45, he second married Martha Aralla HAKEY, in Swanton, VT. Born on 28 Jan 1864 in Franklin, NH. Martha Aralla died in St. Albans, VT on 3 Apr 1939, she was 75.
They had the following children:
      i.   Dorothy Elizabeth [17413412] (1902-)
      ii.   Donald Willard [17413413] (1905-1971)

217. Margaret [1741342] STOCKWELL. Born on 9 Jul 1858 in Pittsford, VT. Margaret [1741342] died in Burlington, VT on 20 Aug 1945, she was 87. Unmarried.

218. Catharine H. [1741343] STOCKWELL. Born in 1864/1865 in Highgate, VT. Catharine H. [1741343] died about 1888, she was 24. Occupation: Albert Williams' 1st wife; he m (2) her sister Anette.
On 12 Jan 1887 when Catharine H. [1741343] was 23, she married Albert C. WILLIAMS, in St. Albans, VT.
m. (2), 2/18/89 at Highgate, VT, Annette "Nettie" V. Stockwell.

219. Daniel [1741344] STOCKWELL. Born on 15 Jan 1869 in Highgate, VT. Daniel [1741344] died in Burlington, VT on 11 Sep 1967, he was 98.

On 23 Jul 1925 when Daniel [1741344] was 56, he married Emma COUTERMANCHE, in Burlington, VT.

220. Samuel A. [1741345] STOCKWELL. Born in 1871/1872 in St. Albans, VT.
On 18 Oct 1896 when Samuel A. [1741345] was 25, he married Elizabeth BERRY, in St. Albans, VT.
They had the following children:
        i.   Beulah Vivian [17413451] (1899-)
        ii.   Harold Samuel [17413452] (1906-1907)

221. David [1741346] STOCKWELL. Born on 4 Jul 1873 in Highgate, VT.

222. Annette V. "Nettie" [1741361] STOCKWELL. Born on 28 Sep 1868 in Highgate, VT. 2nd wife of Albert Williams, who m. (1) her sister, Catherine H. Stockwell.
Annette V. [1741361] married Albert C. WILLIAMS.

223. Millard Arthur [1741362] STOCKWELL. Born on 24 Jun 1872 in Highgate, VT.

224. Jessie Fidelia STOCKWELL,[78] eldest child of Benajah Flavel and Emily Lodiweska (Hyde) Stockwell, was born at Peoria, Peoria County, Illinois, 7 September 1863; died at Clarion, Wright County, Iowa, 12 September 1940. One of her siblings, a brother, was also born in Peoria. The family moved back to Vermont when she was four years old and remained there for three years while her father worked as a school teacher and Methodist preacher. A sister was born during this time in Vermont. In the spring of 1870 her parents moved to Iowa with their three children and homesteaded at Fryeburg, near Rowan, in Wright County, on the upper reaches of the Iowa River. Three more children were born to this family in Iowa. Before her sixteenth birthday her mother died and she became "mother" to her three sisters and two brothers until her father married a widow, Mrs. Lucy Hannings, five months later. Her step brother David Hannings, who was about her own age, lived with the Stockwell family until he became of age, married, and moved to Cerro Gordo County, Iowa, a few miles to the east of Clarion.

    Jessie was married on her nineteenth birthday to George J. Hill, who was the son of a neighboring family. She and her husband farmed near Clarion for thirty years, and had nine children. Seven of the children married and had children; two small daughters died during a diphtheria epidemic in 1894. When she lived on the farm she was a member of the Harvey Community Church. She became a member of the Clarion Methodist Church on 18 April 1915 and was a charter member of the Woman's Society of Christian Service. She was also president of the Foreign Missionary Society of the church in Clarion. It was said that as a midwife she attended the birth of countless babies in Wright County, and of all of her grandchildren.

    Her nephew, the Rev. F. Olin Stockwell, wrote that she was a thin, spare, and terribly energetic person. Her passion was that her youngest son, Gerald Hill, should not be shunted off to a farm job before he was out of his "teens," but that he should have a chance to get an education. It was this determination that enabled him to get a college education. He believed that "she wanted to make a preacher or a missionary out of him, although he ended up a banker."

    Her six living children and many others gathered to celebrate her 77th birthday five days before she died following a short illness. At her funeral, the Rev. H. E. Harvey referred to her as "Sister" Hill, and compared her life to the disciples and heavenly beings who were arrayed in white, quoting St. John the Divine: "They shall walk with me in white; for they are worthy." (Rev. 3:4)

She married, at Fryeburg, Wright County, Iowa, 7 September 1882, George J. Hill, son of Charles W. and Adelia Catharine (Riley) Hill of Wright County. He was born at Caton, Steuben Co., New York, 5 January 1857; died at Clarion, Wright Co., Iowa, 2 June 1952.

George J. Hill and Jessie Fidelia (Stockwell) Hill, undated, probably 1907

George J. HILL,[79] eldest of the three children of Charles W. and Adelia Catharine (Riley) Hill, was born at Caton, Steuben County, New York, 5 January 1857; died at Clarion, Iowa, 2 June 1952. He came to Iowa at the age of four in 1861 with his parents and his older brother, who was born in 1860. The family made the trip by train to Dubuque, Iowa, and then by stage coach to Fryeburg, which was later called Rowan, near Clarion, in Wright County, Iowa. His parents purchased land in Grant Township northeast of Clarion for $10 per acre. In 1994, part of this property was still owned and farmed by the descendants of his son, Myron Hill, Sr. George Hill was for many years manager of the Solberg elevator, to which he commuted from his farm home by horse and buggy. He was a charter member of the Harvey Congregational Church in Grant Township, where he was the church janitor and Sunday school teacher. He was Secretary of the Grant Township School Board in 1895-1898, and he recorded the minutes of the board meetings with a bold and legible hand.

He and his wife moved to Clarion in 1913, where he became an active member of the Methodist church. Meanwhile, his family grew and thrived, some in farming, some in business, and others in the field of education. Following the death of his wife, he lived with his daughter Ruby in Clarion, until he passed away at the age of 95. In his later years he was one of the town's most visible patriarchs, a quiet dignified gentleman with a full white beard and mustache. Following services at the Methodist church in Clarion, he was buried in the family cemetery at Rowan. This cemetery was near or was once part of the original Hill family homestead, on the east bank of the Iowa River, close to where his nine year old brother and his 22 year old uncle had drowned in 1869.

George J. and Jessie (Stockwell) Hill had the following children:
      i.   William Benjamin [145] "Ben" (1883-1924)
     ii.   Harland Eugene [146] (1885-1968)

iii. Leroy George [147] "Lee" (1886-1975)
iv. Myron Emery [148] (1888-1955)
v. Nellie Leola [149] (1890-1894)
vi. Grace Lodawesca [150] (1892-1894)
vii. Ruby Adella [151] (1896-1995)
viii. Adelia Emma [152] (1898-1984)
ix. Gerald Leslie [153] "Gerry" (1905-1979)

George J. and Jessie Hill, Adelia, Leroy, Harland, Myron, Ruby, Benjamin, and Gerald
Clarion, Iowa - 1909

Seven of the children lived to maturity, married, and had children. Nellie and Grace died during a diphtheria epidemic in 1894, and were mourned for the rest of the lives of their parents, and their brothers and sisters.

225. Eugene Sanford STOCKWELL,[80] eldest son of Benajah Flavell and Emma Lodiweska (Hyde) Stockwell, was born at Peoria, Illinois, 21 May 1865; died in a train accident near Norman, Oklahoma, 25 May 1921.

His grandson wrote that, "He was a Methodist preacher, and was admitted to the Illinois Conference of the Methodist Church in 1885. In 1891 he went to the state of Washington where he preached until 1893, when he returned to Illinois. He transferred to the Oklahoma Conference in 1897, where he served in a number of churches until he was appointed District Superintendent in 1913. He strongly opposed the policies of the once slave-advocating southern branch of the Methodist Church, and worked diligently to build the northern branch of the church in Oklahoma."

He married (1), 2 September 1888, Myra E. Bloxham, who died without issue in February 1890.
He married (2), 16 June 1891, Addie Bunnell, daughter of Benjamin and Louise (Schoonmaker) Bunnell; she was born in 1869 and died 30 June 1926.
Eugene and Addie (Bunnell) Stockwell had the following children:
i. Benjamin Paul [17413721] (1892-1975)
ii. Eugene Earl [17413722] (1896-1904)
iii. Bowman Foster [17413723] (1899-1961)
iv. Francis Olin [17413724] (1900-1996)

John Saxe, Loyalist

      v.   Spencer Lewis [17413725] (1902-1986)
      vi.   Emma Louise [17413726] (1904-1904)

226. Ruby Ellen [1741373] STOCKWELL. Born in 1868. Occupation: Mother of 5; lived in Ft. Collins, CO. Ruby Ellen [1741373] married M. L. BENEDICT. Lived in Ft. Collins, CO.

227. Herbert Emory [1741374] STOCKWELL. Born on 6 Oct 1871 in Fryeburg, IA. He was of Seattle, WA. On 7 Dec 1899 when Herbert Emory [1741374] was 28, he first married Lucy HANCOCK.
They had one child:
      i.   Unknown child [17413641]
Herbert Emory [1741374] second married Mrs. Alice BOOKER.

228. Emma Caroline [1741375] STOCKWELL. Born in 1874 in Fryeburg, IA. Occupation: Methodist missionary, Burma; later, Washington, DC.
Emma Caroline [1741375] first married Fred B. PRICE.
Emma Caroline [1741375] second married ? LUM, of Washington, DC.

229. Grace Lymna [1741376] STOCKWELL. Born on 7 Apr 1877 in Fryeburg, IA. Occupation: Missionary, Twante, Burma.
Some of her papers are available for review in the microfilm records of Missionary Files at Drew University, Madison, NJ, on Call #396, Reel 1.

230. Elizabeth M. [1-7-4-1-3-11-1] STOCKWELL. Born in 1880/1881 in Mooers, NY. On 22 May 1901 when Elizabeth M. [1-7-4-1-3-11-1] was 21, she married Lucian S. INGRAHAM Jr., in St. Albans, VT.

231. Ulysses S. [1-7-4-1-3-11-2] STOCKWELL. Born in 1867. Ulysses S. [1-7-4-1-3-11-2] died on 16 Jun 1891, he was 24.

232. Charlie G. [1-7-4-1-3-11-3] STOCKWELL. Charlie G. [1-7-4-1-3-11-3] died on 11 Mar 1892.

233. Ida {1-7-4-1-3-11-2} STOCKWELL. Born in 1867.

234. Gertrude {1-7-4-1-3-11-4} STOCKWELL. Born in 1873 in New York (state).

235. Charles William SAXE.

236. Arthur Griggs SAXE.

237. Charles Edward SAXE.

238. Eugene Crump SAXE.

239. Katherine Louise SAXE.

240. Eleanor Burtis SAXE. Eleanor married Howard SACHS, of Goldman, Sachs.

241. John Burtis SAXE.[81] Born on 27 Jul 1902 in Brookline, Mass.; died in 1959. John Burtis married Lorraine BROOKE.
They had the following children:
      i.   John Brooke
      ii.   _____

242. James Burtis SAXE.

243. John Godfrey SAXE [II], LL.D.[82] Born 25 June 1877, at Saratoga Springs, N.Y. Occupation: Lawyer, author of *Genealogy of the Saxe Family* (1930), N.Y. State Senator; On 10 Jun 1909 John Godfrey married Mary SANDS. She was the daughter of Ferdinand and Mary Collender Sands; d.s.p.

244. Laura Huldah SAXE.

245. Charles Merwin SAXE.
246. Sophia Sollace SAXE.
247. Jessie Ellen SAXE.
248. Ellen Mildred SAXE.
249. Rev. Alfred Jacob SAXE.
250. Henry Wisner SAXE.
251. Rowena Keith SAXE.
252. Mary G. SAXE.
253. Maud Elizabeth SAXE.
254. Agnes Esther SAXE.
255. Helen Douglas SAXE.
256. Marguerite SAXE.
257. Theodosia Wead SAXE.
258. Grace Elizabeth SAXE.
259. Mary Franklyn SAXE.
260. Rev. Ralph Godfrey SAXE.
261. Elizabeth D. SAXE.
262. Herbert URMY.
263. Thomas Van Orden URMY.
264. Ralph Brainard URMY Jr.
265. Keith Merwin URMY.
266. Marion Mabel URMY.
267. Ellen Hannah DURANT.
268. Caroline Maria DURANT.
269. Julia Ella DURANT.
270. Homer Eaton DURANT.
271. Grace Drury STEVENS.
272. Elizabeth Frances STEVENS.
273. Franklin Rand STEVENS.
274. Clark Saxe JENNISON.
275. Ralph Drury JENNISON.
276. Robert Farrar JENNISON.
277. Helen Saxe SEAVEY.
278. Harold V. SEAVEY.
279. Malcolm deForest SEAVEY.
280. Frances Drury SAXE.
281. Catherine Officer SAXE.
282. Mary SAXE.
283. Philip SAXE.
284. John Drew SAXE.
285. Katherine Keith KEYES. Born on 12 Dec 1903 in Munich, Germany.
286. Clara Fannie SMITH.
287. Nellie Sophia SMITH.
288. James Fay PLACE.
289. Olive F. PLACE.
290. Clara L. PLACE.

291. Ethel G. PLACE.
292. Ruth Saxe PLACE.
293. Carl O. PLACE.
294. Graham PLACE.
295. Hannah Lucile BOURETT.
296. Hortense V. S. BOURETT.
297. Edmond Calvin BOURETT.
298. Frederick Drury BOURETT.
299. Horace Eugene ALLEN. Born on 18 Jul 1890 in Swanton, Vt.
300. Clarence Keith ALLEN.
301. Dorcas Irene ALLEN.
302. Charles Cox JEWETT. Born on 18 Sep 1863 in Niles, Mich. Occupation: General Agent of Union Pacific R.R. at San Diego, Calif. He first married Rose PLATT. They had one child:
        i.   Elizabeth Cox (1889-)
On 6 Nov 1911 when Charles Cox was 48, he second married Ekeba ATANURBUI, in Los Angeles, Calif. No children.
303. Rear Admiral Thomas Scovell JEWETT U.S.N.[83] Born 20 Aug 1866, Niles, Michigan. On 21 Apr 1891, he married Carrie A. UNDERWOOD, in Kansas City, Mo. They had one child:
        i.   Thomas Scovell (1866-)
304. Harry Erwin JEWETT. Born on 17 Jan 1871. Harry died on 21 Apr 1901, age 30.
305. May JEWETT. Born on 24 Sep 1876 in Kansas City, Mo.
306. Katherine JEWETT.
307. Charles Dean JEWETT.
308. Edward Dickinson JEWETT.
309. Gid Henry Chipman JEWETT.
310. Mabel Platte JEWETT. Occupation: unmarried; evangelist; delivered opening address at World's Convention of Crippled Children's Organizations, Geneva, 1929.
311. Allan Saxe JONES.
312. Katherine Scovell JONES. Mother of 3. Wellesley College, A.B., 1899. Katherine Scovell married Irwin REW. Occupation: "Capitalist; V.P., Board of Trustees, Northwestern University."
313. George Bayard JONES. Occupation: Patent attorney, Chicago, Ill. Education: Massachusetts Institite of Technology, S.B., 1905; George Washington University, LL.B. 1908, Master of Patent Law, 1909.
314. Capt. Roland Jewett JONES, USAR. Unmarried. Amherst College, A.B., 1907.
315. Lieut. Walter Boardman JONES, Air Service, USAR. Amherst College, A.B., 1909; Washington University, LL.B., 1912.
316. Mary Elizabeth Scovell COLT. Born on 1 May 1878 in Lewiston, N.Y. Unmarried; teacher; Executive Secretary, National Board of Y.W.C.A., 1918-1927.
317. James Bernard McCOLLUM. Born on 5 Nov 1875 in Lockport, N.Y. Occupation: Manager of N.Y.C. branch of General Motors Acceptance Corporation in 1930. Lived at 40 W. 77th St., N.Y.C., in 1930.
318. Francis Xavier McCOLLUM. Born on 3 Dec 1887 in Lockport, N.Y. Francis Xavier died on 27 Mar 1918, he was 30. Occupation: Lawyer, N.Y.C. Cornell

University, LL.B., 1899.

319. Hon. Eugene Lawrence McCOLLUM. Born on 4 Aug 1879 in Lockport, N.Y. Unmarried; Lawyer, Lockport, N.Y.; Member of State Assembly, 1913. Cornell University, LL.B., 1905.

320. Hiram McCOLLUM. Born on 2 May 1878 in Lockport, N.Y.; died in Boston, Mass. on 13 Feb 1905, he was 26. Occupation: d.s.p; Spanish-American War veteran and officer in War Department. Education: Georgetown University.

321. Ella Kate McCOLLUM. Born on 27 Sep 1885.
Ella Kate married William Wallace RALSTON M.D. Occupation: Surgeon & eye specialist in Houston, Texas; surgeon in Spanish-American War; Major, U.S. Army Medical Corps, World War I. Education: University of Texas and Vienna, Austria.

322. Josephine McCOLLUM. Born on 30 Aug 1890 in Lockport, N.Y. Education: Pensionat de la Ste. Maria, Namur, Belgium.
Married Dec. 22; 1915, at New York City to Hector Russell CARVETH, electro-chemist and metallurgist, of Niagara Falls; graduated in 1896 with A. B. degree by Toronto and Victoria Universities, and in 1898 with Ph.D. degree by Cornell University; President of Roessler & Hasslacher Chemical Co.; seven children.

323. Camille Scovell McCOLLUM. Born on 7 Apr 1892 in Lockport, N.Y.
90430. CAMILLE SCOVELL McCOLLUM. B. Apr. 7, 1892, at Lockport, N. Y.; Resided at 406 Kitnach, 4 Chome Aoyama, Tokyo, Japan; Education: Pensionat de la Ste. Maria, Namur, Belgium, and at Dominican Convent, Vienna, Austria; Married Sept. 5, 1918, at St. Patrick's Cathedral in New York City to John Richard GEARY; English Representative of General Electric Co. at London, and later its Japanese Representative at Yokohama and Tokyo; two children. .

324. Lieut. Paul GALLAGHER, M.D. Physician. Education: St. Louis University, Chicago University and Rush Medical College, M.D., 1911.

325. Lieut. Hiram GALLAGHER, M.D. Physician. Education: Canisius College, University of Freiberg, Catholic University of America (A.B.), Johns Hopkins (M.D.).

326. Lieut. Leo GALLAGHER, LL.B, Ph.D. Lawyer, Los Angeles; was in Army secret service in World War I. Education: Catholic University of America, A.B.; Yale, LL.B., Innsbruck Philosophical Institute, Austria, 1915, Ph.D.

327. Captain Donald Joseph GALLAGHER. Lawyer, San Francisco; battalion commander, 90th Division, Argonne. Education: Ecole Notre Dame, Namur, Belgium; Harvard, LL.B., 1913.

328. Captain Robert Jameson SCOVELL.[84] Born on 8 Aug 1887 in Terre Haute, Ind. Resided in Antwerp, Belgium, in 1930; Executive Officer of Intelligence Section at A. E. F. Headquarters at Vladivostok, Siberia, in 1918-1910; honorably discharged from Army in 1919 with rank of Captain; Asstant to Managing Director, General Motors Continental. Married March 25, 1925, at Liverpool, England, to Anne Longton HICKS; three children.

Index

ABBOTT
    Caroline   spouse of 173
AGUIRE
    Alice   spouse of 167
ALLEN
    Clarence E. M.D. (1856 -)   spouse of 183
    Clarence Keith   300
    Dorcas Irene   301
    Ella K.   spouse of 191
    Horace Eugene (1890 -)   299
ATANURBUI
    Ekeba   spouse of 302
ATWELL
    Jodelphia Amelia   spouse of 119
BAKER
    Susan Maria (1822 - 1847)   spouse of 33
BALDWIN FLANNERY
    Mrs. Martha   spouse of 193
BASCOM
    Henry   spouse of 136
BENEDICT
    M. L.   spouse of 226
BERRY
    Elizabeth   spouse of 220
BICKFORD
    ?   spouse of 97
    Grace Merwin   spouse of 172
BLOXHAM
    Myra E. (- 1890)   spouse of 225
BOOKER
    Alice Mrs.   spouse of 227
BOSWORTH
    Mary A.   spouse of 113
BOURETT
    Edmond A.   spouse of 182
    Edmond Calvin   297
    Frederick Drury   298
    Hannah Lucile   295
    Hortense V. S.   296
BROOKE
    Lorraine   spouse of 241
BROWN
    John   spouse of 69
BUNNELL
    Addie Sue (1869 - 1926)   spouse of 225
BURROUGHS
    Eliza J. (1823 - 1859)   spouse of 23
    Sarah E. (1843 - 1865)   spouse of 23

BURTIS
    Sara F. — spouse of 111
CAMPBELL
    Nancy Valina (- >1898) — spouse of 62
CARTER
    Anna — spouse of 12
    Ira — spouse of 13
CARVETH
    Hector Russell Ph.D. — spouse of 322
CHAMBERLIN
    Edgar J. — spouse of 177
CHASE
    Elizabeth — spouse of 37
COLT
    Hetzel — spouse of 58
    Josiah Boardman Scovell (1843 - 1914) — 189
    Julia Maria — 92
    Leander — spouse of 31
    Mary Elizabeth Scovell (1878 -) — 316
CONNOR
    Ida May — spouse of 108
COUTERMANCHE
    Emma — spouse of 219
COX
    Amelia Virginia — spouse of 184
COYLE
    Gertrude — spouse of 164
CRUMP
    Louise Wheaton — spouse of 109
DANIELS
    Flora Jane — spouse of 48
DAVIES
    Mary Hawley — spouse of 185
DILL
    Adelia Sophia — spouse of 94
DOUGLASS
    Elizabeth (1823 - 1903) — spouse of 27
DREW
    Abagail — spouse of 45
DURANT
    Caroline Maria — 268
    Ellen Hannah — 267
    Homer Eaton — 270
    Julia Ella — 269
DRURY
    Grace B. — spouse of 45
    Horace S. (1852 - 1871) — 181
    Minerva Saxe (1866 -) — 183
    Sarah C. (1857 -) — 182
    Sarah Keith (1818 - 1896) — spouse of 35
    Zephanaih Keith (- ~1892) — spouse of 54

DUNHAM
    Martin   spouse of 101

DUNNING
    Clarissa (1792 - 1875)   spouse of 9

DURANT
    Fayette   spouse of 157

FAIRBANKS
    Warren S.   spouse of 209

FERGUSON
    Andrew M.D.   spouse of 28

FISHER
    Evelyn Foster   spouse of 154

FOSTER
    Maryette (- ~1900)   spouse of 216

GALLAGHER
    Captain Donald Joseph   327
    Francis Waters M.D.   spouse of 194
    Lieut. Hiram M.D.   325
    Lieut. Leo LL.B, Ph.D.   326
    Lieut. Paul M.D.   324

GEARY
    John Richard   spouse of 323

GIBBS
    Caroline   90
    John   spouse of 18

GODFREY
    Rhoda Ann   spouse of 205

GRAVES
    Betty   spouse of 5

GRIGGS
    Ellen (1824 - 1904)   spouse of 33
    William N.   spouse of 71

HADLEY
    Delia   spouse of 15

HAKEY
    Martha Aralla (1864 - 1939)   spouse of 216

HALL
    Lotta (1884 - 1927)   spouse of 180
    Louisa J. (1840 - 1817)   spouse of 23

HANCOCK
    Lucy   spouse of 227

HANNINGS
    Mrs. Lucy (- 1914)   spouse of 99

HARPER
    Frances M.   spouse of 153

HEFLON
    Emily   spouse of 178

HEWITT
    Mary Lydia   spouse of 189

HICKS

    Anne Longton   spouse of 328

HILL
    Adelia Emma [152] (1898 - 1984)   child of 224
    George J. [68] (1857 - 1952)   spouse of 224
    Gerald Leslie [153] "Gerry" (1905 - 1979)   child of 224
    Grace Lodawesca [150] (1892 - 1894)   child of 224
    Harland Eugene [146] (1885 - 1968)   child of 224
    Leroy George [147] "Lee" (1886 - 1975)   child of 224
    Myron Emery [148] (1888 - 1955)   child of 224
    Nellie Leola [149] (1890 - 1894)   child of 224
    Ruby Adella [151] (1896 - 1995)   child of 224
    William Benjamin [145] "Ben" (1883 - 1924)   child of 224

HILLIARD
    David S.   spouse of 88

HOGABOOM
    Cordelia   spouse of 98
    Eliza Ann (1833 - 1906)   spouse of 98

HOLMES
    John B.   spouse of 123

HOLT
    Charlotte (1787 - 1811)   spouse of 5

HYDE
    Alice Rowena   157
    Emily Lodiweska (Emma F.) (1840 - 1879)   spouse of 99
    George B.   spouse of 44

INGRAHAM
    Lucian S. Jr.   spouse of 230

JAMESON
    Joanna   spouse of 195

JENNISON
    Clark Saxe   274
    Nahum Edward   spouse of 159
    Ralph Drury   275
    Robert Farrar   276

JEWETT
    Ada Anna (1842 - 1907)   186
    Hon. Charles   spouse of 56
    Charles Jr. (1849 - 1850)   187
    Charles II (1854 - 1870)   188
    Charles Cox (1863 -)   302
    Charles Dean   307
    Edward Dickinson   308
    Major Edward Saxe (1842 - 1900)   185
    Elizabeth (1790 - 1880)   spouse of 7
    Elizabeth Cox (1889 -)   child of 302
    Elizabeth2 (- >1869)   spouse of 61
    Capt. Erwin Scovett (1839 - 1910)   184
    Gid Henry Chipman   309
    Harry Erwin (1871 - 1901)   304
    Katherine   306
    Mabel Platte   310
    May (1876 -)   305

Rear Admiral Thomas Scovell U.S.N. (1866 -)	303
Lieut. Thomas Scovell Jr., USAR, (1866 -)	child of 303

JOHNSON
Emma Marie	spouse of 166

JONES
Allan Saxe	311
George Bayard	313
Katherine Scovell	312
Capt. Roland Jewett USAR	314
Lieut. Walter Boardman Air Service, USAR	315
William Edward	spouse of 186

JUDSON
Mary E. (1821 - 1894)	spouse of 40

KEENAN
Margaret	spouse of 190

KEITH
Rowena	spouse of 8

KEYES
Arthur (1864 - 1878)	171
Conrad Saxe (1874 -)	172
Emerson Willard	spouse of 49
Homer Eaton (1875 -)	173
Katherine Keith (1903 -)	285
Rowena Keith (1880 -)	174

KIRSH
Sarah Louise	spouse of 185

LADD
Cora	spouse of 91

LEROY
Rachel	spouse of 3

LOCKWOOD
Maria	spouse of 5

LOVELL
Francis F.	spouse of 92
1st Lieut. Lawrence Colt U.S.A.R. (1894 - 1917)	212

LOWRY
Gertrude	spouse of 108

LUM
?	spouse of 228

McCOLLUM
Anna Fidelia (1848 - 1913)	192
Camille Scovell (1892 -)	323
Ella Kate (1885 -)	321
Hon. Eugene Lawrence (1879 -)	319
Francis Xavier (1887 - 1918)	318
Hiram	spouse of 59
Hiram (1878 - 1905)	320
Hiram Thomas (1845 -)	190
James Bernard (1875 -)	317
John Timon (1850 - 1918)	193
Josephine (1890 -)	322

    Mary Elizabeth (1852 - 1918)   194
    Silas Wright (1846 -)   191

McGUIRE
    Dennis Charles   spouse of 192

McKECHNIE
    James Henry   spouse of 159

MERWIN
    Huldah K.   spouse of 41

MICKLE
    Mary   spouse of 124

MULLOY
    Mary   spouse of 193

OFFICER
    Ellen   spouse of 163

ONDERDONK
    Mary   spouse of 62

OWEN
    Florence   spouse of 168

PARKER
    Caroline Miranda   spouse of 60

PHILLIPS
    Emily (- >1857)   spouse of 14

PLACE
    Carl O.   293
    Charles Henry (1856 - 1907)   180
    Clara L.   290
    Ethel G.   291
    Graham   294
    Harriet Saxe (1848 -)   176
    James Conrad (1854 -)   179
    James Fay   288
    James P.   spouse of 53
    Lizzie Landis (1846 - 1851)   175
    Olive F.   289
    Ruth Saxe   292
    Sarah Griffin (1850 - 1929)   177
    William Aubrey (1852 - 1907)   178

PLATT
    Rose   spouse of 302

PRESCOTT
    Alice May   spouse of 161

PRICE
    Fred B.   spouse of 228

RALSTON
    William Wallace M.D.   spouse of 321

RANKIN
    Augustin   spouse of 169

REW
    Irwin   spouse of 312

RICHARDSON
    Edmund   spouse of 24

RYCARD
    Katy (- <1849)   spouse of 14

SACHS
    Howard   spouse of 240

SAFFORD
    ?   spouse of 95

SANDS
    Mary   spouse of 243

SARTELL
    Luther   spouse of 17
    William   89

SAXE

_____	child of 241
_____ (female)	239a
Agnes (1838 -)	70
Agnes Esther	254
Rev. Alfred (1814 - 1846)	37
Alfred (1852 - 1871)	137
Rev. Alfred Henry (1839 - 1881)	130
Rev. Alfred Jacob	249
Alfred Jenkins (1846 - 1847)	134
Alfred Jenkins (1861 -)	144
Alfred Keith	166
Alfred W. (1870 -)	168
Amelia Elizabeth (1844 - 1845)	105
Anna	18
Anna (?) (?)	spouse of 6
Anna Maria [or W.] (1804 - 1890)	32
Arthur Griggs	236
Arthur M. (1853 - 1855)	151
Dr. Arthur Wellesley (1820 - 1891)	40
Arthur Wellesley (1857 - 1919)	138
Arthur William	147
Caroline (1832 - 1851)	46
Carrie A. (1857 - 1858)	152
Catherine	11
Catherine Officer	281
Cecile (1846 - 1859)	73
Cecile	81
Cecile (1843 - 1868)	88
Cecile	17
Charles Edward	237
Charles Gordon (1848 - 1893)	115
Charles Gordon (1848 - 1893)	spouse of 149
Charles Griggs (1855 - 1862)	107
Charles Hammon (1846 - 1847)	106
Charles Jewett (1870 -)	129
Hon. Charles Jewett (1814 - 1867)	33
Charles Merwin	245
Charles Philip (1867 - 1909)	163
Charles William	235
Charlotte (1836 -)	69
Charlotte (- 1886)	13

Name	Page
Charlotte Holt (1810 - 1811)	25
Clarissa Eliza (1824 - 1870)	53
Conrad (1784 - 1871)	9
DeForest Wead (1858 - 1924)	139
Edward (1818 - 1862)	39
Edward C. (1851 - 1854)	150
Edward Jacob	143
Edward Thomas (1860 - 1924)	109
Edwin A. (1819 - 1899)	52
Eleanor Burtis	240
Elizabeth Catherine (1828 -)	28
Elizabeth D.	261
Elizabeth Wead (1848 - 1877)	136
Ellen B.	133
Ellen Merwin (1850 - 1889)	spouse of 115
Ellen Merwin (1850 - 1889)	149
Ellen Mildred	248
Ellen Sollace (1858 - 1862)	126
Emily (1849 - 1908)	83
Emma Rowena (1873 -)	169
Emmerson Ladd	211
Eugene Crump	238
Fanny Maria (1860 -)	127
Frances Caroline (1856 - 1888)	158
Frances Drury	280
Frances Maria (1847 - 1847)	135
Frank K.	148
Franklin James (1854 -)	124
Frederic (~1823 - <1824)	42
Frederick Judson	145
George (1773 - 1853)	3
George (1827 - 1900)	22
George (1842 - 1863)	72
George (1833 - 1844)	86
George Brown (1846 - 1847)	114
George G. (1864 - 1900)	153
Rev. George Godfrey (1822 - 1896)	41
George J.	19
George W. (1818 - 1854)	26
Godfrey (- c.1742)	father of 1
Godfrey (1778 - 1807)	6
Grace Elizabeth	258
Grace Maria (1865 - 1914)	162
Hannah (1786 - 1859)	10
Hannah (1834 - 1916)	47
Hannah (1827 - 1909)	54
Harriet Sollace (1853 - 1881)	117
Harriet T. (1830 - 1833)	55
Harriett Jane (1862 -)	78
Helen (1836 -)	87
Helen Douglas	255
Heman Allen (1836 - 1915)	48
Henry G. (1819 - 1897)	27
Henry Wisner	250

Herbert Kimball (1868 -)	154
Homer Polk (1844 - 1921)	121
Horace Jacob (1818 - 1874)	51
Howard Martin (1847 - 1863)	122
Ira Charles (1857 -)	77
Jacob (1783 - 1866)	8
Jacob William (1830 - 1883)	45
James (1823 - 1884)	36
James	239c
James Alfred (1863 - >1930)	110
James Burtis	242
Jane	79
Jessie Ellen	247
John (1732 - 1808)	1
John (1772 - 1793)	2
John	14
John	82
John	239b
John Brooke	child of 241
John Burtis (1902 -)	241
John D. (1868 -)	167
John Drew	284
Hon. John Godfrey L.L.D. (1816 - 1887)	34
John Godfrey [II], LL.D. (1877 -)	243
John Matthew (1848 -)	74
John Theodore (1843 - 1881)	113
John Walter (1863 - 1929)	111
Julia Frances (1830 - 1914)	29
Katherine (1882 -)	165
Katherine Louise	239
Laura Huldah	244
Laura Sophia (1856 - 1874)	118
Loan D. (1816 - 1851)	50
Louise Maria	142
Lucy (1840 -)	71
Luther Drury (1861 - 1861)	160
Mabel Wead (1858 - 1925)	159
Marguerite	256
Maria (1826 - 1854)	44
Maria Ann (1807 - 1891)	24
Marion Freer (1871 -)	156
Mary (1854 -)	76
Mary	282
Mary Elizabeth	146
Mary Ellen (1865 - 1903)	112
Mary Franklyn	259
Mary G.	252
Mary Helen (1834 - 1913)	31
Mary R. (1856 -)	84
Mary Sollace "Mollie" (1865 - 1942)	128
Mathew Conrad (1832 -)	30
Matthew (1776 - 1836)	5
Matthew	15

Maud Elizabeth	253
Minerva Drury (1842 - 1851)	120
Nettie (1857 -)	85
Olivia	80
Hon. Peter (SAX) (1779 - 1839)	7
Peter (1801 - 1848)	16
Col. Peter (1819 - 1891)	35
Philip	283
Pierre (Peter) Telesphore (1822 - 1881)	21
Rev. Ralph Godfrey	260
Ralph Jacob (1862 - 1908)	161
Robert Edward (1883 -)	170
Robert Jenkins (1816 - 1894)	38
Robert Jenkins Jr. (1861 - 1876)	140
Rollin Peter (1840 - 1903)	119
Rowena (~1824 - <1825)	43
Rowena	141
Rowena Keith (1839 - 1915)	49
Rowena Keith	251
Sarah Electa	209
Sarah Elizabeth (1850 - 1879)	116
Simon	12
Simon Peter (1850 -)	75
Sophia Sollace	246
Theodore James (1869 - 1870)	155
Theodosia Wead	257
Walter	131
William (1774 - 1840)	4
William (1813 - 1834)	20
William Arthur (1857 - 1917)	108
William F. (1842 - 1884)	132
William H. (1834 -)	68
William Henry (1856 - 1903)	125
William Holt (1809 - 1880)	23
William Holt (1861 - 1917)	91
William Holt (1889 - 1913)	210
William Jenkins (1871 - 1908)	164

SAXE-HOLMES

Elizabeth Lillian "Lillie" Sophia (1852 -)	123

SCOTT

Elizabeth	spouse of 132

SCOVELL

Alice Louisa (1848 - 1852)	198
Anna Saxe (1858 - 1858)	201
Augusta (1843 - 1869)	196
Charlotte Catherine (1814 - 1883)	56
Elizabeth Eddy (1861 - 1876)	203
Elizabeth Shepard (1847 - 1847)	199
Ella Elizabeth (1849 - 1851)	206
Fidelia (1817 - 1853)	59
Frank Thomas (1852 - 1874)	207
Hezekiah Wilcox	spouse of 24
Col. Josiah Boardman (1786 - 1855)	spouse of 10

Josiah Boardman (1869 -)		205
Josiah Thomas (1841 - 1915)		195
Juliette (1816 - 1890)		58
Leonard Shepard (1853 - 1853)		200
Hon. Oliver Perry (1820 - 1912)		61
Oliver Perry (1859 - 1882)		202
Philo Jewett (1865 - 1914)		204
Captain Robert Jameson (1887 -)		328
Rowena (1815 - 1815)		57
Sammons Onderdonk (1866 - 1867)		208
Stephen Decatur (1819 - 1850)		60
Thomas McDonough (1823 - 1898)		62
William Parker (1846 - 1848)		197

SEAGEL

    ———   spouse of 93

SEAVEY

Charles Lewis	spouse of 162
Harold V.	278
Helen Saxe	277
Malcolm deForest	279

SEE

Caroline (1828 - 1882)	67
Charles	65
David (- >1827)	spouse of 11
David (1812 - 1869)	63
Maria Ann Saxe	64
William	66

SEWARD

    Alice May   spouse of 179

SHARTS

    Rev. Derwin   spouse of 29

SHEPARD

    Elizabeth Eddy (- <1855)   spouse of 61

SMITH

Clara Fannie	286
George (1846 -)	spouse of 176
Nellie Sophia	287
Sarah Grace (1864 -)	spouse of 213

SOLLACE

Sarah Storrs (1828 - 1921)	spouse of 36
Sophia Newell	spouse of 34

STEVENS

Rev. Edwin Pitman	spouse of 158
Elizabeth Frances	272
Franklin Rand	273
Grace Drury	271

STEWART

    Martha Jane   spouse of 193

STITT

    Jimmie D.   spouse of 139

STOCKWELL

    Abi R. [174133] (1828 -)   95

Albert [1741322]	214
Annette V. [1741361] (1868 -)	222
Benajah Flavel [174137] (1836 - 1919)	99
Benjamin Paul [17413721] (1892 - 1975)	child of 225
Beulah Vivian [17413451] (1899 -)	child of 220
Bp. Bowman Foster [17413723] (1899 - 1961)	child of 225
Catharine H. [1741343] (1864 - ~1888)	218
Charles H. [1741323]	215
Charlie G. [1-7-4-1-3-11-3] (- 1892)	232
Daniel [1741344] (1869 - 1967)	219
David [174134] (1830 - 1912)	96
David [1741346] (1873 -)	221
Donald Willard [17413413] (1905 - 1971)	child of 216
Dorothy Elizabeth [17413412] (1902 -)	child of 216
Elizabeth M. [1-7-4-1-3-11-1] (1880 -)	230
Emma Caroline [1741375] (1874 -)	228
Emma Louise [17413726] (1904 - 1904)	child of 225
Eugene Earl [17413722] (1896 - 1904)	child of 225
Eugene Sanford [1741372] (1865 - 1921)	225
Francis Olin [17413724] Rev. (1900 - 1996)	child of 225
George J. [1741321]	213
Gertrude {1-7-4-1-3-11-4} (1873 -)	234
Godfrey E. [174132] (1827 - 1878)	94
Grace Lymna [1741376] (1877 -)	229
Harold Samuel [17413452] (1906 - 1907)	child of 220
Harriet S. [174135] (1832 -)	97
Herbert Emory [1741374] (1871 -)	227
Hermit (Kermit) [174138] (1838 - <1898)	100
Ida [1-7-4-1-3-11-] (1867 -)	233
Jessie Fidelia [1741371] (1863 - 1940)	224
Joseph A. (1851 -)	104
Joseph H. [17413] (1802 - 1870)	spouse of 32
Joseph Matthew [174136] (1834 - 1901)	98
L. Albert [17413211] (1900 -)	child of 213
Lucy Ann [174139] (1840 -)	101
Malona Marcia [1-7-4-1-3-10] (1842 -)	102
Margaret [1741342] (1858 - 1945)	217
Mary A. [174131] (1824 - <1898)	93
Merrow [17413411] (1893 -)	child of 216
Millard Arthur [1741362] (1872 -)	223
Ruby Ellen [1741373] (1868 -)	226
Samuel A. [1741345] (1871 -)	220
Samuel S. [1-7-4-1-3-11] (1844 - <1921)	103
Spencer Lewis [17413725] (1902 - 1986)	child of 225
Ulysses S. [1-7-4-1-3-11-2] (1867 - 1891)	231
Unknown child [1741364]	child of 227
Willard [1741341] (1855 - 1913)	216

TIGHS

Margaret (TYE)	spouse of 96

TILLOTSON

Mary Montgomery	spouse of 138

TREMBLY

Mary Ositte (- >1827)	spouse of 4

UNDERWOOD
    Carrie A.   spouse of 303

URMY
    Herbert Urmy   262
    Keith Merwin   265
    Marion Mabel   266
    Rev. Ralph Brainard   spouse of 156
    Ralph Brainard Jr.   264
    Thomas Van Orden   263

VOSBURGH
    Kate C.   spouse of 39

WEAD
    Rebecca Munson (1819 - 1887)   spouse of 38

WEAVER
    Catherine (1744 - 1791)   spouse of 1

WICK
    Mary Alfred   spouse of 110

WIGHT
    John   spouse of 11

WILLIAMS
    Albert C.   spouse of 222
    Albert C.   spouse of 218

WILSON
    Anna   spouse of 16

WISNER
    Phoebe   spouse of 130

WOODLEY
    ?   spouse of 102
    Susan A. (1846 - 1921)   spouse of 103

WOODWARD
    J.   spouse of 70

Annotated Bibliography

**The two principal sources for this history of the Saxe family are
J.G.S., *Genealogy of the Saxe Family* and Bunnell, *The New Loyalist Index***

J. G. S. [John Godfrey Saxe II]. *Genealogy of the Saxe Family.* **n.p., n.d. [Privately published by John Godfrey Saxe II, New York City, 1930].** The principal source of information about John Saxe and his descendants is a book entitled *Genealogy of the Saxe Family* that was compiled and privately published by John Godfrey Saxe II (who is identified only as J.G.S. in the book), in 1930. John Godfrey Saxe II utilized notes that he had acquired or borrowed from other members of the Saxe family, some of whom are acknowledged in his Foreword (p. 2). J.G.S. says that he began with a manuscript prepared by Hannah Saxe Drury [1827-1909, #805] in her eighty-first year [i.e., about 1908], which was sent to him by her grandson, Horace Eugene Allen [b. 1890, #80531]. J.G.S. says that he edited Hannah Drury's MS and added "much information ... some as to the earlier generations, and a great deal as to the later ones." The only part of the work that J.G.S. cites with respect to its source is the final section (pp. 62ff), on the descendants of the youngest child of John Saxe, Hanna (Saxe) Boardman (1786-1859, #90). This section was prepared by her grandson, Josiah Boardman Scovell (1869- , #9067). J.G.S. (b. 1877) is #60211 in this genealogy; his autobiography appears on pp. 40-43. He died without progeny.

One important source of information that J.G.S. did not mention was a collection of letters that he borrowed from John Walter Saxe (1863-1929, #6017), who was his older first cousin, one generation removed. Andrew Saxe, a great-grandson of this John Walter Saxe, says that John Walter Saxe died in 1929 shortly before J.G.S. published the *Genealogy*, and that the letters and other documents were not returned to John Walter's son John Burtis Saxe (1902- , #60172). The papers that J.G.S. assembled for his research have since disappeared, much to the distress of Andrew Saxe's branch of the family. The descendants of John Burtis Saxe believe that J.G.S. was a stubborn man who for unknown reasons refused to acknowledge the contributions of John Walter Saxe and may have discarded the papers rather than returning them to John Walter's family. The missing documents include the original will of John Saxe, which J.G.S. quoted. John Saxe's will was not submitted for probate in his home county (Franklin County, Vt.) and no copy of it is now known to exist.

There are many obvious minor errors in the text of *Genealogy of the Saxe Family*, most of which can easily be corrected. These include typographical errors, dates that are impossible, and places that are obviously incorrect, such as the incorrect placement on p. 5 of the town of Langensaltza (which J.G.S. misspelled by adding the letter "t") on the Salza River (which is actually nowhere near Langensalza). There are also some transcription errors. The most important of these, from our perspective, is that the name of the husband of Godfrey Saxe's daughter Anna Saxe (#501, p. 24) is shown as Joseph Stockville instead of Joseph Stockwell, undoubtedly as a result of someone's misreading the handwritten letters at the end of Stockwell as "ville" instead of "well."

Genealogy of the Saxe Family was mentioned appreciatively in the *New England Historic Genealogical Register* in 1930, and the name of the author – John Godfrey Saxe II – appears in this article in the *NEHGR*. The *Genealogy of the Saxe Family* is available on CD from Quintin Publications, viz.: "Genealogy of the Saxe Family 1930. Saxe S3278 / 92 / $10.95" © 2006, Quintin Publications, P.O. Box 65546, Orange Park, Florida 32065 (www.QuintinPublications.com).

I downloaded, printed, and then scanned this CD into text, after which I edited the text to correct obvious errors. The author, J.G.S., is #60211 in the *Genealogy*. He appears on p. 40, b. 25 June 1877.

The Will of John Saxe appears on pages 10-11 as it was transcribed by J.G.S. The original copy of the will has since disappeared and this is all that we know of it.

Bunnell, Paul J., A.G., U.E., *The New Loyalist Index* (Bowie, Md.: Heritage Books, Inc., 1989), pages unnumbered. This book is the principal source for the oft-repeated statement that John Sax(e) was a Loyalist. This book is about 600 pages long, arranged alphabetically.

John Saxe appears twice on the same page (about p. 500):
   Sax, John / Source: FHLD / 5 typed pages / Fr: / Stl: Eastern Township, Quebec, Canada / Reg: Cl:
   Saxe, John / Source: FHLD / b: 10 Nov. 1732. d: 12 Mar. 1808. m:NY Cath. Weaver, b: 10 Jan. 1744, Phila. Pa. / Fr: Langensaltza, Germany/Rhinebeck, NY Stl: Philipsburg, Quebec, Canada / Reg: Cl:

The abbreviation FHLD refers to "Family History of Loyalists & Their Descendants Index of the Non-Lending Library. Holdings at the United Empire Loyalist Association, Toronto, Ontario, Canada." Reg. & Cl. refer to Regiment and Rank if any claims were made (and since they are blank, he made no claims).

Unfortunately, the "5 typed pages" that Bunnell cites could not be located in the archives of the United Empire Loyalist Association of Canada in 2007 (e-mail from the President of the UELAC to George Hill). However, the UELAC believes the information in Bunnell is correct, and it has been accepted by the Sir John Johnson Branch of the UELAC as satisfactory evidence that John Saxe was a Loyalist.

Other sources are listed below in alphabetical order

Census Records for Highgate, Vermont

Census records for Highgate, Vt., in 1790 and 1800 show John Sax as the head of a family. No other Saxe or Saxe names are in those U.S. censuses for Highgate, and there is no one named Saxe in the 1810 census.

John Saxe, Loyalist

In 1790, Highgate was in Chittenden Co. There were then 17 families in Highgate. John Sax was head of a family of 11: 3 free white males over age 16, 6 free white males under 16, and 2 free white females. This accounts for the entire family. John 58, John Jr 18, George 17, William 16, Matthew 14, Godfrey 12, Peter 11, Jacob 7, and Conrad 6. The ages of the women were not recorded in the census; Catherine was 46 and Hannah was 4.

In 1800, Highgate was (and still is) in Franklin Co. There were then 77 families. John Sax was head of a family of 7: Free white males - 5 aged 16-25 (who would be Matthew 24, Godfrey 22, Peter 21, Jacob 17, and Conrad 16), 1 age 45+ (John Sr.), and one free white female age 10-15 (Hannah 14). By this census, we can see that oldest three sons were not recorded in this census. They were John Jr, who died in 1793, and two who had moved to Quebec, George 27 and William 26. Their mother, Catherine, had died in 1791, so she is not in this census.

There are no families named Saxe or Sax in Highgate in the census of 1810. This confirms what appears in the *Genealogy of the Saxe Family*, in which it is stated that Godfrey died in 1807, John Sr. died in 1808, and the other sons had all moved away. Hannah was not married until 1813, but she must have been living in another family in 1810. However, we know that Conrad Saxe was in a Highgate military unit in the War of 1812, and he is back in Highgate in the Census of 1830 and 1840. Matthew appears to have moved to Chazy, Clinton Co., N.Y. between 1800 and 1810 and he is shown in the 1810 census in that town. He does not appear in the U.S. census thereafter. Peter Sax was in Highgate in the census of 1820 and 1830. The surname Saxe disappeared from the census records of Highgate by the time of the census of 1850.

Although for unknown reasons, they were not listed in the censuses, Conrad Saxe and his wife and family continued to live in Highgate for many years. Conrad died in 1871 and although the place of his death is not recorded, his widow Clarissa died in Highgate in 1875, and it therefore likely that Conrad died there, too. His sons Horace Jacob (d. 1847) and Edwin (d. 1899) apparently did not marry and although they do not appear in census records we may presume that the lived somewhere in Highgate. If so, Edwin Saxe would be the last named Saxe to live in Highgate.

The last member of the Saxe family who is known to have lived in Highgate was Hannah (Saxe) Drury. She was Conrad's daughter Hannah (1827-1909), who married Zepahnaih Drury. Hannah Drury lived in Highgate until about 1882, when she moved to the nearby town of Swanton, Vt. Her notes, prepared from Highgate town records (Zephanaih was the Town Clerk), became the principal source of information for John Godfrey Saxe II when he compiled the *Genealogy of the Saxe Family* (1930).

Highgate, Vermont:

There are two good summaries of the early history of Highgate, Vermont, up to 1891. Both of these histories draw upon notes that were made by Amos Skeels of Highgate, who died in about 1861. These summaries are Warren Robinson, *History of the Town of Highgate* (1871), and Lewis Cass Albright, *History of the Town of Highgate* (1891):

Robinson, Hon. Warren (ed.). *History of the Town of Highgate*, **1871**, in "The Vermont Historical Gazeteer: A Magazine Embracing A History of Each Town, Civil, Ecclesiastical, Biographical and Military." Vol. 2, *Franklin, Grand Isle, Lamoille &*

Orange Counties. Ed. and published by Miss Abby, Maria Hemenway (Burlington, Vt., 1871), pp. 254-275. Transcribed by Karima Allison, 2004. On http://www.rootsweb.com/~vermont/FranklinHighgate_2.html (28 pp., 10/27/2005).

This is the principal source for information about the history of Highgate, Vermont. Robinson credits Amos Skeels as the author of much of this history, saying on page 2 that he has edited the papers of Skeels, who recently died in his 45th year of age. This was apparently in 1861. Other papers and poems were added to what Amos Skeels wrote and Robinson's edited version was published in 1871. Robinson's work was apparently the main source for a shorter history of Highgate that appeared in Lewis Cass Aldrich's history of Franklin County, Vermont, in 1891.

Aldrich, Lewis Cass. "History of the Town of Highgate" (Chapter 31), in *History of Franklin and Grand Isle Counties Vermont* **(Syracuse, N.Y.: D. Mason & Co., 1891),** 593-611 (accessed from Google Books).

Aldrich's work adds details about the service of Highgate men in the Civil War, but his early history of Highgate is essentially unchanged from what Amos Skeels compiled and which was published by Robinson.

I have also spoken on the telephone with the Highgate Town Historian, Charles Nye (P.O. Box 51, Highgate Center, VT 05459. 802-868-4619). Mr. Nye has nothing to add to the story of John Saxe and his descendants, other than what is in the Saxe *Genealogy* and is on the historical marker by the Saxe farmhouse at Saxe's Mills.

Kinship - Sources for Kith and Kin. Correspondence from Nancy Kelly to George Hill, 2007.

Arthur and Nancy Kelly are the premier genealogists of the mid-Hudson Valley. Their business address is Kinship, 305 Cedar Heights Road, Rhinebeck, NY 12572 (845) 876-4592. E-mail: kinship@hvc.rr.com

Nancy Kelly to George Hill, 9 September 2007, quotes the United Empire Loyalist Association's Index, which confirms the information in Saxe, *Genealogy*, and adds a specific date of birth. Kelly believed the information is credible, although the source of the information in the UELA files was not stated. Kelly quoted *The New Loyalist Index: Loyalist Lineages of Canada 1783-1983, Toronto Branch of UEL Association*
     SAXE, John, b. 11.10.1732 d 3.12.1808; married NY Catherine WEAVER, b. 1.10.1744;   Philadelphia, PA; from: Langensaltza, Germany / Rhinebeck, NY; settled in Philipsburg, Quebec.
     Kelly provided images of documents that I cited in my biography of John Saxe: Map of Rhinebeck, prior to 1812; and Livingston Rent Book of 1766.

Kelly also provided the following source that shows John Sax was "suspected" of Loyalist activities: Roberts, *New York in the Revolution as Colony and State*. Vol. 2. (n.d.), p. 230-1:

Kelly found the following source that documents John Saxe's relocation to Quebec: C. Thomas, *Contributions to the History of the Eastern Townships* (1866), 15.

[Misissquoi] Missisquoi Museum and Historical Society: www.townshipsheritage.com (accessed 5/4/2009), www.geocities.com/Heartland/Lake/8392/en_society.html (10/28/2005), and other sites from Google. These websites appear to be credible.

Reynolds, Cuyler (ed). *Genealogical and Family History of Southern New York and the Hudson River Valley: A Record of the Achievements of Her People in the Making of a Commonwealth and the Building of a Nation.* **Vol 3. New York: Lewis Historical Publishing Company, 1914.** Five generations of the Saxe family in the line of Peter Saxe to John Godfrey Saxe II are on pp. 1094-1098, with a portrait of John Godfrey Saxe (II) between pp. 1096-7. Godfrey Saxe is mentioned in generation 2 as a son of John and Catherine (Weaver) Saxe, who died "at twenty-eight." This volume was downloaded from Google Books on 11 July 2009, from a copy in the Harvard University Library.

Saxe, Andrew. E-mail correspondence and phone conversations in 2008-2009. Andrew Saxe is a descendant of John Saxe in the line of his son Peter (who deleted the terminal "e" from his surname). Andrew Saxe is the most knowledgeable and interested descendant of John Saxe in his generation. He was largely responsible for commissioning the official Vermont historical marker that identifies the Saxe farmhouse at Saxe's Mills in Highgate, and he spoke at the dedication of that marker.

Andrew Saxe worked with Nancy Kelly of Kinship (*q.v.*) and he has done independent work on the Saxe and Weaver families in Rhinebeck, N.Y.
Andrew Saxe was my source for information about the Saxe family Bible, which is now in the hands of his uncle Walter Saxe, and about some of the documents that were used by John Godfrey Saxe II in preparing the *Genealogy* and which have since disappeared.

Skaaren, Lorna. "Robert R. Livingston and the American Revolution" from "The Livingston Legacy: Three Centuries of American History," Symposium at Bard College, 6-7 June 1986. Skaaren documented the business of profiteering by the Livingstons and others in the mid-Hudson Valley during the Revolutionary War. "Throughout the years of the Revolution, merchants developed an almost fanatical pursuit of profit, and John [Livingston] was not an exception. [In 1778] John made an agreement in Rhinebeck with Samuel Hake, a former New York Loyalist merchant. Hake was to purchase goods in New York City. Concerned about the frequent shipment of articles from the enemy in New York City to points upstate, Governor George Clinton sought to end this traffic. He had Hake's ship stopped and Hake placed under arrest. John's sister Janet Montgomery expected goods from Hake's ship and wrote Clinton asking for them." http://www.ulster.net/~hrmm/steamboats/livingston/prt~skaaren.html, accessed 8/6/2005.

Shields, Addie – Historian, Clinton County, N.Y.
Mrs. Shields provided very useful information about Anna (Saxe) Stockwell, who was the granddaughter of John Saxe, and about other members of the Saxe family. Enclosures to her letter included cemetery records that provide proof of the marriage of Anna Saxe and Joseph H. Stockwell. Mrs. Shields provided, incidentally, the only contemporary record that I have seen of the existence of Godfrey Saxe. His name appears on a list of sponsors of a resolution to establish a ferry on Lake Champlain in November 1804. The list also includes his brother Matthew Saxe and Conrad Barr, who would have been either his uncle or his first cousin (depending on whether he was Conrad Sr. or Jr.). The sponsors are said to men from Highgate, so we can see that Godfrey Saxe was living in Highgate three years before he died, although he was buried in Quebec. The petition signed by Godfrey Saxe was "Passed by the General Assembly, 1 Nov 1804 (Ms. Vt. State Papers, Vol. 44, pg. 150.) (Laws of Vt., 1804, pg. 56.)" (see below). Mrs. Shields died in October 2009.

Mrs. Shields enclosed copies of many pages from books, and other documents, viz.:
1. "McLellan Cemetery Records of Clinton County with Index" including "Old Mooers Cemetery - Town of Mooers - Clinton County - New York": Anna M. / Saxe Wife of Jos. Stockwell / Died / Feb. 4, 1890, AE. 86 Ys.
2. Nell Jane Barnett Sullivan and David Kendall Martin, *A History of the Town of Chazy, Clinton County, New York* (n.p., n.d.)
3. *History of Clinton and Franklin Counties, New York* (Philadelphia: J. W. Lewis & Co., 1880), p. 203:
4. Allen L. Stratton, *History of the South Heroe Island Being the Towns of South Hero and Grand Isle, Vermont ... in Two Volumes.* Vol. 1 (North Hero, Vt., n.d.), 151, the Petition in Highgate, Vt., 12 August 1804, is signed by Godfrey Sax.
5. _____ Hurd, a map of Clinton Co., N.Y. (1880)
6. Mrs. George Fuller Tuttle, *Three Centuries in Champlain Valley* (Plattsburgh, N.Y.: Saranac Chapter, D.A.R., 1909), 99: "April 6 1862 Was killed in battle Capt. Edward Saxe, grandson of the pioneer John Saxe ..." [This was the Battle of Shiloh]
7. Allen L. Stratton, *History Town of Alburgh, Vermont, in Two Volumes.* Vol. 1 (Barre, Vt.: Northlight Studio Press, 1986), pp. 32-33: "We ... establish a probable dating (1786) of the list of names of Loyalists whose names appear on this list. This Petition and list is found in the Public Archives of Canada, 'Lower Canada Land Petitions,' Vol. 190) ... Claimants Name   Sax, John"
8. Allen L. Stratton, *History Town of Isle La Motte, Vermont* (North Hero, Vermont, n.d.), on which Saxe family names appear on pp. 189, 294-5, 418-9.

The letter from Mrs. Addie L. Shields to George J. Hill, 12/21/05, is as follows. Regarding Anna (Saxe) Stockwell, wife of Joseph H. Stockwell:
  "Anna was a Saxe, probably the daughter of Saxe who migrated from Europe and following the Rev migrated north settling in Hygate. (He of British persuasion thought he was under British Rule in Canada.) Following the Rev, she met this Stockwell coming from the Eastern Seaboard across Vermont and they migrated inland. Using the Cemetery Records you will note that ... Anna is buried in Mooers in the Woodley Lot. I believe that she may have been living with her sister [actually, daughter] - who may have

been the Woodley. ... Note that she died in February in the year of 1890 ... and the Woodley Family were respectful of her and placed her name on the stone as Stockwell's widow. Whereever and when ever he died there may not have been money for a stone. As a widow lady she endeared herself to this family ... and there is no stone for Joseph. Widows had a difficult time in that time frame. This was a wilderness for a long time. ..." The letter from Addie Shields enclosed eight pages of double-sided copies of typed pages with hand-drawn illustrations from "McLellan Cemetery Records of Clinton County with Index" including "Old Mooers Cemetery - Town of Mooers - Clinton County - New York" on which in alphabetical order (unpaginated) appears "WOODLEY Stockwell [drawing of WOODLEY monument] (front) WOODLEY / (on base) --- (side) Wilbur M / 1872-19 / Jennie L. / His Wife / 1872-1939 / (side) Anna M. / Saxe Wife of Jos. Stockwell / Died / Feb. 4, 1890, AE. 86 Ys. / hs. Wilbur / Jennie"

The letter from Mr. Shields also enclosed pages from Nell Jane Barnett Sullivan and David Kendall Martin, *A History of the Town of Chazy, Clinton County, New York* (n.p., n.d.) in which the Woodley family is mentioned on pp. 55, 107, and 313. "Samuel Woodly came to Chazy from South Hero, Vermont, about 1790."

Also enclosed, *History of Clinton and Franklin Counties, New York* (Philadelphia: J. W. Lewis & Co., 1880), p. 203: "Town of Altona ... Sarah Stockwell, who afterwards became the wife of George McFadden, is said to have taught the first school in the town in 1804. But this is believed to be a mistake, for at that date there were but two or three settlers in the town. Miss Stockwell probably taught over the line, and within the town of Chazy, although that locality too was then sparsely settled." [This Sarah Stockwell was a third cousin of Joseph H. Stockwell]

Also enclosed: Allen L. Stratton, *History of the South Heroe Island Being the Towns of South Hero and Grand Isle, Vermont ... in Two Volumes.* Vol. 1 (North Hero, Vt., n.d.), 192: "Samuel Woodley & Family were ordered to depart from Grand Isle, 26 Feb. 1806 under the state Poor Law." On p. 269, a photocopy and transcription of the advertisement for sale of "Joseph S. Mott's Patent Plaining and Jointing Machine" in Highgate, Swanton, and Milton, Vt., by Peter Sax of Highgate or Matthew Sax of Chazy, N.Y., 30 March 1808. On p. 172, records of the signature in Alburgh, Vt., on 13 April 1805 of Peter Sax, Seletman, and Matthew Sax, Justice of the Peace. On p. 151, the Petition of Elisha Reynolds & Christopher Pickle for **a Ferry (1804) in Highgate, Vt., 12 August 1804, is signed by 37 Subscribers, including John Irish, Cornelius Irish, Matthew Sax, Conrad Barr, and Godfrey Sax.** The petition was "Passed by the General Assembly, 1 Nov 1804 (Ms. Vt. State Papers, Vol. 44, pg. 150.) (Laws of Vt., 1804, pg. 56.)" The petition proposed a ferry across Missisquoi Bay from "Hog Island in Highgate to Alburgh in Franklin Co. [N.Y.] it being the most direct route from this part of Vermont to Montreal ...We sincerely hope and pray that by the correct information that may be given by our Representatives Mr. E. Reynolds & Matthew Sax, Esqr. ..." On p. 173, "On 20 Oct. 1791, Ira Allen, the prime proprietor of Alburgh, petitioned the Vt. General Assembly, for a 'half-penny Tax' on each acre of land in Alburgh for making and repairing roads."

Other items sent by Ms. Shields include **a map of Clinton Co., N.Y. (1880, from Hurd)**, showing the towns on the Canadian border, from East to West: Champlain, Mooers, Clinton; the next tier, from East to West: Chazy, Altony, Ellenburgh. Plattsburgh and Schuyler Falls are further to the south.

Also, Mrs. George Fuller Tuttle, *Three Centuries in Champlain Valley* (Plattsburgh, N.Y.: Saranac Chapter, D.A.R., 1909), 99: "April 6 1862 Was killed in battle Capt. Edward Saxe, grandson of the pioneer John Saxe and son of Jacob who first engaged in business in Sheldon, Vt., and afterwards with his brothers Matthew and Peter at West Chazy. At the beginning of the war of 1812, Jacob removed his merchandise to the storehouse at Chazy Landing, and on the approach of a large force of British, took the same on batteaux to Orwell, Vt., where the only sister of the Saxe brothers cared for them. The war over, there was a short period spent in Chazy before removal to the mouth of the Salmon river (Port Gilliland) where he built a blast furnace, sawmill, dams, charcoal kilns, etc., employing forty men. The freshet of 1830 swept all these buildings and dams into the lake, but the stone dwelling which he built still stands. He spent the closing years of his life in Sheldon to which his wife had gone during the British invasion and where she plainly heard the booming of cannon during the battle of Plattsburgh."

Also, Allen L. Stratton, *History Town of Alburgh, Vermont, in Two Volumes*. Vol. 1 (Barre, Vt.: Northlight Studio Press, 1986), pp. 32-33: "We ... establish a probable dating (1786) of the list of names of Loyalists whose names appear on this list. This Petition and list is found in the Public Archives of Canada, 'Lower Canada Land Petitions,' Vol. 190) ... Claimants Name Sax, John / Present Place of Abode Missisquoi Bay" [Beside his name there are no entries in the columns for "In What Corps Served" and "Time of Residence in Canada"]

Also, Allen L. Stratton, *History Town of Isle La Motte, Vermont* (North Hero, Vermont, n.d.), on which Saxe family names appear on pp. 189, 294-5, 418-9. The book of accounts of Ira Hill (no relation of ours), Tavern and Inn keeper in his large Stone House at the Isle La Motte "Corners", p. 189, shows on 15 June 1835, a bill to "Matthew Saxe (of Chazy Landing, N.Y.), Making Map of this Island per your Order...$1.80." On pp. 294-5 and 418-9 the complicated genealogy of three families is shown, in which multiple marriages took place between siblings in the families of Hiram Hall, Rowland Thomas, and Matthew Saxe. One of the Thomas children was named, inexplicably, Matthew Saxe Thomas, though he was not directly related to the Saxe family. However, he married Louisa J. Hall (thereafter known as Louisa Thomas), who married, as her second husband, William Holt Saxe, son of Matthew Saxe. She thus became the third wife of this William Holt Saxe, who had previously married Eliza J. Burroughs, and then Eliza's sister Sarah E. Burroughs, by whom he had a son William Holt Saxe (II).

Stockwell, Foster Paul. "Genealogy of the Stockwell Family and Other Related Families." Typed MS, ca. 1970, with computer-printed addendum 10 Dec 1988. "The members of the various branches of the Stockwell family, like most early settlers in New England, were farmers with strong religious preferences. One came to America as early as 1629. John Saxe . . . came to America in about 1750, and was jailed in the Revolutionary War as a British Loyalist. His fifth son, Godfrey Saxe, was born on Jan. 28, 1778. It is not known who he married but he lived in Vermont where his one child was born. He died Aug. 16, 1807. His daughter, Anne Saxe, was born Feb. 13, 1804. She married Joseph H. Stockwell on July 8, 1823."

Stockwell, Mabel Kennedy. *The Stockwell Genealogy* (Lebanon, N.H.: Stockwell Family Association, 1983), 463-4: "Joseph Stockwell / born – April/May 5, 1802 at Bennington, Vt. / married – July 8, 1823/25, Anna M. Saxe (Sachs) / died – Sept. 22, 1870, Ae 68 yrs., 5 (4) mos., 17 dys. At Bennington, Vt. / Wife, Anna, daughter of ___ / born – Feb. 10, 1804 / died – Feb. 4, 1890, Ae 85 yrs, 11 mos., 22 dys. / Joseph was a farmer. After his marriage, he moved to Stanbridge, Que, Can., then later back to U.S., where he lived at Mooers, N.Y. Then follows a list of 11 children of Joseph and Anna (Saxe) Stockwell, with birth dates, and some death dates and marriages.

Tuttle, Charles E. *A Partial Record of One Branch of the Hyde Family* (Rutland, Vt.: Tuttle Co., 1931). Emily L. Hyde is person IV in 8th generation (page 25).

United Empire Loyalist Association of Canada.
An e-letter from the President of the UELAC said that "more than a half dozen people have proved to John Saxe since 1971 [in] the Sir John Johnson Branch ... We recently had another request from someone else using a Paul Bunnell reference for a 30 page document. We have no record of it. So, I do not know if there were things in the library that are no longer there ... as the index directory is out at the moment having some work done with it ..." (Douglas Grant to George Hill, 18 August 2005).

The Sir John Johnson Branch has accepted the claim that John Saxe was a Loyalist. The summary of his life that appears in the records of this Branch of the UELAC is similar – though not quite identical – to the biography of John Saxe in Saxe, *Genealogy*. This suggests that stories about John Saxe began to diverge as they were remembered and passed on by his children and their children, perhaps as far back as the early nineteenth century, and that the story of his life in the *Genealogy* was not fiction that was concocted by John Godfrey Saxe II. Correspondence with the Sir John Johnson Branch began with a letter from Jean McCaw, UE, Sir John Johnson Centennial Branch Genealogist, to George Hill, 19 Aug 2005. Mrs. McCaw enclosed a page that showed "John Saxe, Loyalist" with 2 paragraph biography of Saxe (b. 1732, Langensaltza) and list of his 9 children by Catherine Weaver (b. 1744, m. 1771) with b. and d. years for each: John, George, William, Matthew, Godfrey (1778-1807), Peter, Jacob, Conrad, and Hannah. Mrs. McCaw, who subsequently died, wrote that John Saxe's biography has been accepted as qualifying him and his descendants for membership in the UELAC.

George Hill became an Associate Member of the Sir John Johnson Branch of the UELAC in 2005 after submitting his line of descent from John Saxe, and he has continued to be a member on a yearly basis since then.

Information about Mary Sollace Saxe is from http://www.rootsweb.com/qcmtl-w/SaxeMaryS.html (accessed 7/31/05). This information appears to be credible.

John Saxe, Loyalist

Notes

[1] Paul J. Bunnell, A.G., U.E., *The New Loyalist Index* (Bowie, Md.: Heritage Books, Inc., 1989), ca. 600 pp., pages unnumbered. This book is the principal source for the oft-repeated statement that John Sax(e) was a Loyalist, and it shows his date and place of birth, his death date, and his marriage. John Saxe appears twice on the same page (about p. 500):

Sax, John / Source: FHLD / 5 typed pages / Fr: / Stl: Eastern Township, Quebec, Canada / Reg: Cl:

Saxe, John / Source: FHLD / b: 10 Nov. 1732. d: 12 Mar. 1808. m:NY Cath. Weaver, b: 10 Jan. 1744, Phila. Pa. / Fr: Langensaltza, Germany/Rhinebeck, NY Stl: Philipsburg, Quebec, Canada / Reg: Cl:

The abbreviation FHLD refers to "Family History of Loyalists & Their Descendants Index of the Non-Lending Library. Holdings at the United Empire Loyalist Association, Toronto, Ontario, Canada." Reg. & Cl. refer to Regiment and Rank if any claims were made

John Saxe's birth year and birth place are also in J.G.S. [John Godfrey Saxe II], *Genealogy of the Saxe Family* (1930), 12. The birth year and place have been restated in many publications since 1930. Saxe, Genealogy, gives his birth year and birth place & death date and place (p.12), and burial location (p.9).

A letter from Nancy Kelly, of Kinship, to George Hill, 9 September 2007, quotes the United Empire Loyalist Association's Index, which confirms the information in Saxe, *Genealogy*. Philipsburg is now part of the town of St. Armand. It is known as St. Armand-West, and it is immediately north of Highgate, across the border in Missisquoi County, Quebec.

John Saxe was a Lutheran, and those who accompanied him to Canada were also Protestants, according to the sign on the United Church in Philipsburg. The "town cemetery of Philipsburg, Canada" where John Saxe was buried is therefore the one known as the Old Protestant Cemetery in the southern part of town, rather than the newer Roman Catholic Cemetery which is now usually referred to as the town cemetery. The earliest gravestone that I could find in the Old Protestant Cemetery in 2008 has a death date of 1813. The Catholic Cemetery's gravestones in the northern part of Philipsburg all appear to be much more recent than those in the Protestant Cemetery.

I will spell his name as "John Saxe" throughout this work, except when I am quoting from a document in which it is spelled differently.

[2] Saxe, *Genealogy*, 5, 6, 64. Although it remains to be seen if it is correct, John's success in America suggests that he did indeed begin life as a child of privilege, and that he had a good early education. In Saxe, *Genealogy*, J.G.S. speculates that John Saxe may have been related to the princely family of Saxony, perhaps a descendant in the Ernestniche line of Von Sachsen, "an ancient Thuringian family name." J.G.S. says that others with this surname include the German poet Hans Saxe, born in Nuremburg in 1494 and Maurice Saxe (1696-1750), who was Marshal of France in 1746. Andrew Saxe discounts this legend, saying that he "would remove the reference to Hans Saxe and Maurice de Saxe. Maurice de Saxe was the illegitimate child of the King of Saxony, August the Strong, and the Countess of Konigsmark . . . [H]is real name is Moritz von Sachsen, which was gallicized to 'de Saxe.' Being of royal lineage Maurice is of no relation to this Saxe family (Sachse). . . . As for Hans Saxe and Maurice de Saxe and the connection to Prince Albert, these were all efforts by Hannah Saxe to puff up the family lineage."

[3] The history and geography of Bad Langensalza and Thuringia are from various websites including those of the town and the state, the Hainach National Forest, and Wikipedia.

[4] Saxe, *Genealogy*, 5-6. The Saxe family Bible, dated 1732 (the year of John Saxe's birth) passed down in the line of his son Peter Sax and in 2008-9 it was owned by Walter Saxe, an uncle of Peter's descendant Andrew Saxe of Boston (e-mails from Andrew Saxe to George Hill, 4 December 2008 and 17 May 2009).

The date and place of John Saxe's arrival in America has not yet been conclusively identified. Nevertheless, I believe that "our" John Saxe could be the "Johan Adam Sachs" who arrived on the ship *Edinburgh* from Rotterdam on 15 September 1749. Nancy Kelly found records of the arrival of several men named John Saxe (with various spellings) in the years surrounding 1750 (e-mail from Kelly to Hill, 9 September 2007). Kelly found the following arrivals in Philadelphia:

Pennsylvania German Pioneers: vol. 1, p567 - courthouse 9.28.1753:

came over on "Two Brothers" from Rotterdam: SECK, Johannes

Names of Immigrants in Pennsylvania, 1727-1776:
    p202 - Palatines in ship "Edinburgh" from Rotterdam 9.15.1749: SACHS, Johan Adam
    p299 - ship "St Michael" from Hamburg - 9.8.1753: SAXE, J. George
    p306 - ship "Richard and Mary" from Rotterdam - 9.17.1753: SACK, Johannes
    p351 - ship "Snow Chance" from London - 11.10.1756: SACK, Johan

[5] Saxe, *Genealogy*, 6-7. The marriage record was found by Nancy Kelly (correspondence, op. cit): *Marriages Prior to 1784*: SAX, John, married WEAVER, Catherine on 11.18.1771. *Marriage Bonds*, vol. 17, p258. The baptismal records and the account book record are from Nancy Kelly (letter, op. cit.). Kelly also found that John Saxe and Catherine Beber (presumably Weaver) witnessed a baptism in 1777.

There are many Weaver tombstones in the churchyard of the Reformed Church, Rhinebeck, N.Y., e.g.: Rhoda Weaver, d. Ap 17, 1810, aet. 59. [i.e., b. ca. 1751]
Hannah Weaver, widow of Christopher, b. Apr 15, 1770; d. 23 Dec 1818.

[6] The original records of the old Reformed Church of Rhinebeck for the eighteenth century were summarized long ago on typed card files. The original records were then transferred to some other place, a location that is now unknown. In 2007, I examined these card files looking for records of John Saxe, to no avail. No old records exist in the new Lutheran Church of Rhinebeck. There are no relevant records in the National Archives of the Reformed Church, in New Brunswick, N.J. (personal communication with the Archivist, 2007). The baptismal records of six of the Saxe children have been found. The records are in five different churches, both Lutheran and Reformed, between 1772 and 1784. Nancy Kelly says this is probably the result of having different pastors traveling to serve the Germans who lived in this area, and that the baptisms were recorded in the principal church of each pastor. John and Catherine Saxe also served as sponsors of record for a baptism in Kingston, N.Y., in 1777.

[7] Saxe was Livington's mill operator. *Robert Gilbert Livingston Rent Book* shows Saxe, 1781-83. Nancy Kelly (op. cit.). "Note how the John SAX page was previously that of William Weaver. Was that Catherine Weaver's father? brother?" E. Livingston Collection - Princeton University Library: *Isaac Davis Account Book - Tole Ground,*" p. 8 (1781ff). SAX, Catherine, 1781, 1783. SE(S)T, John, 1783. Kelly enclosed a map of Rhinebeck before 1812, saying "The Robert G. Livingston land on which I mentioned as lists John Saxe as a tenant, was located in Rhinebeck NY and in Beekman, southern Dutchess County, NY. The Rhinebeck land, where I believe he would have lived, is Lot 3 & 4 on the attached map."

"John Sachs" in "Acc't of a miller" in "Sax Denker / Beekman … account book" for 1765-1775, copied from NYHS, Account page 94. From Rhinebeck History Consortium, printed 10/9/2006.

[8] The Livingston family's involvement in the complex relationships between Loyalists and those who favored the Revolution was presented by Lorna Skaaren, "Robert R. Livingston and the American Revolution" at a symposium on 6-7 June 1986 on "The Livingston Legacy: Three Centuries of American History," 7 pp. http://www.ulster.net/~hrmm/steamboats/livingston/prt-skaaren.html, accessed 8/6/2005. (Copyright, Bard College, 1987).

Many documents, including those of the Daughters of the American Revolution, show that another man named John Saxe lived in the mid-Hudson Valley and was a Patriot during the American Revolution. Information about this other John Saxe is included in the letter from Kelly to Hill (op. cit.) but it is not relevant to the biography of "our" John Saxe and will not be elaborated upon here.

[9] Saxe, *Genealogy*, 7-8. John Sax on the list of "suspected persons" whose property was sold, in *New York in the Revolution as Colony and State*. Vol 2. (New York State Comptroller, n.d.), 230-1 (title page and 2 pp. copied, with letter of Kelly to Hill, 9 September 2007).

[10] Although John Saxe was surely a Loyalist, the details of his service to the Crown are unknown. His activities as a Loyalist are described somewhat vaguely in Saxe, *Genealogy*, 7-8, which cites the MS of his son William, written in Quebec in 1824 – a manuscript which later disappeared. Sax appears as a Loyalist is in Atten L. Stratton, *History of the Town of Alburgh Vermont*. Vol. 1 (Barre, Vt.: Northlight Studio Press, 1986), 32-3: "Loyalists whose names appear on this … Petition and list … in the Public Archives of Canada, "Lower Canada Land Petitions," Vol. 190: …Claimants Name - SAX, JOHN. Present Place of Abode – Missisquoi Bay." (Copy of pages enclosed with letter from Addie Shields, Clinton County, N.Y. Historian, to George Hill, 21 December 2005).

John Saxe is also seen as a Loyalist in the following secondary sources:
Bunnell, *The New Loyalist Index: Loyalist Lineages of Canada 1783-1983* (see above, Footnote 1); and C. Thomas, *Contributions to the History of the Eastern Townships* (Montreal: John Lovell, 1866), 16: "All were loyalists, and most, if not all of them, had been in the British service in the American revolution. …

They purchased their land of the Hon. Thomas Dunn, at the price of two shillings an acre. Page 17: "Philipsburg ... The first party of white men ... came in the fall of 1784 [including] John Sax" (copy with letter from Kelly to Hill, op. cit.). Thomas also says an "exploring party" visited this area in 1783, so it may be that Saxe made his first visit to Canada at that time. Saxe, *Genealogy*, says "In June 1786, John moved with his family to Missisquoi Bay ..." (p.8). I suspect that the *Genealogy* probably is correct. John Saxe probably made one or two visits to Canada and may have constructed a dwelling there, but he waited until his youngest child was two and the weather was warm before he moved his whole family to their new home.

No record of Saxe's actual service with the Ansbach Jaegers has been found, and he is not mentioned in the *Diary of Two Ansbach Jaegers* (translated and published by Heritage Books). However, the Jaeger unit in which these two officers served did not come to the mid-Hudson Valley so it is not surprising that there is nothing in this book about Rhinebeck or Saxe. Andrew Saxe has searched in vain for the name of a Major Cautine of the British Army. It appears therefore that John Saxe probably served as a scout rather than as a soldier under arms.

[11] "John Sax" is in the Robert G. Livingston Rent Ledger in Nov. 1779 (microfilm from N.Y. Historical Society, NYC, copy with letter from Kelly, op. cit.). "Cath Sax" is shown as "land, rent" in an account "for Mrs. Livingston C0208" in "1781, 1783" in the records of Isaac Davis, RTH D1781, from Rhinebeck History Consortium, printed 10/9/2006. The move to Quebec is from Saxe, *Genealogy*, 8.

[12] For Missisquoi Museum and Historical Society, see www.townshipsheritage.com (accessed 5/4/2009), www.geocities.com/Heartland/Lake/8392/en_society.html (10/28/2005), and other sites from Google.

[13] Saxe, *Genealogy*, 8. Also, the names of the nineteen men who were the first settlers in Philipsburg appear in "Philipsburg," in Thomas, *Eastern Townships*, 16. The names include "John Sax" and "Jacob Barr" (copy with letter from Kelly, op cit.). Jacob Barr is unknown to me. Conrad Barr, who was married to John Saxe's sister-in-law Elizabeth Weaver, does not appear on this list, although other records show that Conrad Barr migrated to Missisquoi Bay with the Saxe family. Conrad may therefore also have been known as Jacob. Records in the Sir John Johnson Centennial Branch of the United Empire Loyalists' Association of Canada confirm the loyal service and migration to Canada of John Saxe. Files in the line of John Saxe's son George (1773-1853) show that "John Saxe, Loyalist" was born in "Langensalza, Kingdom of Hanover, Germany in 1732 ... in 1771 he married, at Rhinebeck, NY, Catherine Weaver, born of German parents in 1744. When the Revolution broke out he swore allegiance to the King and was put in prison ... escaped and served in Yager's' Loyalist Corps ... In 1783 ... there were several settlers who wished to settle in the Missisquoi Bay area of Lake Champlain. John Saxe is listed on a petition dated 1783 and another in 1786. He bought land in the Seigniory of St. Armand from Thomas Dunn ... in a place that became known as Saxe's Mills. When the boundary line was drawn this became part of Vermont" (typescript from Jean Darrah McCaw, UE, Branch Genealogist, 14 August 2005. Also see Paul J. Bunnell, A.G., U.E., *The New Loyalist Index* (Bowie, Md.: Heritage Books, Inc., 1989), unnumbered. John Saxe appears twice on the same page (about p. 500).

An e-letter from the President of the UELAC (Douglas Grant to George Hill, 18 August 2005) said that "more than a half dozen people have proved to John Saxe since 1971[in] the Sir John Johnson Branch."

See also Hon. Warren Robinson (ed.), *History of the Town of Highgate*, 1871, in "The Vermont Historical Gazeteer: A Magazine Embracing A History of Each Town, Civil, Ecclesiastical, Biographical and Military." Vol. 2, *Franklin, Grand Isle, Lamoille & Orange Counties*. Ed. and published by Miss Abby, Maria Hemenway (Burlington, Vt., 1871), pp. 254-275. Transcribed by Karima Allison, 2004. On http://www.rootsweb.com/~vermont/FranklinHighgate_2.html (28 pp. accessed 10/27/2005). Robinson (on p. 5) credits the work of Amos Skeels (p. 2), who had recently died at age 44. This *History of the Town of Highgate* says John Saxe and Conrad Barr and six other men arrived in 1787 (p. 2), that Catherine died in 1791 (p. 3), and it mentions the Saxe family and related families on many additional pages, most notably a brief biography of John Saxe on pp. 13-14. Some items in this biography are incorrect, but portions of the story later appeared in J.G.S., *Genealogy*, published in 1930. In this *History of the Town of Highgate*, it is said that when Saxe and Barr arrived in 1787, they joined six others including C. and L. Drury, who had arrived in 1785-6.

[14] Saxe, *Genealogy*, 7-9.

[15] Robinson, *History of the Town of Highgate*, 2-11. Ebenezer Stockwell had lived in Bennington prior to his arrival in Highgate, and his son Joseph H. Stockwell (who later married John Saxe's granddaughter

Anna Saxe), was born in Bennington in 1802. The Potter, Allen, and Stockwell families would eventually become joined in the marriage of Joseph Stockwell's granddaughter Jessie Stockwell to Emma Hyde. Emma was a granddaughter of Luther Hyde, whose sawmill in 1820 gave its name to what was then called Hyde's Falls, now known as East Highgate. Emma Hyde was also a descendant of Freeborn Potter, brother of Andrew and Noel; and of Jemima Allen, who was a third cousin of Ira, Ethan, and Heman Allen.

In 1790, Highgate was in Chittenden Co. There were then 17 families in Highgate. John Sax was head of a family of 11: 3 free white males over age 16, 6 free white males under 16, and 2 free white females. This accounts for the entire family. John 58, John Jr 18, George 17, William 16, Matthew 14, Godfrey 12, Peter 11, Jacob 7, and Conrad 6. The ages of the women were not recorded in the census; Catherine was 46 and Hannah was 4.

In 1800, Highgate was (and still is) in Franklin Co. There were then 77 families. John Sax was head of a family of 7: Free white males - 5 aged 16-25 (who would be Matthew 24, Godfrey 22, Peter 21, Jacob 17, and Conrad 16), 1 age 45+ (John Sr.), and one free white female age 10-15 (Hannah 14). By this census, we can see that oldest three sons were not recorded in this census. They were John, Jr., who died in 1793, and two who had moved to Quebec, George 27 and William 26. Their mother, Catherine, had died in 1791, so she is not in this census. The name of Saxe as head of a family does not appear in Highgate after the census of 1800.

[16] Saxe, *Genealogy*, 9-11. John Saxe's Bible is now owned by Walter Saxe, according to Walter's nephew Andrew Saxe of Boston (e-mail to Hill, 17 May 2009). It is puzzling that John Saxe did not name his son Godfrey in his will, which was written in March 1807, inasmuch as Godfrey was still alive at that time. Godfrey died in August 1807. Nor, for unknown reasons, did John Saxe make any provision for Godfrey's daughter, Anna, who was born February 1804, and was then only three years old. Anna later married Joseph Stockwell, son of Ebenezer, who came to Highgate in 1809 (Robinson, *History of Highgate*, 12-13).

[17] Saxe, *Genealogy*, 8-9.

[18] Saxe, *Genealogy*, 7 (Catherine Weaver, her birth, parents, and family; marriage to John Saxe; and births of their first eight children in Rhinebeck and vicinity), 8 (movement to Missisquoi Bay, death of Catharine and John; and a brief statement about each of their sons – John, George, William, Matthew, Godfrey, Peter, Jacob, and Conrad), 9 (her burial location), and 12 (outline of b. and d. dates and places of John and Catherine (Weaver) Saxe and of their nine children, including Hannah, b. at Highgate).

Letter from Kelly to Hill (op. cit.) names the churches in which baptisms were recorded for six of the sons of John Saxe and Catherine Weaver: John (1772), George (1773), William (1775), Matthew (1776), Peter (1779), and Conrad (1784). Three siblings of Catherine Weaver are Margaret (m. John Merkle), Elizabeth (m. Conrad Barr), and ___ (m. George Fellows). Elizabeth and ___ are in Saxe, *Genealogy*, 7; Margaret is in Kelly to Hill, letter (op. cit.), as witnesses to bp. of George Saxe.

See also Robinson, *History of the Town of Highgate*, op. cit.

And also see Lewis Cass Aldrich, "History of the Town of Highgate" (Chapter 31), in *History of Franklin and Grand Isle Counties Vermont* (Syracuse, N.Y.: D. Mason & Co., 1891), 593-611 (accessed from Google Books). Aldrich refers to "to papers of the late Amos Skeels" (p. 598) as he restates, summarizes, and adds to the publication edited by Robinson and published in 1871 (previous paragraph). Aldrich does not, however, add anything new about John Saxe.

[19] Mary Sollace Saxe is at http://www.rootsweb.com/qcmtl-w/SaxeMaryS.html (accessed 7/31/05).

[20] Saxe, *Genealogy*, 24: "50. Godfrey Saxe. / 501. Anne Saxe, m. Joseph Stockville [sic]." The rendering of Stockwell as "Stockville" in the *Genealogy* can easily be explained by a misreading of the second syllable in a handwritten document, which the reader must have interpreted as "ville" instead of "well." Each of these groups of letters is comprised of three sharp upward strokes, followed by three rounded upward strokes.

The history of Highgate, Vt., shows "Anna Saxe" was one of the founding members of the Congregational Church of Highgate on 28 October 1811. There is no single adult named Anna Saxe (either as a maiden name or as a married name) alive at that time in the Saxe *Genealogy*, so we can presume that she was the widow of Godfrey Saxe. See Robinson (ed.), *History of the Town of Highgate*, Part 2, p. 8 of 22, which shows 15 original members of the Highgate Congregational Church, including several who were undoubtedly members of the families of John Saxe and Conrad Barr: "Conrade Barr," John Barr, Anna Saxe, Martha Barr, and Sarah Drury.

[21] From *Genealogy of the Saxe Family*:

page 12
1. JOHN SAXE.
 B. 1732 at Langensalza, Germany,
 D. March 12, 1808, Highgate, Saxe's Mills,
 M. Catherine Weaver Nov. 18, 1771, Rhinebeck, N. Y., B. 1744, Philadelphia, Pa. D. Jan. 10, 1791.
10. John Saxe, B. April 17, 1772, D. Aug. 22, 1793, at Saxe's Mills, without issue;
20. George Saxe, B. Aug. 31, 1773, D. Sep. 18, 1853, at Stanbridge, Quebec;
30. William Saxe, B. Dec. 16, 1774, D. Jan. 13, 1840, at Quebec, Canada;
40. Matthew Saxe, B. Mar. 16, 1776, D. Aug. 2, 1836, at Chazy, N. Y.;
50. Godfrey Saxe, B. Jan. 28, 1778, D. Aug. 16, 1807;
60. Peter Saxe, B. Dec. 15, 1779, at Woodstock, N. Y., D. May 27, 1839, at Cambria, N. Y.,
70. Jacob Saxe, B. Aug. 2, 1783, D. Nov. 12, 1866, at Sheldon, Vt.;
80. Conrad Saxe, B. Oct. 18, 1784, D. July 5, 1871, at Highgate, Vt.;
90. Hannah Saxe, B. Nov. 5, 1786, at Highgate, Vt., D. March. 20, 1859, at Cambria, N.Y.

[22] John Saxe, Jr., is mentioned in J.G.S.,*Genealogy of the Saxe Family* (1930), 8, 12. His baptismal record is transcribed in a letter from Nancy Kelly, of Kinship, to George J. Hill, 9 September 2007. Kelly cites documents from "Church- RAP/MAR Pre 1790."

[23] George Saxe is mentioned in J.G.S., *Genealogy*, 8 ("George was a hunter and drover") and 12-14. Baptismal record transcribed in letter from Nancy Kelly, of Kinship, to George J. Hill, 9 September 2007. Kelly cites documents from "Church- RAP/MAR Pre 1790."

[24] William Saxe is mentioned in J.G.S., *Genealogy of the Saxe Family*, 8, 12, 15-19. Baptismal record transcribed in letter from Nancy Kelly, of Kinship, to George J. Hill, 9 September 2007. Kelly cites documents from "Church- RAP/MAR Pre 1790."

[25] William Saxe's manuscript was transcribed and published in *Genealogy of the Saxe Family*, 15-17.

[26] In *Genealogy of the Saxe Family,* she is named Mary Osiette Trembly.

[27] Matthew Saxe is mentioned in J.G.S., *Genealogy of the Saxe Family*, 8, 12, 20-23. Baptismal record transcribed in letter from Nancy Kelly, of Kinship, to George J. Hill, 9 September 2007. Kelly cites documents from "Church- RAP/MAR Pre 1790."

[28] Matthew and Jacob in Saxe, *Genealogy*, 20.

[29] Matthew Sax is in the U.S. Census of 1810 in Chazy, Clinton Co., N.Y. He does not appear in the U.S. Census after that year.

[30] A letter of 12/21/05 from Addie L. Shields, Historian, Clinton County, N.Y., enclosed the following pages from Allen L. Stratton, *History of the South Heroe Island Being the Towns of South Hero and Grand Isle, Vermont ... in Two Volumes.* Vol. 1 (North Hero, Vt., n.d.). On p. 269, a photocopy and transcription of the advertisement for sale of "Joseph S. Mott's Patent Plaining and Jointing Machine" in Highgate, Swanton, and Milton, Vt., by Peter Sax of Highgate or Matthew Sax of Chazy, N.Y., 30 March 1808. On p. 172, records of the signature in Alburgh, Vt., on 13 April 1805 of Peter Sax, Selectman, and Matthew Sax, Justice of the Peace. On p. 151, the Petition of Elisha Reynolds & Christopher Pickle for a Ferry (1804) in Highgate, Vt., 12 August 1804, is signed by 37 Subscribers, including John Irish, Cornelius Irish, Matthew Sax, Conrad Barr, and **Godfrey Sax**. The petition was "Passed by the General Assembly, 1 Nov 1804 (Ms. Vt. State Papers, Vol. 44, pg. 150.) (Laws of Vt., 1804, pg. 56.)" The petition proposed a ferry across Missisquoi Bay from "Hog Island" in Highgate to Alburgh in Franklin Co. [N.Y.] it being the most direct route from this part of Vermont to Montreal ..."We sincerely hope and pray that by the correct information that may be given by our Representatives Mr. E. Reynolds & Matthew Sax, Esqr. ..." On p. 173, "On 20 Oct. 1791, Ira Allen, the prime proprietor of Alburgh, petitioned the Vt. General Assembly, for a 'half-penny Tax' on each acre of land in Alburgh for making and repairing roads."

Mrs. Shields also enclosed Allen L. Stratton, *History Town of Isle La Motte, Vermont* (North Hero, Vermont, n.d.), on which Saxe family names appear on pp. 189, 294-5, 418-9. The book of accounts of Ira Hill (no relation of ours), Tavern and Inn keeper in his large Stone House at the Isle La Motte "Corners", p. 189, shows on 15 June 1835, a bill to "Matthew Saxe (of Chazy Landing, N.Y.), Making Map of this Island per your Order...$1.80" On pp. 294-5 and 418-9 the complicated genealogy of three families is shown, in which multiple marriages took place between siblings in the families of Hiram Hall, Rowland Thomas, and Matthew Saxe. One of the Thomas children was named, inexplicably, Matthew Saxe

Thomas, though he was not directly related to the Saxe family. However, he married Louisa J. Hall (thereafter known as Louisa Thomas), who married, as her second husband, William Holt Saxe, son of Matthew Saxe. She thus became the third wife of this William Holt Saxe, who had previously married Eliza J. Burroughs, and then Eliza's sister Sarah E. Burroughs, by whom he had a son William Holt Saxe (II).

[31] Godfrey Saxe is mentioned in J.G.S., *Genealogy of the Saxe Family*, 8, 12, and 24. On page 8, it is said that "Matthew, Godfrey, and Peter kept the first store" in Highgate, Vermont. He is shown as a son of John Saxe, born in 1777 and died in 1807 in a letter of 19 August 2005 to George J. Hill from Jean Darrah McCaw, Sir John Johnson Centennial Branch, United British Empire Loyalist Association of Canada. Godfrey Saxe is named as a son of John Saxe in *History of Highgate, Vt.*, in which he is said to have died at age 28. His date of death appears in J.G.S., *Genealogy*, 12. The place of his death and burial is not given in any printed reference that I have seen, but an unsourced internet page stated that he died at Philipsburg, P.Q., and was buried at the Old Philipsburg Cemetery. From www.oneworltree.com, accessed 21 Oct 05.

[32] The first store in Highgate, Vermont, was kept by Matthew, Godfrey and Peter Saxe (J.G.S., *Genealogy*, 9; the words "and tavern" and the year, 1801, were added to this statement in Warren Robinson, *History of Highgate, Vt.* (1871), p.3. Letter from Addie Shields, op. cit., in which the Laws of Vermont (1804), p.56 are cited for the petition signed on 12 August 1804 by Godfrey Saxe and others.

[33] The formation of the Congregational Church in Highgate is described in Robinson, *History of Highgate* (op. cit.), Part 2, page 8, viz.: "The first Congregational Church of Highgate was organized in a school-house in the N. W. part of the town, Oct. 28, 1811, Rev. Benjamin WOOSTER officiating. The names of the 15 original members were, as follows: Conrad **BARR**, Hezekiah HARNDEN, John JOHNSON, John STINEMATS (STINETS in modern times), John **BARR**, Henry LOUK, Eunice TICHOUT, Anna **SAXE**, Martha **BARR**, Catherine STINEHOUR, Rachael JOHNSON, Sarah **DRURY**, Sarah WILLIAMS, Hannah STINEMATS, and Rachel HARNDEN."

[34] *Genealogy of the Saxe Family*:

page 24

50. GODFREY SAXE.

501. Anne Saxe, M. Joseph Stockville [sic].

We suggest that the transcriber of this record misread the last syllable, which has three sharp upward strokes and three rounded upward strokes, seeing "ville" instead of "well." Joseph Stockwell was a son of Ebenezer Stockwell, who arrived in Highgate in 1811. Ebenezer Stockwell and his family lived near the Saxe family and he managed the mill of Andrew Potter.

Her name was spelled "Anna Maria" on the baptismal record of her son Benajah Flavel Stockwell, on 16 November 1856 at the Methodist Church, Clarenceville, Quebec (from Quebec Vital and Church Records, Drouin Collection, 1621-1967. A photocopy of the original was seen and printed from Ancestry.com, 24 June 2009). Anna Maria is a typically German form of the name which usually appears in English as Ann Mary and in French as Anne Marie. This suggests that her mother may have been of German origin.

A letter of 12/21/05 from Addie L. Shields, Historian, Clinton County, N.Y.: "Anna was a Saxe, probably the daughter of Saxe who migrated from Europe and following the Rev migrated north settling in Hygate. (He of British persuasion thought he was under British Rule in Canada.) Following the Rev, she met this Stockwell coming from the Eastern Seaboard across Vermont and they migrated inland. Using the Cemetery Records you will note that ... Anna is buried in Mooers in the Woodley Lot. I believe that she may have been living with her sister [actually, daughter] - who may have been the Woodley. ... Note that she died in February in the year of 1890 ... and the Woodley Family were respectful of her and placed her name on the stone as Stockwell's widow. Whereever and when ever he died there may not have been money for a stone. As a widow lady she endeared herself to this family ... and there is no stone for Joseph. Widows had a difficult time in that time frame. This was a wilderness for a long time. ..." The letter from Addie Shields enclosed eight pages of double-sided copies of typed pages with hand-drawn illustrations from "McLellan Cemetery Records of Clinton County with Index" including "Old Mooers Cemetery - Town of Mooers - Clinton County - New York" on which in alphabetical order (unpaginated) appears "WOODLEY Stockwell " [drawing of WOODLEY monument] "(front) WOODLEY / (on base) --- (side) Wilbur M / 1872-19 / Jennie L. / His Wife / 1872-1939 / (side) Anna M. / Saxe Wife of Jos. Stockwell /

Died / Feb. 4, 1890, AE. 86 Ys. / hs. Wilbur / Jennie" [We can see that Mrs. Shields missed a generation in the Saxe family, as she assumed that Anna's father was the Tory who emigrated from "the Eastern Seaboard" although in fact, the Tory was Anna's grandfather.

    The Stockwell genealogy says that Anna (Saxe) Stockwell was born on 10 February 1804. Her tombstone record shows that she was 86 years old when she died on 4 February 1890, so by that reckoning she would have been born between 5 Feb 1803 and 4 Feb 1804. See Mabel Kennedy Stockwell, *The Stockwell Genealogy* (Lebanon, N.H.: Stockwell Family Association, 1983), 463.

    Also, a single page showing Stockwell births, deaths, and marriages, written in longhand, was found in the Hill Family Bible in Clarion, Wright County, Iowa, where it was photographed by George J. Hill in 1962. The page of Stockwell births that is laid into the Hill Family Bible shows "Joseph H. Stockwell was born May 5th, 1802 … Anna M. Saxe was born February 10th, 1804," and "Joseph Stockwell was married to Anna M. Saxe July 8th, 1823." The births of eleven children are then given, ending with Samuel S., and two additional lines which appear to be deaths of children. Although the entry for Anna Saxe is very faint, the birth date does appear to be February 10th, 1804. That Bible is now in the possession of Myron Hill, Jr., of Clarion.

[35] Woodstock, N.Y., where some say that Peter Saxe was born, is across the Hudson River from Rhinebeck and about 20 miles to the west. The baptismal record of Peter Saxe in the Lutheran Church, West Camp, was located by Nancy Kelly of Kinship. See the attachment to her letter to George Hill of 9 September 2007. West Camp is also on the west side of the Hudson River, across the river from Rhinebeck and about 20 miles to the north. It is unknown if Peter Saxe was baptized there or if the minister of that church baptized him and made a record of the event there.

    The probate record of Peter Sax was seen by George J. Hill on 10 October 2008 in the Franklin County Courthouse, St. Albans, Vermont. The card catalogue shows that it is In Book Z, p. 135. His name is spelled without a terminal "e" and he is referred to as Hon. Peter Sax. He made his will on 13 May 1839. Probate was on 30 October 1839. He named his wife Elizabeth and four sons: Charles J., John J. [sic], Peter, and James. Peter Sax(e)'s burial site is in Saxe, *Genealogy*, 63.

[36] Saxe, *Genealogy*, 12 (birth place and date & death place and date). The birth date and death place in the *Genealogy* are not consistent with other records, and the birth place is dubious.

[37] Peter Saxe's section of the *Genealogy* extends from page 23 to page 45, largely because of the long section about his son, the poet John Godfrey Saxe, in which many lines of poetry are quoted.

[38] The twin sons of Charles Jewett Saxe are James and John, born in Troy, N. Y. on December 2, 1863.

[39] Robinson, *History of Highgate* (op. cit).

    On 10 October 2008, I saw the following entries in the Franklin County Probate Office in St. Albans: Sax, Peter / Guardianship Elizabeth Saxe, Guardian / 1838, December 17 / Application and citation, V 349. Hon. Peter Sax, late of Highgate, now of Cambridge, Vermont, made his will 13 May 1839, naming his wife Elizabeth and sons Charles J. Sax, John J. Sax, Peter Sax, and James Sax. No other heirs were named. Bequests included a gift to the Methodist Episcopal Church (Book Z, page 135).

[40] Saxe, *Genealogy*, 12, 46-56. Shields, Addie – Historian, Clinton County, N.Y. Letter to George J. Hill, 12/21/05.

[41] John Saxe's will in Saxe, *Genealogy*, 10-11.

[42] Matthew and Jacob in Saxe, *Genealogy*, 20. Also see Shields to Hill, letter with enclosures (op. cit.)

[43] Marriage to Rowena Keith and their 13 children in Saxe, *Geneaogy*, 46.

[44] Saxe, *Genealogy*, 7 (for his place of birth), 12 (for his parents' names, and for his date of birth and date and place of death), 56-65 (for wife's name, date of marriage, date of death, and for his biography). The statement "nineteen years" is surely incorrect, inasmuch as John Saxe and Catherine Weaver were married in 1771 and they left for Canada no later than 1786 (and perhaps as early as 1784). It may be that Catherine Weaver lived in Rhinebeck for 19 years, however. Baptismal record for Conrad Saxe and other information about the Saxe family from Kinship - Sources for Kith and Kin. Correspondence from Nancy Kelly to George Hill, 2007.

[45] Saxe, *Genealogy*, 56-7.

[46] Robinson, *History of Highgate*.

[47] Ibid.

[48] Saxe, *Genealogy*, 6.

[49] Saxe, *Genealogy*, 12 (for her birth date and birth place, and death date and death place), 59 (for her marriage date and the name of her husband and his ancestry), 59-60 (for her life), and 60-88 (for her descendants). J. G. S. wrote that, "The ... record of the Scovell branch of the Saxe Family has been prepared for this *Genealogy* by Josiah Boardman Scovell of Lewiston, New York, a grandson of Hannah Saxe Scovell."

[50] Saxe, *Genealogy*, 64. The quotation from Oliver Perry Scovell continues as follows: "Mr. Scovell adds: 'The descendants of Duke Ernest of Saxe-Coburg-Gotha, as shown in the Almanach de Gotha, published since 1764 at Gotha, have occupied the thrones as Kings or Queens of Great Britain, Germany, Russia, Spain, Belgium, Norway, Prussia, Bulgaria and Roumania, and as rulers of many principalities and dukedoms. The striking personal resemblances of Rev. Peter Saxe (302), Charles Jewett Saxe (601), Oliver Perry Scovell (906), Lilian Elizabeth Baxe Colt (4093), Erwin Bcovell Jewett (9011), Josiah Boardman Scovell (9067), and Howard Atwell Saxe (60311) . . . to certain of the ruling descendants of the House of Saxe-Coburg-Gotha, leads to the conclusion that the story of Hannah Saxe, as to her father's connection with that royal house, is more than mere tradition'." Andrew Saxe discounts this legendary connection of John Saxe's family to these royal houses as unproved and unlikely to be true.

[51] Except where otherwise referenced, all of the information in the next generations is taken directly from, or paraphrased from, Saxe, *Genealogy*.

[52] Anne Saxe is person #501 in Saxe, *Genealogy* (p.24). She is said to be the daughter and only child of Godfrey Saxe (#50), son of John and Catherine (Weaver) Saxe. The Saxe *Genealogy* says that "Anne Saxe, M. Joseph Stockville." The incoreect spelling of Stockwell is presumably due to a misreading of this surname in a handwritten record.

Her name was spelled "Anna Maria" in the baptismal record of her son Benajah Flavel Stockwell (1856 Methodist Church Register, Clarenceville, Quebec; from Quebec Vital and Church Records [Drouin Collection]), 1621-1967, downloaded and printed from Ancestry.com on 24 June 2009.

Additional details from Mabel Stockwell Kennedy, *The Stockwell Genealogy* (Lebanon, N.H.: Stockwell Family Assoc., 1983), 463-4: "Joseph Stockwell / born – April/May 5, 1802 at Bennington, Vt. / married – July 8, 1823/25, Anna M. Saxe (Sachs) / died – Sept. 22, 1870, Ae 68 yrs, 5 (4) mos., 17 dys. At Bennington, Vt. / Wife, Anna, daughter of ___ / born – Feb. 10, 1804 / died – Feb. 4, 1890, Ae 85 yrs, 11 mos., 22 dys. / Joseph was a farmer. After his marriage, he moved to Stanbridge, Que, Can., then later back to U.S., where he lived at Mooers, N.Y. Then follows a list of 11 children of Joseph and Anna (Saxe) Stockwell, with birth dates, and some death dates and marriages.

[53] Anna Stockwell's burial in Old Mooers Village Cemetery, Mooers, N.Y., is also given by "Davisons of Clinton County, New York State" <http://awt.ancestry.com/cgi-bin/igm.cgi?op> accessed 8/4/05. This website also says: "1860 Federal Census, Clinton County, Mooers Township, Mooers Forks, N.Y., recorded 8/20/1860, shows Joseph (58) Stockwell living with wife Ann W. (56), children Lucy Ann (20), Marvina M. (18) and Samuel J. (16) and a Joseph A. Shedwell (9). Joseph born in New Hampshire, Ann in Vermont and everyone else in household born in Canada. Family real estate valued at $800 and personal estate at $200. Joseph is a farmer."

[54] Ms. Shields also enclosed a page from *History of Clinton and Franklin Counties, New York* (Philadelphia: J. W. Lewis & Co., 1880), p. 203: "Town of Altona ... Sarah Stockwell, who afterwards became the wife of George McFadden, is said to have taught the first school in the town in 1804. But this is believed to be a mistake, for at that date there were but two or three settlers in the town. Miss Stockwell probably taught over the line, and within the town of Chazy, although that locality too was then sparsely settled." [This Sarah Stockwell was a third cousin of Joseph H. Stockwell]

Ms. Shields also enclosed several pages from Allen L. Stratton, *History of the South Heroe Island Being the Towns of South Hero and Grand Isle, Vermont ... in Two Volumes.* Vol. 1 (North Hero, Vt., n.d.). On page 192, Samuel Woodley & Family were ordered to depart from Grand Isle, 26 Feb. 1806 "under the state Poor Law."

Addie Shields' new book, *Survival of Families in Beekmantown, N.Y., in the First Half of the 20th Century*, was featured at the Northern New York American Canadian Genealogical Society Family Festival in Plattsburg, N.Y., in August 2009. Sad to say, Ms. Shields died on 31 October 2009, at the age of 93 (from *Newsletter* of Sir John Johnson Centennial Branch, UELAC, Fall 2009).

[55] The birth date of Joseph H. Stockwell appears in various sources as 5 April or 5 May 1802. If his gravestone record is accurate, it would be 5 May 1802, for he is said to have died on 22 Sep 1870 at the age

of 68 y, 4 m, 17 d (from Cassano, Lynne M., ed., *Bennington, Vermont Cemetery Inscriptions* [database online], Orem, Utah: Ancestry, Inc., 1999) accessed 8/4/2005).

[56] "The Stanbridge, Quebec, Canada, Stockwells," by Foster Stockwell (letter to George Hill, 10 Dec 1988): "For some time I have been struggling with the problem of the Stanbridge Stockwells, partly because I am on their direct line. I have checked all the records I can find (both family records and public records) and I have written several times to the city records department at Stanbridge, Quebec, Canada. Several things stand out in relation to this line. They are as follows:

A. It seems to be a consensus in all branches of this line that the Stockwells of Stanbridge came there from the United States rather than England and then came back later to various parts of the U.S.

B. Stanbridge is a very small town in French-speaking Canada and so it is highly likely that all Stockwells who were there in the 1800s were related to one another. In fact it would be a miracle if two unrelated English-speaking Stockwell families were living in this tiny town at the same time.

C. It seems most likely that they were a part of the Ebenezer Stockwell line (Kennedy page 459).

D. The case for the Ebenezer Stockwell line is clearer [than for the Asa Stockwell line] and the public record has been better established. The reason that Joseph (son of Ebenezer) Stockwell went to Canada was apparently because of his wife's family. Members of this family supported the British during the American Revolution and so were not welcomed in the United States. Some moved to Canada. There were thus Canadian contacts that would have assisted the Joseph Stockwell family in their emigration."

[57] Charles Jewett Saxe's great-great-grandson, Andrew F. Saxe, wrote to George J. Hill, 4 December 2008, by e-mail: "Much of the [*Genealogy of the Saxe Family*] was based upon documentation gathered by [my] great-grandfather, John Walter Saxe, and loaned to JGS II. As I may have mentioned this collection of letters were not returned to my grandfather when John Walter Saxe died suddenly of heart-attack just before the genealogy was published. What I would really like to do is find that tranche of letters.

"However, I have a short life of Charles Jewett Saxe, written in 1914 by John Walter Saxe (his son), and he too refers to the same elements of the story. There is no reason to assume he had not come from Bad Langensalza." [N.b. George Hill believes Andrew Saxe meant to write "written in 1914 by John Burdis Saxe (his son)," inasmuch as Burdis was the middle name of the son of John Walter Saxe.]

"The Saxe Family bible is in the hands of my uncle, and I will take a look at it again. It was published in 1732 and was most likely given to John (Johannes) when he left Thuringen (where Bad Langensalza is located). I will copy and send to you (can you provide your address)." Andrew later wrote that he believes the Bible was actually printed prior to 1732 and was given to John when he left home.

[58] From *Genealogy of the Saxe Family*, 29:

"602. JOHN GODFREY SAXE, M. Sophia Sollace, Sept. 9, 1841.

"The following sketch of the life of John Godfrey Saxe is based in part on an article in the *Bookman* of June, 1916, written by John, a grandson, and Mary Sollace Saxe, a niece, of Montreal.

Give me English, the aptest tongue to paint

A sage or dunce, a villain or a saint,

To lend fantastic Humour freest scope

To marshal all his laughter-moving troop

Give Pathos, power, and Fancy, lightest wings,

And Wit, his merriest whims and keenest stings.

　Progress.

"John Godfrey Saxe, State's attorney and twice candidate for Governor of Vermont, lawyer, editor, lecturer, and poet, still lives through the wit and humour which characterised his poems. He was born at Highgate, Vermont, then known as Saxe's Mills. The frame house in which he was born, built by his pioneer grandfather, is still standing, and the old mill-wheel is now used as its door step. Saxe's ballad, 'Little Jerry, the Miller,' is reminiscent of his boyhood days. It begins:

Beneath the hill, you may see the mill

With wasting wood and crumbling stone;

The wheel is dripping, clattering still,

But Jerry, the miller, is dead and gone.

"Saxe's early studies were at the St. Albans Academy, and in 1839 he was graduated from Middlebury College. In 1850, when Middlebury College celebrated its semi-centennial, Saxe recited his

'Carmen Laetum,' celebrating his Alma Mater's refusal to accept Vermont University's offer to consolidate with it. In 1916, Middlebury College celebrated his centenary, by conferring the degree of doctor of laws on his grandson and namesake [i.e., J.G.S., author of *Genealogy of the Saxe Family*], who made an address, the subject of which was the grandfather and his writings. In 1843, he was admitted to the bar, but he soon developed his literary tastes and in 1846 published his first volume: 'Progress; a Satirical Poem.' In 1850, he assumed management of the *Burlington Sentinel*. During the next decade, he became a prominent figure in Vermont public life. He was Attorney General of the State and in 1859 and 1860 candidate for Governor. Later, he gave up politics and devoted himself wholly to writing and lecturing.

"In 1853, Saxe was initiated into the Psi Upsilon Fraternity at the Alpha (Harvard) Chapter. In 1863, his son, John Theodore Saxe was initiated at the Theta (Union) Chapter, and in 1898, his grandson, John Godfrey Saxe, was initiated into the Lambda (Columbia), Chapter, becoming the first three-generation member of that Fraternity. Herbert K. Saxe and James A. and John W. Saxe were also Psi U's, Herbert at the Delta (New York University) and the "Twin Saxes" at the Xi (Wesleyan). As poet of the fraternity, Saxe, at its banquet in 1853, read a poem, the closing lines of which are read at nearly every Psi U. reunion:

Success to 'Psi Upsilon!'--Beautiful name!
To the eye and the ear it is pleasant the same;
Many thanks to old Cadmus, who made us his debtors,
By inventing, one day, those capital letters,
Which still, from the heart, we shall know how to speak
When we've fairly forgotten the rest of our Greek! . . .
Remember 'tis blessed to give and forgive;
Live chiefly to love, and love while you live;
And dying, when life's little journey is done,
May your last, fondest sigh, be Psi Upsilon!

"In September, 1841, the young poet was married to Sophia Newell Sollace, a daughter of Judge Calvin Sollace. There were three intermarriages between the Sases and the Sollaces. Calvin Sollace married Sophia Bascome, daughter of Susannah Stetson Bascome; Calvin's sister, Hepsibeth, married Nathaniel Bosworth; Calvin's daughters Sophia Newell Saxe and Sarah S. Saxe married John Godfrey Saxe and James Saxe, respectively; Nathaniel Bosworth's son, Justice Joseph Sollace Bosworth, married Frances Pumpelly. John and Sophia's son, John Theodore, married Justice Bosworth's daughter, Mary Bosworth.

"One of Saxe's early contributions to the Knickerbocker was the 'Rhyme of the Rail,' which was reprinted all over the United States, appeared in London Punch and was known to generations of school children. 'In reading it,' says one commentator on Saxe, 'one can close his eyes and almost hear the varied sounds that form an undersong to the monotonous rumble of the cars.' It ran thus:

Singing through the forests,
   Rattling over ridges,
Shooting under arches,
   Rumbling over bridges,
Whizzing through the mountains,
   Buzzing o'er the vale,-
Bless me! this is pleasant,
   Riding on the Rail!
Men of different 'stations'?
   In the eye of Fame
Here are very quickly
   Coming to the same.
High and lowly people,
   Birds of every feather,
On a common level
   Travelling together! . . .
Ancient maiden lady

    Anxiously remarks,
That there must be peril
    'Mong so many sparks!
Roguish-looking fellow,
    Turning to a stranger,
Says it's his opinion
    She is out of danger!
Singing through the forests,
    Rattling over ridges,
Shooting under arches,
    Rumbling over bridges,
Whizzing through the mountains,
    Buzzing o'er the vale,--
Bless me! this is pleasant,
    Riding on the Rail!

"Among Saxe's longer poems are 'The Money King' and 'The Proud Miss McBride.' The latter is exceedingly humorous and full of satire upon the pretensions of would-be aristocrats in this country, as when he writes:

Of all the notable things on earth,
The queerest one is pride of birth,
    Among our 'fierce Democracie'!
A bridge across a hundred years,
Without a prop to save it from sneers,--
Not even a couple of rotten Peers,--
A thing for laughter, fleers, and jeers,
Is American aristocracy!
 Depend upon it, my snobbish friend,
Your family thread you can't ascend,
Without good reason to apprehend
You may find it waxed at the farther end
    By some plebeian vocation;
Or, worse than that, your boasted Line
May end in a loop of stronger twine,
That plagued some worthy relation!

"And also the following, peculiarly appropriate to November and December, 1929, and frequently printed in the press at that time:

Alas! that people who've got their box
Of cash beneath the best of locks,
Secure from all financial shocks,
Should stock their fancy with fancy stocks,
And madly rush upon Wall Street rocks,
Without the least apology;
Alas! that people whose money affairs
Are sound beyond all need of repairs,
Should ever tempt the bulls and bears
    Of Mammon's fierce Zoology!

"As early as May, 1853, William Cullen Bryant wrote of 'Proud Miss McBride,' – 'This delightful poem shows an uncommon facility of versification. You will not find a single nonsensical or slovenly line in the entire book, no slipshod English and no rough edges or loose ends. Saxe's heroic couplets, we are inclined to think, are the best of their kind that America has yet produced, and quite lately, with other of Saxe's measures, they have had much currency given them by the English and the Scotch papers.'

    "When a candidate for Governor of Vermont on the Democratic ticket, Saxe, of course, had virtually no chance of election, and in accepting his first nomination he wrote a short letter closing with the words: 'For further political views and opinions, I will refer you to my inaugural message.' An incident of the campaign gave rise to the following:

When John was contending (though sure to be beat)
In the annual race for the Governor's seat,
And a crusty old fellow remarked to his face,
He was clearly too young for so lofty a place,-
'Perhaps so,' said John; 'but consider a minute
The objection will cease by the time I am in it!'

"In or about 1860, Mr. and Mrs. Saxe moved to Albany, New York, and Saxe now devoted himself wholly to literature and lecturing.

Now I am a man, you must learn,
   Less famous for beauty than strength,
And for aught I could ever discern,
   Of rather superfluous length.
In truth, 'tis but seldom one meets
   Such a Titan in human abodes,
And when I walk over the streets,
   I'm a perfect Colossus of roads.

"Thus he described his personal appearance, which was in reality most attractive, and, with his skill in speaking, won great popularity as a lecturer and reader of his own verses. In the palmy days of the old lyceum system he attracted brilliant and overflowing audiences and was popular everywhere.

"It is chiefly as a poet that Saxe will be known to fame, and more especially as a humourous poet. He has often been styled the Tom Hood of America, and he resembled Oliver Wendell Holmes in the finish of his verse, but had the advantage over him in his faculty of punning.

You'll oft find in books, rather ancient than recent,
A gap in the page marked with 'cetera desunt,'
By which you may commonly take it for granted
The passage is wanting without being wanted;
And may borrow, besides, a significant hint
That desunt means simply not decent to print!

"Summer after summer, in the early sixties, the poet was to be seen at Saratoga Springs. One raconteur says, 'There man Saxe, six foot tall, attired from head to foot in white duck, the centre of an admiring group. He was one of the most brilliant talkers of his day. His fine head with its brown flowing locks and deep-set blue eyes towered above his companions. It was during one of Saxe's twenty-three consecutive summers at Saratoga Springs that he answered the question, 'Pray, what do they do at the Springs?' with his 'Song of Saratoga,' which was reprinted many a summer afterwards:

Imprimis, my darling, they drink
   The waters so sparkling and clear,
Though the flavour is none of the best,
   And the odour exceedingly queer;
But the fluid is mingled, you know,
   With wholesome medicinal things,
So they drink, and they drink, and they drink,--
   And that's what they do at the Springs!
Now, they stroll in the beautiful walks,
   Or loll in the shades of the trees;
Where many a whisper is heard
   That never is told by the breeze;
And hands are commingled with hands,
   Regardless of conjugal rings;
And they flirt, and they flirt, and they flirt,--

And that's what they do at the Springs!
In short,--as it goes in the world--
   They eat, and they drink and they sleep;
They talk, and they walk, and they woo;
   They sigh, and they laugh, and they weep;
They read, and they ride, and they dance;
   (With other unspeakable things;)
They pray, and they play, and they pay!
And that's what they do at the Springs!

"A time-worn clipping in Mrs. Drury's scrapbook, bearing neither date nor authorship, contains a poetical tribute to Saxe, which ends as follows:

And the jokes grow better as they grow old,
And so will continue; and I'll be bold
To say that, a hundred years from now,
Some weary soul, with an anxious brow,
Will smile again, as his cares relax
And thank the Lord for our brother Saxe.

"These 'hundred years' in prospect doubtless seemed longer than they will in retrospect. The American press gave more than passing notice to Saxe's Centenary in June, 1916. An editorial of the *New York Times* of June 4th is written in unusually happy vein, and is entitled and reads as follows:

'JOHN GODFREY SAXE.

The name John Godfrey Saxe, honorably borne by his grandson in this State, has a pleasant sound and savor in many memories. It brings back the scent of old pages of the *Knickerbocker Magazine*, some volume of Mr. Peter Parley Goodrich's annual 'Token' lying by its side on the 'centre table' of our not so remote ancestors who read *Godey's Lady's Book* and *Graham's Magazine* and *The Democratic Review* and *Arcturus* and *BaJlou's Drawing Room Companion* and the *New York Observer*, venerated Mr. Willis and General Morris, had their backgammon boards solemnly bound as 'The Complete Works of Flavius Josephus,' Mr. Rollin's 'History' on their shelves, admired 'The Old Lamplighter' and 'The Lofty and the Lowly,' and too often swapped their fine mahogany old furniture for funereal horsehair and 'whatnots.' Age of innocence, in whose less innocent later days boys and girls, shy worshippers of Mr. Beadle, used to read Mr. Saxe's verses in 'Readers and Speakers,' and singsong them on 'declamation days.' Many of these amateur reciters remember them fondly still. They are worth remembering. In the humorous manner of Tom Hood, the sages tell us. A good manner, simple, clear, effective. Because Mr. Saxe had not the scholarly, clever felicities of Calverley, the taking bang-and-cymbal topsyturviness of Gilbert, shall he be patronized by superior persons? Just as there are multitudes of reactionaries who swear by humble folk like Whittier and Longfellow, no matter how industriously the Vorticists whirl and the Imagists make faces, so divers oldsters will continue to swear by Saxe, a man with 'wit an' humor an' shrewd Yankee sense, more'n there is mosses on an old stone fence.' Some princoxes say he punned too much. Habit of the time, which will recur, like everything else, no matter how wearisome in the mouths of bunglers. One may pun beyond forgiveness, as Henry J. Finn did when he said:

'If my punnish head were pun-i-shed for every pun I shed, I should not have a puny shed to hide my punnish head.'

'This is debauchery. Saxe is a moderate punner. He doesn't offend. He sharpens carelessly antithesis. He is always neat, makes his point, gets his laugh. He must have been a lecturer worth hearing in the prime of 'the Lyceum.' He is often as clever in the humorous vein as Dr. Holmes. But he didn't live in the Boston Pale, though his works were published by its classic house. So he missed accelerated and imputed fame. After he left Vermont, he settled in Albany. So he was not in the Knickerbocker school, albeit his first verses appeared in *The Knickerbocker Magazine* in 1841. He was isolated, without a claque. Mr. Stedman left him out of that exceedingly catholic 'American Anthology.' The pious care of two of Saxe's grandchildren is to be thanked for a charming essay in the June *Bookman* on 'Saxe, the Vemont Poet.' He would have been a hundred years old on June 2. A graduate of Middlebury College – one of those sound, ancient little colleges at the mere name of which you hear elms rustle and almost possess the Latin accidence – he read law, edited a paper, amused himself by running twice as the Democratic candidate for Governor, a test of humor in a State whose Democratic Party could be assembled in George Stearn's back garden. From 1860 till his death, in 1887, he resided in Albany. He was a brilliant and distinguished figure, a man of the world, of great social charm, a successful reader and lecturer. Oldsters brought up on him will be glad to find him so variously accomplished. Among the verses quoted by his grandchildren we miss the lines on Phaethon – we forget the title – son of the gun, joy-riding with papa's team. Papa Helios counsels in vain:

* * * 'The horses are wild,

And when their mettle is thoroughly riled,

Depend upon it, the coach will be spiled.'

"It is a pleasure to many ancients to find that Mr. Saxe's frolic coach of verse is still driving, 'unspiled,' among the moderns."

[59] Quotation from page enclosed with letter of 21 December 2005 from Addie Shields, Clinton County, N.Y., Historian, to George J. Hill, re Anna M. (Saxe) Stockwell

[60] "Zephaniah Keith Drury's ancestry is as follows: Obed Drury, England, B. 1650; 1. Hugh Drury in 1640 came to Boston, Mass., died in 1689, buried in Kings Chapel Cemetery, Boston. Lydia, his wife, B. 1628, D. 1675; 2. John Drury, B. Sudbury, Mass., 1646, D. Boston, 1678; 3. Thomas Drury, B. 1668, Boston, D. Framingham, Mass., 1687; 4. Caleb Drury, B. Sudbury, 1688, D. 1706; 5. Daniel Drury, B. Framingham, 1709, D. Shrewsbury, Mass., 1786; 6. Ebenezer Drury, B. Framingham, 1734, D. Pittsford, Vt., 1818, served in Revolutionary War; 7. Abel Drury, B. 1772, D. 1828, M. Sarah Keith, B. Mch. 24, 1775, D. Aug. 5, 1843; 8. Zephaniah Keith Drury, M. Hannah Saxe, (as above); 9. Horace Saxe Drury; 10. Horace Allen."

[61] From Google 4/12/09: Vermont in the Civil War. Database Search Results

Stockwell, David, cred. Shaftsbury, VT, age 32, enl 9/18/62, m/i 10/21/62, CPL, Co. K, 14th VVI, red 1/30/63, m/o 7/30/63

[62] From Google 4/12/09: Vermont in the Civil War. Database Search Results: Stockwell, Mathew, cred. Highgate, VT, age 25, enl 5/2/61, m/i 5/9/61, PVT, Co. A, 1st VVI, m/o 8/15/61. Mathew [sic] Stockwell's name is inscribed on the Civil War monument in Highgate.

[63] His middle name, Flavel, is the surname of a noted English non-Conformist Presbyterian minister, John Flavel (1628-1691).

Citations for Benajah Flavel Stockwell & Emily L. Hyde & Mrs. Lucy J. Hannings

1. Mabel Stockwell Kennedy, *The Stockwell Genealogy*, Benajah Flavel Stockwell is person 174137.
2. Foster Paul Stockwell, *Genealogy of the Stockwell and Other Related Families*, Typed MS, ca. 1970, with computer-printed addendum 10 Dec 1988.
3. Charles E. Tuttle, *A Partial Record of One Branch of the Hyde Family* (Rutland, Vt.: Tuttle Co., 1931). Emily L. Hyde is person IV in 8th generation (page 25).
4. Benajah Flavel Stockwell Obituary, bound with Funeral of Dr. [E. S.] Stockwell, 11 pp., with covers, n.d., ca. 1921. Photographs of B. F. Stockwell, E. S. Stockwell, Mrs. E. S. Stockwell, and Stockwell Boys (B. Paul, B. Foster, F. Olin, S. Lewis) (copy held by Dr. George Hill)
5. F. Olin Stockwell to George J. Hill, letter, 4 Aug 1963
6. The Oklahoma City Directory for 1918 shows (p. 700):

Stockwell Benajah F h 1624 W 37th

" B Paul eng h 1624 W 37th (USA)

" Eugene S Rev (Addie B) r 1624 W 37th

" F Olin h 1625 W 37th

" S Lewis clk E R Fitch h 1624 W 37th

[copy from *The Oklahoman* sent to George Hill, 24 January 2003]

7. A record of his marriage to Emily Hyde was located by the Town Clerk of Highgate, Vt., in February 2003. In a handwritten response to an inquiry on 17 January 2003 seeking a record of her birth, the Clerk (Cora A. Baker) replied, "No B,D,M <1857 Hyde's / Death Sanford Hyde A45 4-8-1861 / Marriage Emily Hyde A6 B. F. Stockwell."

8. His death certificate from Oklahoma City says that he was buried at Rowan, Iowa.

9. George J. Hill found the following graves in Rowan, Iowa, on July 17, 2006:

Graceland Cemetery, Rowan, Iowa, on the east bank of the Iowa River -

STOCKWELL monument, 50 ft SW of Hill family group
Ranging to the N from the STOCKWELL monument are stones with the following inscriptions:
  Lucy J   Oct 18, 1833 Mar 30, 1914 [Her death date shows she was Mrs. Lucy (Hannings) Stockwell, 2nd wife of Benajah Stockwell]
    Father Aug 14, 1836 Mar 28, 1919 [This is Benajah Stockwell]
    Mother Nov 27, 1840 May 28, 1879 [This is Emily (Hyde) Stockwell]
Facing these, in a row to the W are stones that cannot be identified. Perhaps they are related to Lucy.
  Daughter Emma R. 1891 [She is not in Mabel Stockwell Kennedy, *The Stockwell Genealogy*]
  Mother Lucy L. 1858-1933 [She is not in Mabel Stockwell Kennedy, *The Stockwell Genealogy*]
  Father Ira O. 1856-1930 [He is not in Mabel Stockwell Kennedy, *The Stockwell Genealogy*]
10. A record of his baptism was found on 24 June 2009 on Ancestry.com. The original page was photocopied and printed, from Quebec Vital and Church Records (Drouin Collection), 1621-1967:
1856 Methodist Church Register – Clarenceville, Quebec – Baptism – Stockwell, B.F.
"Benajah Flavel, son of Joseph Stock- / well, farmer of the Siegnory of Foucault / and of Anna Maria his wife was born on / the fourteenth day of August in the year of / Our Lord Eighteen hundred and thirty six; / and was baptized in the sixteenth day of / November in the year Eighteen hundred and fifty six / By me / John Tompkins / Wesleyan Minister / Witnesses / L. Sinfora [?] / John H. Gomland [?]
11. Census records show that Mrs. Lucy (Hannings) Stockwell had at least one and perhaps two or three children by her first marriage. Her son David A. Hannings (1864-1930) was living with the Stockwells as a step-son in the census of 1870 in Blaine, Wright Co., Iowa. He later married, became the engineer of a cement plant in Mason City, Cerro Gordo Co., Iowa, ahd had three children. He was buried in the Elmwood Cemetery, Mason City, Iowa. Both his father (whose given name is unknown) and his mother, Lucy J. Hannings, were born in New York State.

[64] Benajah Stockwell's second wife, Lucy J. Hannings, had at least one son, David A. Hannings, who was living in the Stockwell household in 1880. The census of 1880 does not show Benajah, because his name was illegible – it was transcribed as "Vonigla" by Ancestry.com. Lucy probably also had a daughter named Edith, who was 17 and living with her at the time of the census of 1870 and who cannot be located after that date. She would have been born in about 1853 and may have married and left her mother's home before her mother married again in 1879. David Hannings lived in Iowa until he died in 1930 (see below).

[65] The family photograph of 1909 is carefully labeled to show the names of all who were present. Now that I know of David Hannings, who was about the same age as his step-sister Jessie (Stockwell) Hill, I hope to look at that photograph again to see if he and his mother – Lucy (Hannings) Stockwell – are both in that photgraph. It would seem that although Lucy was a step-mother to the six Stockwell children, by 1909, she had been their "mother" for thirty years and was probably better remembered than their birth mother, who died in 1879.

[66] Her middle initial is on her tombstone, and from the 1900 U.S. census, which shows that she was 66 years old (three years older than her husband, Benajah F. Stockwell). She and her husband and Emma C. Stockwell (26) and Grace L. Stockwell (23) were then living at Murray Village, Troy, Clarke Co., Iowa. The census says, incorrectly, that Lucy and Benajah had been married for 40 years. In the 1870 U.S. census, Lucy J. Hannings (born in New York State) was living in a household of 14 people in Concord, Hancock Co., Iowa (near Mason City). Two others named Hanning were there, too: Edith (17, born in Michigan) and David (6, born in New York but in later censuses was said to have been born in New Jersey). Five named Pritchard were in this household. Also, in Belmond, Wright Co., Iowa, an Ellen Hannings, (14, b. in New Jersey) was living in a family of 5 named Pritchard. It is tempting to think that there is a family relationship between the widow, Lucy J. Hannings and two or three of these children (Edith, 17; Ellen, 14; and David, 6), and that they are all related in some way to the Pritchard family. I do not know what happened to the three Hanning children, but they do not seem to have moved into the Stockwell household with Lucy when she married Benajah. Unfortunately, Benajah is not in the census of 1890, and by 1900 only two unmarried Stockwell daughters were left at home.

[67] References for Emily L. Hyde:
1. A record of her death could not be provided by the Wright County Registrar, because "We do not have records before 1880." (The search was conducted in response to George J. Hill's letter of 11 December 2002; the response by the Wright County Registrar was dated 23 December 2002.)

2. A record of her death could not be provided by the Bureau of Vital Records, Iowa Department of Public Health because "The event occurred before registration began in Iowa (7-1-1880)." The search for this v.r. was initiated by a letter from George J. Hill on 23 December 2002, and the Department of Public Health responded on 27 December 2002.

3. A record of her marriage was located by the Town Clerk of Highgate, Vt., in February 2003. In a handwritten response to an inquiry on 17 January 2003 seeking a record of her birth, the Clerk (Cora A. Baker) replied, "No B,D,M <1857 Hyde's / Death Sanford Hyde A45 4-8-1861 / Marriage Emily Hyde A6 B. F. Stockwell."

4. The origin of her middle name was a puzzle until it was clarified in a search through the "Google" website on 24 November 2003. "Lodiweska" does not appear in Google, but "Lodoiska" (which would be pronounced in the same way) is there. There are about 1840 citations of "Lodoiska" in the world wide web. "Lodoiska" is said to mean "famous battle maid" of Poland. "Lodoiska" apparently became famous as the result of the success of the heroic comedy by that name by Luigi Cherubini (1760-1842), which was first performed in 1791. An unnamed website appearing in the "Google" search states that, "This work, which made its composer famous throughout the world, obliterated in an instant the melodious trifles that had been in vogue since Gluck's departure. Its deep earnestness, its profound learning, its harmonic and melodic richness, and its great dramatic strength won instant approval, and kept the piece on the boards for nearly two hundred times during its first year. Its story, rather poorly arranged, deals with the efforts of Lodoiska's lover to rescue her from the castle of a more powerful rival, and introduces an assault by Tartars at the close, to make a diversion that ensures her final escape." Beethoven is said to have been impressed by Cherubini's "Lodoiska," and it is currently available on a Sony Classical CD.

"Lodoiska" appears as the first or middle name of many American women who were born in the 19th century. It was also a popular first name ("prenom") in France in the early 20th century, peaking in 1914 with an incidence of 2/1,000 births. There were 16 theatre works bearing the name "Lodoiska" written between 1769-1829, and it appears as the title of two pieces of sheet music in the Library of Congress: "Lodoiska" by Arnold Mueller of New York (in "Music for a Nation: American Sheet Music, 1820-1860," LoC MI.A1ZI, vol. 14); and "Lodoiska Overture" by Kreutzer (New York: J. L. Peters, 1875; in "Music for a Nation: American Sheet Music, 1870-1855 [sic]).

Another website appears in the Google search for "Lodoiska": "Giants of Europe," describes the so-called "Countess Lodoiska," a Polish giantess. "Seven feet tall and weighing two hundred and seventy, she could with only one hand and without much strain lift one hundred and seventy pounds. In 1863, at the age of twenty, she exhibited at Saville House, Leicester-square. Writers described the Warsaw woman as 'remarkably well formed,' with a pleasing appearance." There is also a "Lodoiska Rose," which was bred in France.

It now seems likely that in 1840 Harvey and Fidelia Gadcourt (Potter) Hyde decided to give their new daughter, Emily, a middle name that would be culturally significant. The Hydes chose "Lodiwska," having in mind the name which is now (and was then) commonly spelled "Lodoiska," although it may have been a bit pretentious for a rural Vermont community. So we do not need to look for a specific connection with Poland to explain the name "Lodiweska," which is simply "Lodoiska" transliterated into English.

5. From: "Foster Stockwell" <foster@wesleyresident.org>
To: "'George Hill'" <ghill@drew.edu>
Date: Tue, 3 Aug 2004 13:40:03 -0700
Subject: RE: genealogy

I think you are probably right about the Lodiweska name, although this had not occurred to me before. I am, however, familiar the Polish woman. She is listed in my book on American communes. She and her husband ran an intellectual commune designed on the Brook Farm, MA, experiment. She is reputed to have been a great actress, and her husband was a writer of some note. / Foster

[68] Ancestry.com gives his middle initial as J. And his wife first appear in U.S. census records in 1880, living in Mooers, N.Y. Presumably they were in Canada at the time of previous censuses. The 1890 census is available only in fragments, and he is not there.

Census records; and Sullivan, Nell Jane Barnett, and David Kendall Martin, *A History of the Town of Chazy, Clinton County, New York* [copy of pages from Clinton County Historian, 2005], Chapter 11, 55.

Samuel Woodley Jr. was in the 60th Regiment, U.S. Army, in the Civil War (p. 313). Woodley's potash mill operated in Sciota, Chazy, in the 19th century (p. 107).

There is no record to show why Samuel S. Stockwell went to Murray, Iowa, in the 1890s, but there may be a clue in the relationship of the Murray family to the Woodleys in Clinton County, N.Y., where, for instance, a burial in the Rural Cemetery, West Chazy, shows Philip Murray (1861-1927) and his wife Elsie Woodley (1868-1933). Murray, Iowa, is now a town of less than 800 residents, and the origin of the name is not readily available, but it is conceivable that Murray, Iowa, takes its name from a Murray who settled there as a pioneer from Clinton County, N.Y.

Also, it is probably not a coincidence that Woodleys have lived for many decades in Rowan, Wright County, Iowa. This is the same rural township where Benajah Stockwell – Samuel's older brother – moved to in the 1860s, where Benajah Stockwell is buried, and near where the descendants of his daughter, Jessie F. Stockwell, are also still living. The once close relationship between the Woodley and Stockwell families in upstate New York has long been forgotten by their descendants.

[69] Susan A. Woodley's father was probably the son of Samuel Woodly, who was born in England and came to Chazy, Clinton County, N.Y., from South Hero, Vermont, in about 1790, when that area was densely forested. South Hero is an island in Lake Champlain, and Clinton County is on the western side of the lake. Woodly was driven out by rattlesnakes and returned five years later to become one of the earliest settlers in northern Clinton County, just south of the Canadian border. This Samuel Woodly married a woman who was born in New York State, and for many generations their descendants continued to live in Clinton County.

Samuel Woodly's son, Samuel Woodley, born in 1801, married Margaret _____ and probably had at least four children: Samuel Jr., born say 1839, who was a soldier in the 60th Regiment in the Civil War; George L., born ca. 1841, who was a sergeant in the 118th Regiment in the Civil War and who is buried in the Rural Cemetery, West Chazy; Daniel, b. 1843, who had a son Wilbur K. (b. 1872) who married Jennie (1872-1989); and Susan A. (1846-1921). In 1880, this Samuel Woodley, 79, married, white, was head of a household in Chazy, Clinton County, N.Y.

[70] From *Genealogy of the Saxe Family*:
"6016-7. James and John Saxe

The proverb says in sombre tone
'Misfortunes seldom come alone;'
But then, to recompense our cares,
Blessings, too, are sent in pairs;
Thus where a single babe was due,
The grateful father welcomes two.
God bless them, in this world of trouble,
May both find all their blessings double;
And to the joy of sire and mother,
Each prove an honor to his brother.

Dec. 4, 1863.   Jno. G. Saxe"

This poem accompanied a congratulatory letter from John Godfrey Saxe to his brother Charles on the birth of the "Twin Saxes."

[71] His great-grandson, Andrew F. Saxe, wrote to George J. Hill, 4 December 2008, by e-mail:

"... much of the genealogy was based upon documentation gathered by [my] great-grandfather, John Walter Saxe, and loaned to JGS II. ..." (See also Note above for 33. Hon. Charles Jewett SAXE.).

[72] From the *New York Post*, accessed through New England Historic Genealogical Society website, 3 January 2006: 1876 1/19 Tues. Jan. 18, Rev. William Adams, John Theodore Saxe of West Troy, N.Y. son of John Godfrey Saxe to Mary A. dau. of Ex-Judge Bosworth at residence of bride's parents in N.Y.C.

[73] 6042. Frank J. Saxe was a graduate of Norwich University. In 1873, he entered the wholesale lumber business with his cousins John T. and Charles G. Saxe at Troy, New York. In 1881, he moved to Albany, New York, as a partner in the firm of Saxe Brothers. In 1896, he moved to New York City and became Manager of Export Lumber Company in the South American and West Indies trade. In October, 1911, he married Mary (Reynolds) Mickle, whose father was Mayor of New York City in 1846. In 1901, he was

one of the charter members of Atlantic Coast Lumber Corporation with mills in South Carolina. He and his wife reside at Flushing, Long Island, N.Y.

[74] From *Genealogy of the Saxe Family*:
6046. Mary Sollace Saxe for many years has been and now is the Librarian of the Westmount Library at Montreal. She is a member of the A. L. A. Authors' Club, Dickens Fellowship and Professional and Business Women's Club.

Her life and career is profiled in John M. Elson, *National Reference Book on Canadian Men and Women* (5e), 1936, in which she is said to have dates of 1868-1942, viewed in <http://www.rootsweb.com/~qcmtl-w/SaxeMaryS.html> accessed 7/31/2005. This page says her great grandfather was "a United Empire Loyalist."

[75] Author of Lessons in Geography, Lessons in Physiology and Practical Lessons in Science; member of American Society for Advancement of Science; ascended Mt. Orizaba in Mexico in 1894, elevation 18,314 feet; and President of Vigo County Abstract Co.

[76] J.G.S. [John Godfrey Saxe (II)] credits him with compiling the record of the Scovell branch of the *Genealogy of the Saxe Family* (see p. 62). Cornell University in 1891 with LL.B. degree; Sigma Chi; Phi Delta Phi; O. Admitted to Bar of New York in 1892; Editor of Federal Cases for West Publishing Co. from 1892 to 1894; practising lawyer since 1894 in Buffalo, Niagara Falls and Lewiston, specializing in U.S. court practice and corporation law; since 1895 promoter of legislation at Albany, Washington and Ottawa affecting hydro-electric-power developments on Niagara and St. Lawrence Rivers; M. June 16, 1909, at Lewiston, N. Y., to Rhoda Ann Godfrey; three children.

[77] All information in the Fifth Generation is from Saxe, *Genealogy*, unless otherwise specified. Numbers in brackets that follow given names are descendants of Joseph H. Stockwell, and are person numbers in Kennedy, *Stockwell Genealogy*.

[78] References for Jessie Fidelia (Stockwell) Hill, who is person 1741371 in Kennedy, *Stockwell Genealogy*.
1. The record of her death was provided by the Wright County Registrar of Vital Records on 9 December 2002, stating:
STATE OF IOWA County Record Certificate of Death
Certificate No.   Bk 2 #49
DECEDENT'S NAME Jessie Fidelia Hill
DATE OF DEATH November 12, 1940
PLACE OF DEATH Wright County Grant Township
SEX Female   AGE 77 yrs. 0 mos. 5 days   RACE White
MARITAL STATUS Married   SURVIVING SPOUSE Geo. Hill
PLACE OF DISPOSITION Cemetery X   Rowan
IMMEDIATE CAUSE OF DEATH Myocardial Failure
DUE TO X
DATE RECEIVED BY REGISTRAR   X [not shown on record]
NOTATIONS   X
Issued 12-9-02 By Dwight N. Reiland Wright County
C1498880
2. She appears in *Genealogy of the Hill Family in America*, page 8, sheet #7, married to person 68.
3. News story (p.1) and Obituary, Wright County *Monitor*, Thursday, 19 Sep 1940.
4. Funeral Sermon by Rev. H. E. Harvey.
5. F. Olin Stockwell to George J. Hill, M.D., letter, 4 Aug 1963. Jessie (Woodin) Kent to George J. Hill, M.D., 31 Jul 1994: "Grandma Hill was present for all of her grandchildrens' births, even for you and Tom, who were delivered by a doctor in the hospital."
6. Jessie Fidelia Stockwell was the daughter of Benajah and Emily (Hyde) Stockwell. Benajah Flavel Stockwell (1836-1919) was the son of Joseph H. Stockwell (1802-1870; m. Anna M. Saxe [1804-1890]), son of Ebenezer Stockwell (1778-1828; m. Abi Holbrook [1764-1846]), son of Benajah Stockwell (1735-?; m. Hannah Gale [1742- ?]), son of Ebenezer Stockwell (1702-1738; m. Mary Singletary [1707-1749], son of William Stockwell, Sr., (1650-1727; m. Sarah Lambert [1661-1738]). William Stockwell emigrated from England to Ipswich, MA, and later was a founder of Sutton, MA, where the house he built and which

was lived in by his son Ebenezer still stands and is the oldest house in town. Ebenezer's wife's family lived on the adjacent property, which includes Singletary Lake, a large body of water south of Worcester, into which Stockwell Creek flows.

Emily Lodiweska Hyde (1840-1879) was the dau. of Harvey Hyde (1802-1866; m. Fidela Gadcourt Potter [1803-1874]), son of Luther Hyde (1775-1851; m. Phoebe Giddings [1776-1807]), son of Henry Hyde (1748-1813; m. Thrina Ward [1756-1813]), son of Jabez Hyde (1716-1758; m. Hannah Bacon). The Hyde family has been traced back five more generations to Samuel Hyde, the Emigrant. This large family includes many descendants who have intermarried and produce complex intergenerational relationships. They include many early settlers of Vermont, where Emily Hyde was born. Her ancestors include Jemima Allen, a third cousin of General Ethan Allen and his brothers Ira Allen and Heman Allen. She is also descended from the Emigrant William Ward, who founded Shrewsbury, MA, and whose descendants include both George J. Hill and Helene Zimmermann, who are thus half-tenth cousins.

[79] References for George J. Hill, who is person #68 in *Genealogy of the Hill Family in America*:

1. The record of his death was provided by the Wright County Registrar of Vital Records on 9 December 2002, stating:
STATE OF IOWA County Record Certificate of Death
Certificate No.   Bk 4 Pg 210
DECEDENT'S NAME George J. Hill
DATE OF DEATH June 2, 1952
PLACE OF DEATH Wright County   Clarion
SEX Male AGE 95 years RACE White
MARITAL STATUS Widowed SURVIVING SPOUSE X
PLACE OF DISPOSITION Graceland Cemetery   Rowan
IMMEDIATE CAUSE OF DEATH   Cerebral thrombosis
DUE TO   malnutrition and arteriosclerosis
DATE RECEIVED BY REGISTRAR   June 11, 1952
NOTATIONS   X
Issued 12-9-02 By Dwight N. Reiland Wright County
C1498881

2. Memory book of "Jessie F. Stockwell, Fryeburgh, May 19, 1878." (copy from Mrs. Dale Hill's records):
> To Jessie,
>
> Fryeburg,   July 28, 1878,
> "Though many days pass by
> And you I can not see,
> Remember there is still a friend
> Who often thinks of thee."
>   Geo. J. Hill

3. Minutes of Grant Township, Wright County, School Board, 14 Mar 1898. (copy from Mrs. Dale Hill)

4. His family was described as follows in the 1900 census for Iowa, Worth and Wright Counties, Grant Township, Roll #468: (copy from Charles E. Hill to George J. Hill, 17 Sep 1995 -- Household #33: Hill, Geo. J. / Head [of family] / W[hite] / M[ale] / [Date of Birth] Jan 1857 / [Age at last birthday] 43 / M[arried] / 17 [years married] / [Place of Birth] N.Y. / [Father's place of birth] N.Y. / [Mother's place of birth] N.Y. / Farmer / 0 [years not working] / Yes [read, write, speak English] / R[ent] ? / F[arm] / 3 [farm animals]

Hill, Jessie F. / Wife / W / F / Sep 1863 / 36 / M[arried] / 17 [years] / 8 [children] / 6 [alive] / [born] Ill. / [Father born] Canada / [Mother born] Vermont / Yes, Yes, Yes [read, write, speak English]

Hill, William B. / Son / W / M / July 1883 / 17 / S[ingle] / Iowa / N.Y. / Ill. / At School / 5 [months in school] / Yes, Yes, Yes

Hill, Harland E. / Son / W / M / May 1885 / 15 / S / Iowa / N.Y. / Ill. / At School / 5 [months] / Yes, Yes, Yes

Hill, Leroy G. / Son / W / M / Aug 1886 / 13 / S / Iowa / N.Y. / Ill. / At School / 6 [months] / Yes, Yes, Yes

Hill, Myron E. / Son / W / M / Sep 1888 / 11 / S / Iowa / N.Y. / Ill. / At School / 8 [months] / Yes, Yes, Yes

Hill, Ruby A. / Daughter / W / F / Aug 1896 / 3 [years] / S[ingle]

Hill, Adelia E. / Daughter / W / F / Oct 1898 / 1 / S

Hill, Charles W. / Father / W[hite] / M[ale] / [Birth] Aug 1831 / [Age last birthday] 68 / W[idowed] / [Place of birth] N. Y. / [Father's place of birth] Conn. / [Mother's place of birth] Conn. / [Occupation] Farmer / can read, write, and speak English.

5. An undated newspaper clipping, given by Avis [Boyington] Hill to George J. Hill, M.D., 21 Aug 1995: "Mr. and Mrs. George Sheffield returned to Clarion the last of the week, after spending the winter in St. Petersburg, Fla. Mr. and Mrs. George Hill, who accompanied them to Florida and spent the winter months at Orlando, returned to Iowa with them and are spending some time with their son, Gerald, and his family at Lisbon." This must have been sometime between 1936 and 1940.

5. "George J. Hill" Obituary; and "George Hill, 95, County Pioneer, Succumbs Monday" (from Wright County *Monitor*)

6. The descent of George J. Hill in the 10th generation from Edward Fuller, the Pilgrim, as shown in this genealogy, was accepted by the Historian General of the Society of Mayflower Descendants in July 1995, when the application for membership of his grandson, George J. Hill, M.D. was approved; membership number #1856 was assigned to the grandson in the Society of Mayflower Descendants in New Jersey.

7. Recollections from his grandson, Charles E. Hill, 1 October 1995 (by e-mail to George J. Hill, M.D.).

8. The Hill family originally settled on land that was called "Pike's Timber." This property eventually became part of the 3,500 acres of public land in Wright County that in 2000 were managed by the Wright County Conservation Board and the Iowa Department of Natural Resources. In the summer of 2000, Pike's Timber was one of 38 county-maintained recreation and wildlife areas. It was located north of Clarion, one and one-half miles southeast of Lake Cornelia. The Lake Cornelia Edition of the Wright County *Monitor* (Spring 2000) stated that "The heavily timbered 46 acres is a park and wildlife area. It has three shelter houses, one bathroom, electricity, water, and playground equipment. The Iowa river flows along the length of Pike's Timber. There is camping available. . . . [I]t is primitive. In the spring, we have people using the park for musrooming in June. People come to pick the wild beries." Nearby is "Elm Lake, a 466-acre lake marsh, is . . . 2 miles east and 2 miles north of Clarion." Elm Lake was visible from the barn that George J. Hill's son, Leroy, built in about 1910, and that was still standing in 2000.

[80] 1. He is person 1741372 in TSG/MSK; date of birth given 10 May 1865

2. Foster P. Stockwell gives his date of birth as 21 May 1865

3. Benajah Flavel Stockwell Obituary, bound with Funeral of Dr. [E. S.] Stockwell, 11 pp., with covers, n.d., ca. 1921. Photographs of B.F. Stockwell, E.S. Stockwell, Mrs. E.S. Stockwell, and Stockwell Boys (B. Paul, B. Foster, F. Olin, S. Lewis) (copy held by Dr. George Hill)

4. The Oklahoma City Directory for 1918 shows (p. 700):

Stockwell Benajah F h 1624 W 37th
"   B Paul eng h 1624 W 37th (USA)
"   Eugene S Rev (Addie B) r 1624 W 37th
"   F Olin h 1625 W 37th
"   S Lewis clk E R Fitch h 1624 W 37th

[copy from *The Oklahoman* sent to George Hill, 24 January 2003]

[81] Andrew F. Saxe, a grandson of John Burtis Saxe and great-grandson of John Walter Saxe, wrote to George J. Hill, 4 December 2008, by e-mail: "... much of the genealogy was based upon documentation gathered by [my] great-grandfather, John Walter Saxe, and loaned to JGS II. ..." See also Noes above for 33. Charles Jewett Saxe and 111. John Walter Saxe. John Burtis Saxe d. in 1959 (e-mail from Andrew Saxe, 27 June 2009).

[82] From J. G. S. [John Godfrey Saxe (II)], *Genealogy of the Saxe Family* [written in the third person]:
60211. John Godfrey Saxe, B. June 25, 1877, at Saratoga Springs. M. June 10, 1909, Mary Sands, daughter of Ferdinand and Mary Collender Sands.

"John Godfrey Saxe is a lawyer, practicing since 1900 in New York City, and since 1909, as a member of the law firm of Worcester, Williams & Saxe, now Williams & Saxe. He was graduated from

McGill University in 1897, with the degree of Bachelor of Arts and the Prince of Wales Gold Medal, and, in 1914, while President of the New York Graduates' Society, McGill conferred on him the honorary degree of Master of Arts. He was graduated from the Columbia Law School in 1900, with the degree of Bachelor of Laws. He now holds the office of attorney for Columbia University. In 1910-1911, he was State Senator; in 1914, counsel to Governor Glynn; in 1915, a member of the Constitutional Convention and, during the World War, a member of the District Board for the hearing of appeals, of which Charles E. Hughes was Chairman..

"For many years, he has been one of the leaders in the movement for simplified practice and lessening the law's delays. In the Senate, he fathered several useful laws. Later, he was Chairman of the Special Committee of the Bar Association of the City of New York to consider the proposed Practice Act. After that proposal had been enacted into law, he was the lawyer delegate from Manhattan and the Bronx to the Convention of Lawyers and Judges to frame the Rules of Civil Practice. He served from 1913 to 1923 on the Committee on the Amendment of the Law of the Bar Association of the City of New York. Later, he was appointed Chairman of the important State Commission to Investigate Defects in the Law and its Administration. From 1926-1929, he was a member of the Executive Committee of the Bar Association of the City of New York, and in 1928-1929 was Chairman of that Committee. He was also a member of the Joint Committee of all Bar Associations to investigate ambulance-chasing and one of the draftsmen who assisted the Appellate Division in preparing its new Rules to check ambulance chasing.

"He is the author of a Manual on Elections, which is the leading work on New York election law. Some of his articles on governmental topics, which received extensive notice at the time of publication, are 'The Finances of the State,' published in the *Times* of March 21, 1915; 'Taxation to cover Waste,' published in the Sun of March 6, 1916, and 'The Republican Constitution of New York from a Democratic Standpoint,' published in the *World* of November 5, 1922.

"For several years, he was a member of the Executive Council of the Psi Upsilon Fraternity. He has always been an active Democrat, and has served as Chairman of the New York Democratic State Law Committee and of the Tammany Hall Law Committee. He was President of the Manhattan Club in 1925-1927, and in April, 1929, was recalled to the Presidency. In 1916, on the Centennial of his grandfather, who had delivered the poem on Middlebury College's Semi-centennial, Saxe delivered the commencement oration at Middlebury, and Middlebury conferred on him the degree of Doctor of Laws. President John M. Thomas, on that occasion, presented him with the following certificate accompanying his degree: 'You bear, sir, a name familiar to every graduate of Middlebury College – a name they have ever held in high honor and deep affection. You have done credit to that name by your zealous study of the principles of government and by your distinguished services in the practice of the law. On this Centennial of the birth of the genial poet whose name sheds lustre on the roll of our Alumni, I confer upon you the degree of Doctor of Laws.' On the following day, June 3, 1916, the *Brooklyn Standard Union*, in an editorial presumably written by the late Herbert L. Bridgman, long President of the Psi Upsilon Fraternity, said 'Whether ex-Senator Saxe goes down to posterity as a great poet or a great Democrat, his filial and eloquent tribute, yesterday, in connection with the Highgate (Vt.) honors to his distinguished ancestor, whose name he bears, demonstrates that his verse does not suffer by comparison and that his politics have the same originality and independence which marked his service at Albany. "Blood will tell," and the better the blood the better the tale; there's something in the air and waters of the Green Mountains which keeps it pure and strong'."

[83] 90112. REAR ADMIRAL THOMAS SCOVELL JEWETT, U.S.N. B. August 20, 1866, at Nile, Mich.; E. Annapolis Naval Academy, Class of 1887; Appointed Assistant Paymaster, U.S.N. on March 14, 1892; Commissioned Rear Admiral, U.S.N. on June 2, 1923; now stationed at Naval Supply Depot, Brooklyn, N.Y.

[84] 90513. CAPT. ROBERT JAMESON SCOVELL. B. Aug. 8, 1887 at Terre Haute, Ind.; R. 26 Avenue Helene, Antwerp, Belgium; G. University of Indiana in 1909 with A. B. degree; post-graduate student at Johns Hopkins University School of Commerce from 1916 to 1917; at Georgetown School of Foreign Service from 1921 to 1922; O. Teacher of French and German at Jefferson School for Boys at Baltimore from 1909 to 1912; Assistant Professor of French and Spanish at Georgia School of Technology at Atlanta in 1914-1915; Assistant to Managing Director of General Motors Continental at 113 Rue St. Laurent, Antwerp, since 1927; P. Director of Research for Inter-Allied Technical Board, advisors to Trans-Siberian

Railway, at Harbin, Manchuria, in 1919-1920; Assistant Editor of Bulletin for Russian Chamber of Commerce at New York City in 1920-1921; Special Agent and Assistant Trade Commissioner of U. S. Department of Commerce in Washington, Berlin and Brussels from 1921 to 1927; W. Special Assistant to American Ambassador at Petrograd, Russia, in 1916-1917 for administration of relief work for German and Austrian civil prisoners; attended Second Officers Training Camp and was commissioned 2nd Lieut. of Infantry in 1917; commissioned 1st Lieut. and assigned to Positive Intelligence Section in Office of Chief of Staff at Washington in 1917-1918.

Appendices

A = Selected pages from *Genealogy of the Saxe Family* (1930), including
    Will of John Saxe   119
B = Letter from Nancy Kelly of Kinship to George J. Hill, 9 September 2007   125
C = Correspondence and conversations with Andrew F. Saxe   129
D = Correspondence with United Empire Loyalists' Association of Canada
    (UELAC)   130
E = Early Highgate, Vermont: Saxe and Stockwell Connections   132
F = Documents Related to Anna (Saxe) Stockwell   157
G = Summary of Proofs for Generations 1-5 for Jessie Fidelia Stockwell   159

Appendix A
Selected pages from *Genealogy of the Saxe Family* (1930)

Scanned from images on the following CD:
Saxe S3273   92 $10.95
© 2006
Quintin Publications
P.O. Box 65546
Orange Park, Florida 32065
www.QunitinPublications.com

Pages 1-12 (Introduction and entries for John Saxe) and 62-5 (additional information and legends about the Saxe family in Europe)

Scanned into OCR and edited in Word from *Genealogy of the Saxe Family* 1930. Some minor errors in the original text were corrected, and some new errors were probably introduced, inadvertently.

FOREWORD

"There is a moral and philosophical respect
for our ancestors which elevates the
character and improves the heart."

  --DANIEL WEBSTER.

To a descendant of one Jacob Saxe or Sax, a Hessian soldier, who came to America at the time of the Revolutionary War, is due the existence of this Genealogy of the descendants of John. In January, 1929, Hon. William D. Morrow wrote me asking information as to the kinship to our Saxes of Edna Sophia Saxe Morrow, his wife. I communicated with several members of the family and, in the course of my inquiries, Horace Eugene Allen generously sent me a manuscript compiled for him by Hannah Saxe Drury, his grandmother, in her eighty-first year. It was her interesting manuscript, in turn, which suggested the idea of preparing some printed record of John Saxe and his descendants. During July to December, 1929, Mrs. Drury's manuscript has been edited and much information added, some as to the earlier generations, and a great deal as to the later ones. I gratefully acknowledge the active cooperation of many members of the family, including:

Frank J. Saxe.
Mrs. Clarence E. Allen.
Horace Eugene Allen.
Miss Lilian Elizabeth Saxe Colt.
Mrs. Louise E. Jennison.
Miss Mary S. Saxe.
James A. Saxe.

Charles William Saxe.
Herbert K. Saxe.
Howard A. Saxe.
J. Boardman Scovell.
Miss Fannie E. Wead.
Charles Miner Wead.

4

It is also interesting to record that Mr. Morrow and I, after being at very considerable pains to try to establish kinship between the two Saxe families, have been unable to do so-at least up to date. Also, that Jacob Saxe, Mrs. Morrow's ascendant, had a son, Elias Saxe (B. Stillwater, N. Y., July 29, 1794, D. Greenfield, N. Y., September 24, 1831, M. Sally Person); that Elias had six children, Jacob, Polly, Constantine, John (B. June 8, 1823, D. Feb. 27, 1897, M. Sally Sophia Person), Asa and Elias Jr.; that John had two children, Willard Elias Saxe and John Brayton Saxe, and that Mrs. Morrow is the latter's daughter.

This Genealogy, herewith presented to the descendants of John, supplies a printed record where none previously existed. In it is incorporated all material to be found in various records compiled by members of the family, and also all information which could be procured by correspondence during the comparatively brief time available. It may be said to be substantially accurate and fairly complete, "up to now".

 J. G. S.
  [John Godfrey Saxe, II]
New York, January 1, 1930.

5

JOHN SAXE, son of Godfrey, was the first American representative of the family, which: as the name indicates, originated in Saxony. The name, originally "Von Sachsen", is an ancient Thuringian family name, probably, at one time, connected with one of the branches of the house of Saxony [Sachsen], the Ernestniche line, which split up into various families that descended from the younger scions and located in the northern Dutchies of Sachse Coburg, Sachse Gotha, Sachse Weimer, Brunswick and the Kingdom of Hanover. Some family records give the original American spelling as "Sax", with the notation that John Sax subsequently changed the name to "Saxe". Other records give the original spelling as "Saxe" and explain that John later left off the "e", because the French Canadians pronounced the name "Sax-y". The second version finds corroboration in the statement attributed to the Poet Saxe, that: "It was all wrong for the natives to have deprived the old fellow of his 'ease' "and by John's will (post, pp. 10-11), written the year before his death, which spells the name without the "e". Ascendants, according to some records, may have included Hans Saxe, the German poet, born in Nuremburg in 1494, and Maurice Saxe, born in 1696, later Marshall of France (1746), died at Chambord, 1750.

Saxe was born in 1732 at Langensaltza, in the Kingdom of Hanover, Germany, a town nineteen miles north of Erfurt, on the Salza. It is enclosed in walls, defended by a castle and has manufactories of woolen fabrics, paper and salt petre. John was the youngest of a large family of children. His father was a man of influence and the owner of eight acres of land. The son was but ten years old at his father's death and so could give but little account of him except as a stern man of great strength and courage.

6

John attended school until thirteen years of age when it became necessary for him to engage in some occupation to secure a livelihood. The highest peaks of the Thuringian forest are found in Saxe Gotha and the grand mountain scenery, the beautiful valleys and forests of his native Duchy awakened his childish enthusiasm and lingered in his memory like a beautiful picture down to his latest days. At fourteen, he said farewell to his home and with a companion two years his senior went out to seek his fortune. More than three years were spent in their wanderings, when at last they made their way to Amsterdam, where they stayed six months. John, who was then eighteen, was one day visited by his comrade, who said, "John, I am going to America and I want you to go with me". The reply was "I have not money enough to pay my passage". "Well", said his friend, "I have more than enough for myself and putting our savings together there will be enough for both." This settled the matter, and they immediately engaged passage and after a voyage of fifteen weeks landed at Philadelphia, where they took the oath of allegiance to King George of England. John was heavily in debt to the Captain of the vessel, his companion having barely enough to pay his own bills. In accordance with the custom of the times, the Captain bound John out for three years' service to pay the passage money, which was advanced by his employer, a miller. The latter was an intelligent man taking a friendly interest in his apprentice, making him his companion and trusted friend. Besides acquiring a thorough knowledge of milling, John also learned to read, write and speak English. When, therefore, at the age of twenty-one, he had finished his apprenticeship, he was well prepared to begin the battle of life for himself. Later, he learned to speak French fluently. John Saxe was a man of marked characteristics and under more favorable auspices would no doubt have

7

achieved public distinction. He was a man of ability and perseverance in every way calculated to endure the hardship of an early settler and pioneer. He was five feet, eleven inches, in height, broad shoulders and tapering to his feet, which were small. He was long armed, active and athletic, possessed great physical strength and endurance and indomitable courage. In manly sports and in physical contests he was champion, had light brown hair, fair complexion and blue eyes, regular, well defined features, aquiline nose, a mouth and chin indicating great firmness and strength of character, a conscientious man of temperate habits, of a calm sense of justice and integrity. He continued to work at his trade, after leaving his employer, for some years in Philadelphia and vicinity, was superintendent of a flouring mill at Valley Forge. Afterwards his residence for some time was in New York City. While residing there, he was accustomed to travel on horseback to Rhinebeck to visit the lady who afterwards became his wife. On November 18, 1771, at Rhinebeck, when thirty-nine years of age, he married Catherine Weaver, then twenty-seven years old. She was born in Philadelphia, in 1744, of German parents and removed to Rhinebeck with them, where John and she were married. She is described as a beautiful woman, rather below medium height, fair complexion, black eyes and dark curling hair, an excellent housekeeper, a faithful wife and mother. Her sister Elizabeth married Conrad Barr, who moved to Highgate. Another sister married George Fellows. Their daughter married one Shrives.

John and Catherine lived in Rhinebeck and vicinity for nineteen years and had eight sons born to them there. John was a loyal subject to Great Britain and the breaking out of the Revolutionary War wrought no change to him in this regard. He said he had taken the oath of allegiance to the King and, as the King had done

8

him no wrong, he could not in conscience violate his oath. He was arrested and thrown into prison at Esopus, New York, but he eventually was set at liberty or escaped. Some accounts state that he then joined the British standard at New York. According to a manuscript written by his son William in Quebec in 1824, he had assisted a Major Cautine of the British Army to penetrate through the lines of the American troops. In June, 1786, John moved with his family to Missisquoi Bay, on Lake Champlain, in Canada, just north of Vermont line. They proceeded by boat, he and his wife and eight sons, and a man servant, up to the Hudson to Glens Falls, then down Lake George and Lake Champlain. His youngest son was less than two years old, when, on November 15, 1786, was born his youngest child and only daughter, Hannah. After residing two years in Canada, John settled in Highgate, Vermont, where he built mills, which later gave to the settlement the name "Saxe's Mills" and cleared a large farm, making this his home until his death on March 13, 1808. Catherine, his beloved wife, had died on January 10, 1791, at the age of 47, and though Hannah was then only four years old, John never remarried. The following years were times of severe trial to the strong man, he struggled manfully against the harsh unfriendly influences incident to pioneer life in a new country and severe climate. He and his family had many difficulties to endure. They were harassed by Indians, and wild beasts. John, the eldest son, died on August 22, 1793, at the age of twenty-one. George was a hunter and drover. William was a surveyor. Matthew was a wheelwright; later a merchant and Town Clerk. Godfrey died at the age of twenty-eight. Peter remained on the homestead, a farmer, merchant and man of business. He represented the town in the Legislature, and the poorer classes always voted for him, for said they: "'We all know Peter". Jacob was a merchant, Conrad a farmer.

9

Highgate, in the northwest part of Franklin County, was chartered August 17, 1763, by Governor Wentworth to Samuel Hunt and sixty-three others, six miles square. First settlers in 1785-6--Joseph Rycard, John Villaker, Jeremiah Brewster, Thomas Butterfield, John Stinchover, Abram Rycard, Conrad Barr, John Saxe, John Shelters, George Wilson, John Nagle, Peter Wagoner. John Saxe built the first grist mill on a small stream, Rock River, running into Missisquoi River, a mile north of Highgate Springs. The first Post Office was there. A carding mill was built next the mill, also a potashery. There were no other mills nearer than Burlington, thirty-five miles, or Plattsburg, hence the place with its little log mill and one run of stone was a great blessing and brought many settlers into town. Matthew, Godfrey and Peter Saxe kept the first store. The first settlers were Dutch, principally refugees who supposed they had settled in Canada until after the establishment of the boundary line on Latitude 45. At that time, there were no settlers between Highgate and Burlington. In 1786, with no guide but his pocket compass, John Saxe visited Burlington--the first town meeting was held at his house. John was a member of the Lutheran Church and a careful reader of the Scriptures, which he made the rule of his life. He had a German Bible, from which his youngest children were accustomed to read to him in his old age. He gave his children the best education circumstances permitted, and endeavored to imbue them with a noble ambition. The best commentary is the success and elevated position in life which his children attained. His counsel was often sought in cases of dispute among his neighbors and his decisions were a finality. He lived to see his children grow to maturity. Prospered and respected, he died at Highgate at the age of seventy-six years. He and his wife are buried in the town cemetery of Philipsburg, Canada.

10

WILL OF JOHN SAXE.

In the name of God, Amen.
I, John Sax, of the Town of Highgate, in the County of Franklin and State of Vermont., being weak in body but sound in memory, Blessed be God, do this 28th day of March, in the year of our Lord Christ 1807, make and publish this my Last Will and Testament in manner following. Imprimis--I give and bequeath to my three sons, Mathew, Peter and Jacob, all my lands with the mills and buildings standing thereon which I hold and possess in the Town of Highgate aforesaid, under the following conditions that the premises herein demised to the said Mathew, Peter and Jacob to be held by them in equal shares, i.e. one third of the same to each, but subject nevertheless to pay the following legacies, that is to say, to my sons George, William and Conrad--unto George and William, fifty dollars each and unto Conrad one hundred and fifty dollars, and to my daughter Hannah one hundred and fifty, making in the whole four hundred dollars, to be paid by the said Mathew, Peter and Jacob s aforesaid within one year after my decease. Item. I give and bequeath to my son George, Lott No. 8 in the Township of Shefford and half of Lott No. 27 in the town-

11

ship of Clifton, in the Province of Lower Canada. Item. I give and bequeath to my son William, Lotts No. 25 and 26 in the said Township of Clifton in the Province of Lower Canada. Item. I given and bequeath to my son Conrad, Lott No. 7 in the Township of

Shefford, Province of Lower Canada aforesaid. Item. I give and bequeath to my daughter Hannah all the lands which I hold and possess in the Signeiory of St. Armand and the buildings thereon standing, in the Province aforesaid. Item. I bequeath unto my grand son John Sax, a minor, son of my son George, the equal one half of Lott No. 27 in the Township of Clifton, in the Province of Lower Canada aforesaid; and as to my goods, chattels and personal estate, I will and ordain that it shall be disposed of in the following manner, that is to say, I give to my son George all the wearing apparel which I shall own at my decease, and as to the horse which I commonly ride I give the same, together with the saddle and bridle, to my son Conrad and also the sett of blacksmith tools which he now works with. I give to my daughter one feather bed, she having the choice out of all my feather beds, together with the bedding for the same, also the sett of bed curtains; and furthermore I give to my son William and Conrad and to my daughter Hannah one horse each worth forty dollars or the value thereof in some other property. As to the remainder or residue of my goods and chattels or personal estate, it is my will and I hereby give the same to all my children to be divided among them equally without sex or priority, and I hereby appoint, constitute and ordain my son Mathew and my friend Thomas Best, and Charles Miller executors of this my last will and testament.

In witness whereof, I, the said John Sax, have hereunto set my hand and seal, the day and year first above written.

JOHN SAX.

Signed, sealed and published as and
   for his last will and testament, in
   our presence, we here subscribe
   our names in his presence

I. JONES
G. R BYNOLDS
PHILIP RUITER

12

1. JOHN SAXE.
 B. 1732 at Langensalza, Germany,
 D. March 12, 1808, Highgate, Saxe's Mills,
 M. Catherine Weaver Nov. 18, 1771,
  Rhinebeck, N. Y., B. 1744, Philadelphia, Pa.
 D. Jan. 10, 1791.
10. John Saxe, B. April 17, 1772, D. Aug. 22, 1793, at Saxe's Mills, without issue;
20. George Saxe, B. Aug. 31, 1773, D. Sep. 18, 1853, at Stanbridge, Quebec;
30. William Saxe, B. Dec. 16, 1774, D. Jan. 13, 1840, at Quebec, Canada;
40. Matthew Saxe, B. Mar. 16, 1776, D. Aug. 2, 1836, at Chazy, N. Y.;
50. Godfrey Saxe, B. Jan. 28, 1778, D. Aug. 16, 1807;
60. Peter Saxe, B. Dec. 15, 1779, at Woodstock, N. Y.,
     D. May 27, 1839, at Cambria, N. Y.,
70. Jacob Saxe, B. Aug. 2, 1783, D. Nov. 12, 1866, at Sheldon, Vt.;
80. Conrad Saxe, B. Oct. 18, 1784, D. July 5, 1871, at Highgate, Vt.;
90. Hannah Saxe, B. Nov. 5, 1786, at Highgate, Vt., D. March. 20, 1859, Cambria, N.Y.

Appendix B

Letter from Nancy Kelly of Kinship to George J. Hill, 9 September 2007

This letter summarizes Nancy Kelly's research on the Saxe family in the vicinity of Rhinebeck, N.Y. in the 18th century. She cites *The New Loyalist Index*; *Pennsylvania German Pioneers*; *Names of Immigrants in Pennsylvania, 1727-1776*; Kingston Reformed Church baptisms; baptisms at Kaat Ref, Stn Ch, King Ref, W Camp, and RH Luth; *Dutchess County Tax Lists, Rhinebeck Precinct, 1739-78*; *New York in the Revolution*(*); *Public Papers of Governor Clinton*; *Upstate New York in the 1760s*; *Marriages Prior to 1784*; *National Genealogical Society Quarterly*; *Robert Gilbert Livingston Rent Book*(*); *Isaac Davis Account Book*; *History of the Eastern Townships*(*).*Church-Bap/Mar pre 1790*; *Rhinebeck Precinct Map* (with e-mail of 23 Aug 2007); and a copy of Kelly's letter of 22 August 2007.
    Enclosed copies of items marked *

Kelly wrote, "We have the birth of a John [Sax] in 1731 and one born in 1732; one who became a Patriot and one who bacame a Loyalist and neither of them seem to be the John who is born in Germany. Unfortunately, the author of the JS [John Godfrey Saxe] work gives very little, if any, documentation for his assumptions ..." [page 2] "Some items, I assume, may be ascribed to the author's desire to embellish but others may be misinformation.
    "When John Godfrey Saxe II, the author of [JS], tells us that John was born at Langensaltza (sic) (page 5) we discover, on further searching, that what was meant was "Bad Langensalza," presumably is the same as the information in:

The New Loyalist Index:
Loyalist Lineages of Canada 1783-1983, Toronto Branch of UEL Association
SAXE, John, b. 11.10.1732 d 3.12.1808
married NY Catherine WEAVER, b. 1.10.1744 Philadelphia, PA
from: Langensaltza, Germany / Rhinebeck, NY
settled in Philipsburg, Quebec

"The early life of John in Europe is interesting but where is the documentation? His leaving Europe and heading for the port of Philadelphia is again without documentation. In an attempt to resolve that, the following references have been discovered:

Pennsylvania German Pioneers:
vol 1, p567 - courthouse 9.28.1753
came over on "Two Brothers" from Rotterdam
SECK, Johannes
and:
Names of Immigrants in Pennslvania, 1727-1776:
p202 - Palatines in ship "Edinburgh" from Rotterdam 9.15.1749
SACHS, Johan Adam

p299 - ship "St Michael Michael" from Hamburg - 9.8.1753
SAXE, J. George

p306 - ship "Richard and Mary" from Rotterdam - 9.17.1753
SACK, Johannes

p351 - ship "Snow Chance" from London - 11.10.1756
SACK, Johan

Only one of the above immigrants arrived at Philadelphia at or before 1750 and his name was "John Adam" and was not too likely to have been called "John." So we have a problem with the immigration scheme. Where he is later, according to [JS], is at Valley Forge, PA as a flouring mill superintendent, then to New York City, and traveling to Rhinebeck to court his future wife whom he marries there on 11.18.1771 (page 7). None of this seems capable of documentation.

[page 3]
"Once in the Hudson Valley of New York, the confusion really begins to set in. I find John SAXE as a husband of the following ladies:
John Saxe and Margaaret BURGER
John Saxe and Rachel (_____)
John Saxe and Margaret Smith
John Saxe and Catherine BIBER
John Saxe and Anna Maria WEBER/WEAVER
John Saxe and Mary RICE
To reconcile:
    1. Burger and Smith may be the same lady since they have the same given name. If she was married before one reference could be to a maiden name while the other to her married name.
    2. Biber and Weber are probably the same lady ... But that leaves a John SAXE with a Rachel (_____), and Anna Maria WEAVER and a Mary RICE. Multiple marriages may solve some of the quandry but there seems to be a limit to how many times a person has wed.

Of all these Johns, let us consider the two that cause the most confusion:

       John, the Patriot
John SAXE and Margaret BURGER/SMITH
    John Sax married Margaaret Smith 1762 Catskill Reformed Church ...
"More information on the above may be obtained through the DAR.
DAR Patriot Index: p2575 SAXE, John ... mar Margaret Smith ... ...

[page 6]
       John, the Loyalist
"The other John in close proximity age wise and geographically to the above John(s) is the family of:
John SAXE and Catherine WEAVER
Kaat Ref 823 John, bp 6.23.1772
   Spon John Merkle & Margaret Weaver
Stn Ch 1095 George, b. 8.30.1773
   Spon George Ring and Catherine Tremper
King Ref 7692 William, bp 3.23.1775
   Spon Philip Hotaling & wife, Janet Elting
King Ref 7772 Matthew, bp 4.21.1776
   Spon Matthew Smith & wife, Catherine Wagner
W Camp 544 Peter, b 9.3.1779
   Spon John Kraft & wife
RH Luth 2205 Conrad, bp 11.28.1784
   Spon Conrad Bahr & wife, Elizabeth Weaver

John Saxe, Loyalist

[The names of the churches listed above in abbreviated form are spelled out by Kelly in a narrative enclosure with a copy of one page from "Church- RAP/MAR Pre 1790": Kaatsban Reformed Church; Stone Church; Kingston Reformed Church; St. Paul's Lutheran; West Camp; and St. Paul's Lutheran, Red Hook]

Kingston Reformed Church: baptisms
#7871 John Sax & wife, Catherine Beber (probable mistake for Weaver) were sponsors on 8.10.1777 at baptism of the child of Elias Ostrander and Rachel Van Etten

"As you are aware, all of the children that [JS] ascribes to this family were not found and some of the dates that [JS] uses are not correct. Also note that the Conrad BARR that [JS] mentions on page 7 is likely the Conrad BAHR showing up as a sponsor in 1784 above.

John, the Loyalist appears in:

Dutchess County Tax Lists:
Rhinebeck Precinct, 1739-1778
SAXE, John, 1765-1771
where his surname is variously spelled SIX, TES and SEA, and also in:
[page 7]
Roberts: New York in the Revolution:
vol. 2, page 231 - Tories and Suspected Persons, various dates 1776-1785
SAX, John - suspected person

Public Papers of Governor Clinton: vol 7, p409 [copy enclosed] where a Court Martial is convened at the house John Saxe [George Hill believes this is more likely the house of John Saxe the Patriot inasmuch as there is no indication that John Saxe was tried at the Court Martial]

and probably in:

Upstate New York in the 1760s:
p97 Catskill, NY Tax List, 1766
   2.13.1766 SAX, John - taxed 6
   2.13.1767 Signed at Loonenburg (Athens)
p189 Capt Cornelius Dubois Company - 4.9.1767 at Catskill
SAX, John
(New York Colonial Muster Rolls has a duplicate of preceding entry)

"His marriage is probably recorded in:
Marriages Prior to 1784:
SAX, John, married
WEAVER, Catherine
on 11.18.1771
Found in Marriage Bonds, vol 17, p258

"An attempt to identify this John as a miller was not successful. He was found in:
National Genealogical Society Quarterly:
Dutchess County, NY Early Residents
Henry Denker ledger, miller - record of customers from @ 1735 through 1772 included:
   SACK, John, from 1766 through 1772 … with no mention of him being a miller …

Robert Gilbert Livingston Rent Book:
Photocopy of page attached to this report. Note how the John SAX page was previously that of William Weaver. Was that Catherine Weaver's father? brother?

"A ledger item that may substantiate that John was indeed confined for a time during the Revolutionary War is in:
E. Livingston Collection - Princeton University Library:
Isaac Davis Account Book - Tole Ground
[page 8]
begun in 1781
SAX, Catherine, 1781, 1783
SE(S)T, John, 1783
Here we see that Catherine's name is being posted on the account book rather than John, in 1781 and 1783 and then follows a return to John at the close of 1783. This may indicate that John was incarcerated. Also note, that we have no evidence of Catherine bearing children from the birth of Peter in late 1779 through sometime in 1784 perhaps because John was 'away'."

An entry for John occurs in:
Lutheran Churches of Rhinebeck, Dutchess County, NY area:
p33 St Peter's Lutheran Church (Stone Church)
___.___. 1786 SEX, John (possibly joined)
This might not be your John since it occurs about the same time that your John appears in VT/CAN. The Canadian John is found in:
The New Loyalist Index:
Unnumbered page - alphabetical
SAX, J - 5 typed pages in the archives of Family History of Loyalists and Their Descendants
Index of the Non-Lending Library - UEL Association, Toronto, Canada
Settled in Eastern Township, Quebec

And is also written about in:
History of the Eastern Townships:
p15 The first party of white men as settlers into the trackless wilderness known as the Eastern Township in the fall of 1784 included:
SAX, John
All were Loyalists and most had been in British service. Nearly all were Dutch. (copy attached)

[page 9] "In summation, - I must admit that I have not seen enough documentation or evidence from the family report to feel comfortable with its accuracy. I understand that you feel it has been handed down through generations of the family and find it hard to judge inaccuracies which might be included. What is the correct line for your John SAXE? I assume that you are convinced that John's son Godfrey was closely enough associated with the family in Canada to accurately be identified as a member of the family ..."

Copies included:
Robert G. Livingston Rent Book p. 194
NY in the Revolution Vol 2 p. 231
Sylvester - History of Ulster County, NY p. 274-5
Public Papers of George Clinton Vol VII p. 409
Contributions to the History of the Eastern Townships by C. Thomas p. 15
Checklist - search for Godfrey Sax b. 1778

Appendix C

Correspondence and conversations with Andrew F. Saxe

4 December 2008 (e-mail): "John Saxe was the miller for the Livingstons. I had the curator at Clermont look through the records there and he found several references in the ledger books that said "X bushels paid to John Saxe." There is also a letter from Chancellor Livingston to the Trustees of Kingston following the burning of Kingston in which "Mr. Saxe" is mentioned. The miller was the rent collector on the patroon estates (typically) because rents were often paid in wheat or rye, etc., which were then processed at the Livingston mills. The Old Stone Church was the Lutheran church. It is now St. Peter's Episcopal. I understand Nancy [Kelly]'s skepticsm, however much of the genealogy was based upon documentation gathered by great-grandfather, John Walter Saxe, and loaned to JGS II. As I may have mentioned this collection of letters were not returned to my grandfather when John Walter Saxe died suddenly of heart-attack just before the genealogy was published. What I would really like to do is find that trance of letters.

"However, I have a short life of Charles Jewett Saxe, written in 1914 by John Walter Saxe (his son), and he too refers to the same elements of the story. There is no reason to assume he had not come from Bad Langensalza.

"The Saxe Family bible is in the hands of my uncle, and I will take a look at it again. It was published in 1732 and was most likely given to John (Johannes) when he left Thuringen (where Bad Lanensalza is located). I will copy and send to you ..."

2 December 2008: "I believe that John Saxe was arrested in 1777, but not exactly sure when. And I saw one reference that he served with the 'Hanspect Yagers,' which I assumed was the Ansbach Jaegers -- a regiment active in NY and CT in 1777 (until December, when that regiment was sent to South Carolina). In the genealogy there is also a reference that John Saxe assisted a Major Cautine through the enemy lines. I have looked at Harvard, and there is no British officer named Cautine in the Revolution. There may however been a Major of the Ansbach Jaegers who had a similar name, but I have seen that spellings are quite diverse."

27 October 2008: "I drafted the plaque at Saxe's Mills ...

"From what I have found, John Saxe was arrested as a Loyalist in 1779 (I believe) or escape and then joined the Ansbach Jaegers (probably as a scout), which was active on the Hudson and in Connectict in 1779. In December 1779 that regiment was transferred to South Carolina, so he was probably discharged at that point.

"Peter Saxe was born early December 1779 -- and probably conceived February-March. This timing suggests John was arrested sometime in the spring of 1779, spent a few months in prison at Esopus, and then joined the Ansbach Jaegers in the summer time.

"He and his sons received several land grants in the Eastern Townships of Canada from 1795 (I think) to 1801, so he clearly could establish his credentials as a Loyalist."

April 14, 2009: Re: Ansbach Jaegers - a reference in a history of Misissquoi Bay: "John Sax, settler Hanspect Yager 1779" "I realized that was an effort by some English official to spell "Ansbach Jaeger"

Appendix D

Correspondence with United British Empire Loyalists' Association of Canada

e-Letter 17 August 2005 from George J. Hill to Douglas Warner Grant, UE, President, United Empire Loyalists' Association of Canada,
"I believe that I am the great (x4) grandson of John Saxe, who has been said to be a United British Empire Loyalist. I am hoping to verify the information in secondary sources that describe his life and his family. My goal, if it is possible, is to qualify for membership in the United British Empire Loyalists Association, to honor the memory of my brave and determined ancestor"

e-Letter 17 August 2005 from Douglas Warner Grant to George J. Hill
"Thank you for your note and for your interest. We would certainly like to work through your ancestry with you and get you your UE post-nominal ...
    "I think the closest branch for you would be the Sir John Johnson Branch east of Montreal. The President there is Adelaide Lanktree <adelaidel@sympatico.ca> ..."

e-Letter 17 August 2005 from George J. Hill to Douglas Warner Grant,
" ... I am hoping that Bunnell's reference to '5 typed pages' in 'FHLD' [Family History of Loyalists & Their Descendants Index] related to John Saxe may provide information about John and his family ... Would it be a deposition from Saxe, or whatever else is in these '5 typed pages'?"

e-Letter 18 August 2005 from George J. Hill to Douglas Warner Grant,
" ... Any help that your Dominion office or Adelaide can provide will be greatly appreciated. Bunnell must have seen something in order to refer to '5 typed pages,' and I hope those pages may turn up. ..."

e-Letter 18 August 2005 to George J. Hill from Douglas Warner Grant,
" ... A very cursory glace at some records at the office showed that more than a half dozen people have proved to John Saxe since 1971, and it is the Sir John Johnson Branch ...
    "We recently had another request from someone else using a Paul Bunnell reference for a 30 page document. We have no record of it. So, I do not know if there were things in the library that are no longer there, or if they were items in a branch rather than the Association. We were not able to check for your information as the index directory is out at the moment. ..."

e-Letter 19 August 2005 to George J. Hill from Jean Darrah McCaw, UE, Branch Genealogist, Sir John Johnson Centennial Branch,
"Thank you for your interest in the United Empire Loyalists' Ass'n of Canada. ... I will send you the necessary applications for joining our Branch ... The Certificate Membership Application is to be filed with proofs. ..."

Letter 19 August 2005 to George J. Hill from Jean Darrah McCaw,
    " ... You have most of the data on John Saxe which I have in my files,"
with a two-page enclosure, viz.:
Page 1-----
JOHN SAXE, LOYALIST
Born in Langensaltza [sic], Kingdom of Hanover, Germany, in 1732. At age 18 he sailed for America from Holland with a friend and landed in Philadelphia where he swore allegiance to King George III in   [sic] He was in service for three years in order to pay off his debt for passage to the captain. He, as a bound servant, worked for a miller, where he learned the trade

also to write and speak English. He was employed later at Valley Forge and in 1771 he married, at Rhinebeck, NY, Catherine Weaver, born of German parents in 1744.

When the Revolution broke out he swore allegiance to the King and was put in prison from which he escaped and served in Yager's' Loyalst Corps. Many of the Loyalist Regiments saw service in the Fort of St. John on the Richelieu. In 1783, when the settlements in western Quebec (Upper Canada) were prepared for settlement there were several settlers who wished to settle in the Missisquoi Bay area west of Lake Champlain. John Saxe is listed on a petition dated 1783 and another in 1786. He bought land in the Seigniory of St. Armand from Thomas Dunn, south of the Peter Miller, in a place that became known as Saxe's Mills. When the boundary line was drawn this became part of Vermont.

CHILDREN

JOHN   1772-1793
GEORGE   1773-1853
WILLIAM   1774-1840
MATTHEW 1776-1836
GODFREY   1778-1807
PETER   1779-1880
JACOB   1783-1866
CONRAD   1784-1871
HANNAH   1786-1859

[N.b. by George Hill: All of the above years are the same as the years that are given in many other sources, including the Genealogy of the Saxe Family by J.G.S. (John Godfrey Saxe II), except that Peter Sax, who spelled his name without a terminal "e" died in 1839. His will was made on 13 May and his estate was probated on 30 October 1839. The Genealogy by J.G.S. says that he d. on 27 May 1839 and there is no reason to dispute this statement.]

Page 2 ----- DESCENDANTS OF GEORGE, SON OF JOHN SAXE, LOYALIST

GEORGE SAXE .. RACHEL LEROY
JOHN SAXE ... KATE RHICARD
CATHERINE SAXE ... JOHN WEBSTER SNYDER
VIOLA SNYDER ... JOHN WILKINS
ADA CATHERINE WILKINS ... CLIFFORD NELSON CHAMBERLIN

PERSONS IN OUR FILES WHO DESCEND FROM THIS LINE
Royce Edwaell Chamberlin
Patricia Chamberlin
Cora Natalie Chamberlin Hazard
Barry Royce Chamberlin
Cathy Hazard Chamberlin
Wesley Larocque (Mother Iris Chamberlin Larocque)

George J. Hill submitted an Associate Member Application on 28 September 2005. It was approved by Jean Darrah McCaw, Branch Genealogist (copy in correspondence with UBELAC).
He became an Associate Member of the UELAC, Sir John Johnson Branch in 2005.

Appendix E

EARLY HIGHGATE, VERMONT: SAXE AND STOCKWELL CONNECTIONS

ANCESTORS, RELATIVES, and IN-LAWS OF JESSIE FIDELIA STOCKWELL (1863-1940) IN THE *HISTORY OF HIGHGATE*, ABBREVIATED AND ANNOTATED

INCLUDING NOTES ON THE FAMILIES OF ALBEE, ALLEN, BARR, DRURY, FREEBORN, HERRICK, HYDE, KEITH, POTTER, SAXE, STOCKWELL, WEAVER, and WINTERS

Prepared by
George J. Hill, M.D., D.Litt.
April 6, 2009

Based upon

History of Highgate, Vermont
Edited and published by Miss Abby, Marian Hemenway, 1871

John Saxe, Loyalist

HISTORY OF HIGHGATE, VERMONT*

The original text was downloaded on April 5, 2009, from
http://www.rootsweb.ancestry.com/~vermont/FranklinHighgate.html

The website appears to have been developed from a publication of 1871 entitled:

"The Vermont Historical Gazetteer:
A Magazine Embracing A History of Each Town,
Civil, Ecclesiastical, Biographical and Military."
Volume II, Franklin, Grand Isle, Lamoille & Orange Counties.
Including Also The Natural History of Chittenden County.
Edited and Published by Miss Abby, Maria Hemenway.
Burlington, VT. 1871.
Page 254-275.

Transcribed by Karima Allison 2004

The text (below) refers to notes made by Amos Skeels, but never published, and by additions made by others, including the anonymous "writer" who edited Amos Skeels' work and added to it. At the end of Part II is a poem by a Mrs. M. R. W. Skeels, presumably a relative or in-law of Amos Skeels, followed by poems by John Godfrey Saxe that were apparently selected by Mrs. Skeels. Clues left by the anonymous "writer" suggest that Amos Skeels died in the 1860s. The "writer" is apparently Hon. Warren Robinson, whose name appears above the Prefatory section, below. The citation to "Miss Abby, Maria Hemenway" on the web page has been brought forward and appears above.

ABBREVIATED AND ANNOTATED TO SHOW RELATIONSHIPS TO THE ANCESTORS, RELATIVES and IN-LAWS OF JESSIE FIDELIA STOCKWELL, WIFE OF GEORGE J. HILL, OF WRIGHT COUNTY, IOWA

HIGHGATE
Township Information

"The Missico River enters this township from Sheldon, and after running some distance in the south part of it, passes in Swanton . . . About six miles above Swanton Falls is a fall in the river of about forty feet, affording some excellent mill privileges . . . The first settlers in this town were Germans, mostly soldiers who had served in the British army

---

* Document downloaded from http://www.rootsweb.ancestry.com/~vermont/FranklinHighgate.html, 5 April 2009, and edited by George J. Hill, M.D., 3 Silver Spring Road, West Orange, NJ 07052

during the revolution, but the time of their settlement is not known. The town was chartered in 1763."

Gazetteer of Vermont, Hayward, 1849.

HISTORY OF THE TOWN OF HIGHGATE

PART ONE

INTRODUCTION TO THE HISTORY OF HIGHGATE. FROM THE PAPERS OF AMOS SKEELS

Highgate, in the north-west part of Franklin County, bounded N. by Canada, E. by Franklin, S. by Swanton and Sheldon, W. by Lake Champlain and Swanton; was chartered Aug. 17, 1763, by Gov. Wentworth to Samuel HUNT and 63 others, 6 miles square. Later surveys extended its boundaries in the form of a diamond on the S. E. nearly half through and between Sheldon and Franklin. None of the original grantees ever settled in town.

FIRST SETTLERS

In 1785-6, Joseph **REYCARD**,[*] on the Canada line, on the farm now owned by C. and L. **DRURY**[†]; John HILLIKER on Missisquoi River below Swanton; Jeremiah BREWSTER and Thomas BUTTERFIELD on the west side of Rock River, near the lake shore; in 1787, Conrad **BARR**,[‡] John **SAXE**,[§] John STINEHOUSE, John SHELTEE, George WILSON, John Hogle, _____ LAMPMAN and Peter WAGGONNER.

1787, Henry STINEHOUSE, Abram **REYCARD**[*] and Catherine SHELTEE were born -- the first children supposed to have been born in town, and the same year, John **SAXE** built the first grist-mill on a small stream in the N. W. part of the town, where a mill has ever since been running, still called "**SAXE**'s Mill." Before this there were no mills short of Burlington, 35 miles distant, a part of the way through pathless woods, or

---

[*] A Katy Rycard was the first wife and mother of four children by John Saxe, son of George, who was a son of John Saxe, the Loyalist. Katy Rycard's ancestry is unknown, but she is presumably in a later generation of the family of Joseph and Abram Reycard. The children of John, the Loyalist, lived on both sides of the U.S.-Canadian line, and George, who married Katy Rycard, lived on the Canadian side.

[†] These Drurys were undoubtedly related to the descendants of Abel and Sarah (Keith) Drury who married descendants of John and Catherine (Weaver) Saxe (see details in later references).

[‡] Conrad Barr was married to Elizabeth Weaver, sister of Catherine Weaver, who was married to John Saxe.

[§] John Saxe was the great-great grandfather of Jessie Fidelia Stockwell.

Plattsburgh, where the lake must be crossed by the settler with his grist in a canoe in addition to carrying it a great distance oh his back; hence the little log-mill, with its one run of stone, was a great blessing, and brought many settlers into town soon after it was built …

1791, Catherine, wife of John **SAXE**, died; supposed to be the first death in town.

1791, the first school was taught by Simeon FOSTER, in a house on Conrad **BARR's** farm, near **SAXE's** mill ….

1797, Andrew **POTTER**[*] built the first saw-mill at Highgate Falls, and a grist-mill, soon after.

1799, Conrad **BARR**, and W. MOULTE built the first framed barns in town.

1801, Matthew, Godfrey and Peter **SAXE**[†] kept the first store and tavern.

1802, the first framed houses were built by Elijah ROOD, on Missisquoi river; ____ NEWCOMB, at Highgate Springs and Conrad **BARR**, near **SAXE**'s Mills.

1804, the first proprietors' meeting held in town, was at the house of John **SAXE**, the second Monday of January.

1805, the town was organized; Mathew **SAXE**[‡] being the first town clerk. …

1807, Abel **DRURY**[§] built the first furnace. …

The first settlers were principally Dutch [sic] refugees who supposed they had settled in Canada till after the establishment of the line between Canada and the States, and at the time there were no settlers found between Highgate and Burlington. John **SAXE** visited Burlington in 1786 with no guide but his pocket compass, and, when there was no house between **SAXE**'s Mills and Burlington.

---

[*] Andrew Potter was the older brother of Freeborn Potter, who was a great-grandfather of Jessie Fidelia Stockwell. Andrew was therefore Jessie's great-great uncle. His brother Noel Potter and his sister Sarah (Potter) Winter(s) also lived in Highgate.
[†] Matthew, Godfrey, and Peter Saxe were sons of John Saxe.
[‡] Matthew Saxe was the fourth son and fourth child of John Saxe.
[§] Abel and Sarah (Keith) Drury were the parents of Sarah Keith Drury, who married Col. Peter Saxe Jr., grandson of John Saxe, and of Zephaniah Keith Drury, who married Hannah Saxe, daughter of John Saxe's youngest son, Conrad Saxe.

At Highgate Falls is one of the most powerful waterfalls in the State. Heman **ALLEN**,[*] brother of Ethan, purchased the mills of Andrew **POTTER**, and the title to numerous lots of land in town which were held subject to annual rent, to which the right of title has been purchased in many instances.

Indians frequented the settlement and sometimes pitched their wigwams near the settlers' cabins, and the children of the Indian and the white man have often played and frolicked together during the Indians' short sojourn. Encounters with wild animals were too numerous to be of much interest, and our early settlers pretty generally believed in spooks (as they called the apparitions of the departed) and would much rather have faced any wild animal of this region than to have seen a Jack O'Lantern in the night-time; they had also great confidence in the influence of the moon upon almost everything they undertook to do, and so far as the putting in of some kinds of crops is concerned, the moon is a ill consulted.

This township is, geographically, very pleasantly situated, and, in picturesque scenery and sporting grounds, cannot be surpassed in the State. Champlain bounds it principally on the west with its silvery waters, its bold or level, gravelly shores, its charming islands, with now and then a white sail glimmering as it passes between or beyond them, -- on the seat, wooded hills, for many miles, dotted here and there with the dwellings and clearings; these hills are some 20 miles from the nearest range of the Green Mountains, and are the last range of hills between the Green Mountains and Lake Champlain. They continue southerly as far as Chittenden, about 6 miles, on an average, from the lake, giving, in many places, a beautiful descending grade from their bass to the lake. A large marsh near the lake, too wet for the farmer, grows a quantity of blueberries that the people from the neighboring towns, from miles around, come to gather, every season.

The nearest depot, on the Vermont and Canada railroad, is at Swanton Falls, 4 miles from Highgate Falls, near the lake shore. Some 3 miles from Swanton depot is located Highgate Springs.

HIGHGATE
BY HON. WARREN ROBINSON.

PREFATORY.

The writer regrets exceedingly the decease of our friend and townsman who had commenced the history of Highgate, and justice to whose memory requires the publication of his papers, so far as he had progressed at the time of his demise, although

---

[*] Heman Allen was a third cousin of Jemima Allen, who was a great-great-great grandmother of Jessie Stockwell. He was the brother of Ira Allen and Ethan Allen (see other references).

he had made only a beginning before the rapid decline which terminated in death, so sadly, in the 45th year of his age; so well known was his character for energy, we have reason to believe that, had he lived in the enjoyment of health to have completed the account, he would have made a far more acceptable history than the writer may be able to do. But as the history is thus left for some one to finish, and no other man has been found willing to undertake, -- and Highgate is my adopted, if not my native town, -- at the solicitations of the projector of this work, I have put my hand to the task so difficult even for one born and reared in the locality; feeling my disadvantages, yet preferring to do what I can for the town rather than see it go undone. [Robinson evidently refers to his "friend and townsman" Amos Skeels, referred to on page 1 and on the next page]

I find, first, on examination of the early records, many imperfections and a want of system which makes it extremely arduous and difficult to glean the desired facts from them, and if some important facts are found wanting it may be charged to the fact that I have not been able to find them, and the memory of our venerable ancestors could not supply them.

ORIGINAL GRANTEES

Samuel HUNT, Jonah ELMER, Eleazer POMROY, Elisha HUNT, Nehamiah HUGHTON, Samuel MARBLE, Hilkiah GROT, John BEAMAN, Josiah WILLARD, Samuel BENNET, Philip ALEXANDER, Elisha HARDING, Henry BOND. Nathaniel DART, Hophni BING, Joseph Loro, Benjamin DIKE, Joseph ASHLEY, Jeremiah HALL, Peter BELLOWS, Josiah POMROY, Jonathan HUNT, Arad HUNT, Elijah WELLS, Samuel HUNT, jr., Ebenezer POMROY, Samson WILLARD, Ebenezer MATTOON, Joseph SPENCER, William SHATON, John HUNT, Josiah STEBBINS, Josiah STEBBINS, jr., Elisha STEBBINS, Josiah HIDE, Samuel WILLIAMS, Thomas TAYLOR, William SYMS, Hezekiah ELMER, Elisha SMITH, John FARRAR, Savage TRESCOTT. Israel KNOWLS, John FISH, Benoni SMITH, Isaac ROBINSON, Caleb NOBLE, James MATTHEWS, John WILLIAMS, Nathan WILLIAMS, Joseph PROSE. Leonard WILLIAMS, Nathan WILLIAMS, Samuel HENSDALE, Thomas WILLIAMS, Barnabas HENSDALE, Capt. Thomas BELL, Hon. Theodore ATKINSON, Mark H. G. WENTWORTH, James NEVEN, Theodore ATKINSON, John FISHER, Esq., Daniel BING, Moses EVENS, William WHITE.

"The 1st condition of the grant was that every grantee, his heirs, or assigns, shall plant and cultivate 5 acres of land within 5 years, for every 50 acres of land contained in his or their share, or forfeit his right, which condition evidently was not complied with in a single case. The second condition was,

That all white and other pine fit for roasting the royal navy be carefully preserved for that use.

3d, before any division of the land be made, as near the center of the town as convenient, shall be reserved and marked out for town lots, one acre to each grantee.

4th, Yielding and paying to us (Gov. WENTWORTH), for the space of ten years the rent of one ear of Indian corn on the 25th day of December, annually, and after the ten years to pay as above one shilling proclamation money for every hundred acres."

From the conditions of the grant it is evident the original proprietors forfeited all right held under the grant, as not one of the above conditions was ever complied with, and it does not from the records appear that any one of these proprietors ever received any consideration for his interest therein. But in all the proceedings of the proprietors' meeting they seemed to respect the original grant as though it had been fulfilled to the letter on the part of the settlers. The first settlement, however, it appears was 23 years from the date of the grant, and without permission of Governor WENTWORTH or King George; and it is a question if King George III, or King George IV., his successor, had not been disturbed in his American possessions, whether Gov. WENTWORTH or his heirs might not disturb the peaceable possession of the present proprietors. However I am of the opinion that our land titles in Highgate are good and valid.

Mr. SKEELS makes the statement that Highgate was not organized until 1805. I have not as yet seen any proof of the same, but find in the early records that Highgate held regular meetings in March of each year, and a freeman's meeting to September also. They regularly elected their town clerks, selectmen, grand jurors, treasurer, fence viewers, constables, and all other town officers as early as 1791, when they made choice of John WAGONER, moderator; Jonathan BUTTERFIELD, town clerk; Isaac ASSELTINE and Minard TEACHOUT, constables; John WAGONER, Mikel LAMPMAN and John HILLIKER, selectmen; Jacob HILLIKER, Peter LAMPMAN, fence viewers, and agreed that hogs might run at liberty. A meeting was legally warned and held Sept. 4, 1792, the record of which reads:

"In obedience to a warning dated 24th August, 1792, signed by the first constable of Highgate, met and the meeting was opened, and the freemen made choice of John KNICHABOKER to represent them in the General Assembly for the year ensuing. Then brought in their votes for governor, lieutenant governor, 12 counsellors. Then brought in their votes for treasurer. Then nominated Jonathan BUTTERFIELD and George WILLISON, justices of the peace."

At this meeting there were 15 votes cast.

In 1793-4 Jonathan BUTTERFIELD was chosen representative. In 1794 there were 45 names entered upon the grand list. In 1795 there were but 13 votes cast for any officer, and the same year 55 names entered upon the grand list. On the 23d of March, 1795, a tax was raised of 3d. on the pound of all ratable estate in town.

In the first book of records and the first record made upon the book, is a bond from Ira **ALLEN**[*] to John **SAXE**, dated July 31, 1792; and reads as follows:

*"To all peple to whome these presents a hall come Know yea that I Ira **ALLEN** of Colchester, County of Chittenden and State of Vermont am holden and firmly bound unto John **SAXE** County and State aforesaid in the penal sum of one hundred pounds L. M. which payment well and truly to be dun, I bind myself, my heirs, Executors, Administrators farely by these presents I witness whereof here hereafter set my hand and seal. The condition of the Bond is as follows (viz) said Ira **ALLEN** on his part acknoleges the rec't of forty pounds of sd **SAXE** has paid sd **ALLEN** in consequence of a former agreement, the true intents and meaning of this agreement is that sd All tis to give sd **SAXE** good Deed of a land on or before the first of May next, or give sd **SAXE** a Lease of sd Lot; No. 45 in Highgate the terms of ten years from this date rent free and pay back to sd **SAXE** forty pounds already Rec'd of him In witness whereof I have set my hand and Seal this 31st day of July, 1792.*
*Signed, IRA **ALLEN**. (Seal.)*

In presents of Thos. BUTTERFIELD.
Recorded 14th Sept., 1793"

In 1792, Caleb HENDERSON, collector, sold nearly the whole township of Highgate to Ira **ALLEN** for £93, which deed was acknowledged Feb. 11, 1794, and appeared upon the record of 1803. Again the township was sold to Ira **ALLEN**, at vendue, by Noah CHITTENDEN, sheriff of Chittenden Co., for £9, and the deed recorded in 1803. In 1798, by the authority of the selectmen, the township was sold by Timothy **WINTER**,[†] collector, to Isaac BISHOP for $3.15 for each share, to pay the one cent tax. This tax was levied by an act of the General Assembly Nov. 10, 1797, to be paid to the State treasurer for public, private and charitable uses. ... ...

The first marriage on record was that of Isaac and Sally ASSELTINE, January 14, 1800, by Sylvester COBB, justice of the peace. Mar. 19, Andrew WILSON and Rachel WILSON were joined in wedlock and lawfully married by Matthew **SAXE**, J. P.

---

[*] Ira Allen, brother of Ethan and Heman, was a third cousin of Jessie Stockwell, 5 times removed.
[†] Timothy Winters was the husband of Sarah Potter, one of the six children of Oliver and Mary (Colvin) Potter. Sarah Potter's brother Freeborn Potter was a great-grandfather of Jessie Stockwell, and Sarah was therefore Jessie Stockwell's great-great aunt. His name is spelled as Winter and as Winters in this History of Highgate, but it is consistently spelled Winters in the census records.

In 1800, Matthew **SAXE** was again elected town clerk, … Mar. 27, 1799, Matthew **SAXE** was elected town clerk; … John **SAXE**, town treasurer; Matthew **SAXE**, lister; … Voted that hogs may run in the road with good yokes on.

On the first Tuesday of September, 1800, there were 19 votes cast for Governor, 23 for Lieut. Governor, 22 for treasurer and 31 for member of Congress.

In 1801, there were 49 votes cast for state officers, and Matthew **SAXE** was again elected representative. In 1802, 62 votes were polled for governor. February 17, 1803, Ira **ALLEN** executed a quit-claim deed of the 23,040 acres to Heman **ALLEN** for the nominal sum of $5,000; and February 25, Heman **ALLEN** executed a deed to Silas HATHAWAY.

The principal actors in town business from 1793 to 1803 were Cornelius WILSON, Jonathan BUTTERFIELD, John **SAXE**, Matthew **SAXE**, Timothy **WINTERS**, Hercules LENT, Sylvanus COBB, Gordon GRAY, George STINEHOUR, Shadrack NORTON, Andrew **POTTER**, Thomas BEST, James WELCH, Nathan OLDS, Henry HUGHMAN, Asa HOLGAT, Thomas BUTTERFIELD, Jacob ELMER, John WAGONER, Jacob CRAY, John HILLIKER, Peter LAMPMAN, John STINETS, John CRAY, Jeremiah BREWER, Jacob HOSTET, Conrad **BARR**,[*] John **BARR**,[*] Levi HUNGERFORD, Samuel FOSTER, Minord TEACHOUT, George WILSON, John CLOW, Elias BERRY, Abraham ASSELTINE, Solomon PERCY, Peter MOULTE, Noel **POTTER**,[†] Peter **SAXE**. The eleven first named held alternately the most important offices in the town, nearly every year, the remainder of the list holding the less important offices occasionally.

The first proprietors' meeting of which there is any record to be found, was 41 years from the date of the grant in 1804, at the dwelling-house of John **SAXE**, Matthew **SAXE**, proprietors' clerk, Shadrach HATHAWAY, moderator. After repeated adjournments from time to time, without accomplishing any important business, April 12, 1805, a committee of three were appointed, to lay out, survey and return a plan of 3 lots of 103 acres, each, to each original share in due form of law. Matthew **SAXE**, Levi HENDERSON and John JOHNSON were appointed that committee, and made their report at a subsequent meeting; having accomplished the business assigned them. Their charge for the survey of the 1st, 2d and 3d divisions was $485.75, which was allowed by vote of the proprietors, no one opposing.

At the above meeting, a vote was also taken to quiet the rights of the actual settlers, some 40 or 50 in number, and after the 4th and 5th division a vote of the proprietors confirmed these rights as in the 1st, 2d and 3d division.

---

[*] John Barr was the eldest son of Conrad and Elizabeth (Weaver) Barr, and therefore a first cousin of Jessie Stockwell, twice removed.
[†] Noel Potter, brother of Andrew, was a great-great uncle of Jessie Stockwell.

The town from 1805---the date of its regular survey---up to 1820 made rapid strides in population, wealth and improvement. Previous to 1805 the settlements were mainly in the N. W. part of the town, where the town-meetings had been mostly held up to 1820, when a town-meeting was called "at the school-house near Arwin P. **HERRICK**'s[*] at **Allen**'s Falls." The central village growing up around this beautiful waterfall, was just beginning to have its influence in town, and from this date the town clerk's office was mostly at the Falls. The grand list of 1794 was £.980 10s.; 1795, £1061 15s.; 1796, £1122 14s.; the grand list of 1820 was $14,851.26, which was 6 per cent of the appraised value. At this date and upon the above list there is 1 saw-mill appraised to Danforth AINSWORTH at $2000 located on the north side of the river at East Highgate, called **Hyde**'s Falls, about 3 miles east of Allen's Falls; also 1 fulling-mill and carding machine to Lorin CARPENTER at Allen's Falls for $1500; 1 saw-mill and store to Abel **DRURY** in the N. W. part of the town at $800; 1 saw-mill to Luther **HYDE**,[†] East Highgate, $1000; 1 furnace to **KEITH**[‡] and **DRURY** in the north part of the town at $2000; to S. W. and S. S. KEYS, 1 grist-mill, saw-mill, distillery, store and blacksmith's shop, at Allen's Falls assessed $10,100; 1 shop and factory to P. P. PAYNE and Diah RICHARDSON for $200; to **SAXE** and POWERS 1 grist-mill and machine, in the west part of the town, at $2000; to Conrad **SAXE**, 1 black-smith's shop, $100; to James STEARNS, 1 smith's shop $200 and to George WAIT 1 saw-mill, supposed to be on Rock river at $400.

Hundreds if not thousands of acres of the township were originally covered with a dense forest of the most valuable white pine that ever graced a forest, -- often one hundred or more large and stately trees standing upon a single acre, which if standing to-day, $50 the single tree, amounting to $5,000 to the acre, would not be an over estimate. Could Highgate have remained untouched until the present time, with its lofty pine plains, in its primeval grandeur, it is doubtful whether it would not he worth more dollars than it now is with all its improvements, and it would, moreover, have been one of the wonders of the world. But the pioneers, with reckless haste, destroyed its beautiful forests and dispersed from their native haunts the numerous herds of deer which fed upon its spicy foliage and drank with such peculiar liking from the mineral springs with which this township abounds. …

HIGHGATE VILLAGE

---

[*] Arwin Herrick is probably a distant relative of Jessie Fidelia (Stockwell) Hill's husband, George J. Hill. George was the grandson of William P. and Sarah (Herrick) Hill. Most if not all of the early Herricks of New England and New York State were descendants of Henry Herrick of Salem, Massachusetts. Arwin P. Herrick does not appear in the Herrick family genealogy. His relationship to Daniel Herrick (see below) is therefore unknown but it is likely that they were kinsmen.

[†] Luther Hyde was a great-grandfather of Jessie Stockwell.

[‡] Jessie Stockwell's first cousins, twice removed, Col. Peter Saxe and Hannah Saxe, were married to two children of Abel Drury and Sarah Keith. The name of Sarah Keith's father is not given in this record, but it is clear that he was a partner of some kind of one of the Drurys, probably Abel.

Highgate Village is about one mile south and a little to the east of the geographical center of the town, upon a waterfall of the Missisquoi river. This fall is one of the best (if not the best), to be found in the State. The bed of the river lies some 75 feet below the handsome pine plain land on which the village is built; the barks being high and rocky make it a convenient and safe water privilege with no possible danger of the river overflowing its banks and carrying off buildings and machinery; any desirable head and fall can be obtained; the bed of the river descends rapidly for ¼ of a mile or more, and at the foot of the fall must be about 80 feet lower than the level of the water above the dam. There are several good privileges as yet unoccupied, upon which factories, shops and mills might be built on either side of the river. I believe there are no mills or machinery on the north side of the river now in use, although it is one of the best and safest water privileges in Vermont. Directly above this privilege the river is spanned by the arch-bridge, before alluded to, which is some 50 feet above the water. The village is divided by the river and the road from the bridge, both to the north and south, is quite ascending -- the north part of the village lying on higher ground than the south, but both portions upon pine-plain land. A more handsome tract of land upon which to build a city can hardly be found in any country; the same on the north, east, west and south, extending for miles, affording any number of desirable building lots-such a privilege as at the West would become a city in 10 years.

There is a waterfall upon the Missisquoi river about 1 mile above the lower village called Keep's Rapids, with good banks, where a head and fall of 16 feet can be realized with no serious expense; it is thought that this fall is as valuable and safe as any upon the river for factory or mill purposes, though it has not as yet been occupied.

If there is any importance attached to the early history of the settlement of the different towns in the State, we have not commenced writing it a day too soon. I find the memory of our oldest inhabitants somewhat treacherous; they have distinct recollections of important events, yet it is next to impossible to arrive at exact dates. I have consulted the very best authority to be found in town, and have, at least, an approximate to the true dates.

Andrew **POTTER**, it has been already stated, built the first house and barn-in the limits of the village, in about 1795, and the first gristmill, of logs, about 1800. It was carried by an over-shot wheel and the water conducted to the wheel by a spout, there being no dam at the time across the river. In 1804 or '05, Andrew **POTTER** and a Mr. PHELPS built the first saw-mill and also a dam across the river, which soon went off. In 1811 or '12 Heman **ALLEN** built a framed gristmill which was burned down about 1 year after. In 1815, Mr. **ALLEN** built a grist-mill of brick, which, after standing 10 or 11 years, was taken down and rebuilt by S. W. and S. S. KEYES, in 1826; this mill is now standing, owned and occupied by Stephen KEYES, the oldest son of S. S. KEYES. The first bridge across the river here was a trestle-bridge, near the foot of the falls, about 40 rods below the present bridge. This bridge was built by **ALLEN** and EVARTS in 1812, and was a toll bridge and went down in the fall of 1822 or '23. The present bridge which is an arch bridge, built by S. W. & S. S. KEYES, in 1824 or '25 is perhaps the best bridge of the kind in the State. The timbers for the arch were hewn out of tall crooked pine trees, and such timbers as, I presume, cannot now be found in the State. The bridge was built by private, enterprise, was a toll-bridge several years, but bought by the town some 15 years since, and from that time has been a free bridge, as are all of our bridges now. KIBBE and HATCH were the master builders, and the bridge, apparently, may stand for yet a half century more. The present mill-dam was built by Heman **ALLEN** in 1811 or '12.

Ebenezer **STOCKWELL**[*] came into town in 1809, moved into the **POTTER** house, and was the principal agent, or foreman, for Mr. **ALLEN** until 1819, when Heman **ALLEN** sold out the water privilege to S. W. & S. S. KEYES. Ira **ALLEN** built the first store in the village (time in doubt). Nathan WHITE and PHELPS built the first saw-mill on the Hungerford Brook … …

The Episcopal Church edifice, an honor and ornament to the village, is situated upon the east aide of the green, in connection with which is the cemetery of the south village. … On the north side of the river there are three meeting-houses, the Congregational, Methodist and Catholic, all comfortable and commodious, to which the church-going people of the town resort for worship -- the 4 houses referred to, being all the meeting-houses in town; whether all the members of these churches are enjoying a good degree of spiritual welfare or not, it is not my province to say. … There is no danger that any communities will have too much religion; that there are more professors than true and genuine possessors of that charity which thinketh no evil, I sometimes think. However, I conclude that the people of Highgate are as morally and religiously disposed, as are those of other localities enjoying the same religious privileges. Total abstinence or temperance is not yet quite universal; there have been repeated spasmodic efforts to reform the people in this particular, with but partial success.

There are 3 hotels in the village, and, although I cannot of my own knowledge convict either of them of violating Vermont law, I have reason to suppose that neither of them is kept strictly upon total abstinence principles. … The two stores are kept by J. B. CROSS, who had been in the mercantile business many years at East Highgate, and, about 4 years since, established himself here, and A. P. **HERRICK**, who had been engaged in trade many years at the south village; but something more than 1 year since removed his trade here. Both keep a general assortment of dry goods and groceries.

Above the arch-bridge some 40 rods, on the north bank of the river, are N. A. WAIT's chemical works … Mr. JOHNSON has refitted his buildings, the past season, for the accommodation of boarders, who resort to the Champlain spring about ½ mile east of the village, and… I. S. JENISON, Esq., has purchased the beautiful residence of the late

---

[*] Ebenezer Stockwell was the great-grandfather of Jessie Fidelia Stockwell. His son Joseph H. Stockwell married a granddaughter of John Saxe. Ebenezer Stockwell's grandson Benajah Stockwell married Emma Hyde, whose father was descended from Hydes and Allens, and whose mother was a Potter.

Heman **ALLEN**, and added thereto a commodious building, for an extensive boarding-house ....

Seldom, if ever, has a mineral spring, in so short a time, gained so enviable a reputation, which the healing virtues of its water richly merit. This fact taken in connection with the healthy locality, makes the village a most agreeable, quiet summer resort. ... .

THE OLD HIGHGATE SPRING

The Old Highgate Spring is in the west part of the town, near Missisquoi Bay. Its curative properties have been known and appreciated for half a century or more. Although there are several other mineral springs in the county of Franklin, the old Highgate spring sustains not only its old high reputation, but is gaining ground every year ... ...

EAST HIGHGATE VILLAGE.

As near as can be ascertained, the settlement commenced in 1807; or '08. Stephen POWELL and Peter MILLER received a lease of 50 acres from Ira **ALLEN** on the north side of the Missisquoi River, at the Falls in 1807, and built the dam across the river at that place and erected a saw-mill. Soon after, a small grist-mill was built upon the same side of the river. The place, for many years, was known as Powell's Falls. Some years from this date, I am informed that Stephen POWELL died, and the water privilege and saw-mill passed into the hands of Danforth AINSWORTH, who was in possession in 1820. About 1813, it is probable that Luther **HYDE** made a purchase upon the south side of the river, and built another saw-mill, and continued his residence there until his death, which was in 1847. The farm and saw-mill remained in the hands of the family until 1865, when it was sold to Freeborn E. **BELL**,[*] the son-in-law of Harvey **HYDE**,[†] Esq. -- the oldest son of Luther **HYDE**. Until 1837, the falls were known as **Hyde**'s Falls, and now takes its name from its post-office. There is no descendant of Luther **HYDE** now in Highgate, and but few of his numerous family are now living. Mr. **HYDE** was somewhat noted in town, and well known through the county. ... ...

DROWNED

---

[*] Freeborn Bell was married to Jessie Stockwell's aunt Harriet A. Hyde. Although his ancestry is unknown, it appears likely that he was also related to the Potters. Several Potters were married to members of the Freeborn family, and whose name thus appears as a given name as well as a surname in the Potter family – most notably Jessie Stockwell'a great-grandfather, Freeborn Potter.

[†] Harvey Hyde was the eldest son and third of the fourteen children of Luther Hyde. The writer suggests that Luther Hyde was better "noted" (i.e., known – or perhaps he means respected) in the county than he was in his home town, for reasons known only to those in the community.

... ... Daniel **HERRICK**[*] -- a man past middle age, was drawn up another time by the rope used for elevating grain to the 2d and 3d stories of the grist-mill, which was carried by water, and met in motion by Derriah **HOGABOAM**,[†] who did not understand its management. Mr. **HERRICK** was drawn up to the pulley under the ridge-pole about 30 feet, and the rope being drawn out of his hands, he fell to the platform (a plank-floor) below. Some of his bones were broken, but he recovered again and lived many years afterwards. ... ...

LONGEVITY

Names of persons who died over 80 years of age [22 are named, of whom four are related to the Stockwells]:

Name	Died	Aged
Conrad **BARR**	1845	92 years
Elkana **ALBEE**[‡]	1856	81 years
Abi **STOCKWELL**[§]	1846	82 years
Daniel **HERRICK**	1860	84 years

REPRESENTATIVES

John KNICKERBOCKER, 1792; Jonathan BUTTERFIELD, 1793, '94, 96; Orange SMITH, 1795; John CRAY, 1799; Matthew **SAXE**, 1800-'02; Sylvanus COBB, 1803, '04; Peter **SAXE**, 1806, '18, '27; Simeon HUNGERFORD, 1811; Abel **DRURY**, 1812, '23; Eben HILL, 1815; John AVERILL, 1820, '21, '22, '24, '25; Thomas BEST, 1827; John **BARR**, 1829, '30, '31, '37; Jesse CARPENTER, 1832-'35; Charles H. JENISON,

---

[*] This Daniel Herrick, one of several bearing the same name in the Herrick genealogy, was the first cousin four times removed, of George J. Hill, the husband of Jessie Stockwell. He is known to have two sons, Daniel Jr., and Luther.

[†] Although his surname is spelled differently, we may assume that this Derriah Hogaboom was in some way related to the two wives of Joseph Matthew Stockwell (1834-1901), third son and sixth child of Joseph H. and Anna (Saxe) Stockwell. Joseph Matthew Stockwell was born and died in Highgate; he was a soldier in the Civil War. He married (1) Cordelia Hogaboom; and (2) Eliza Ann Hogaboom, daughter of Samuel Hogaboom and Catherine Bryce.

[‡] Elkana Albee was the husband of Andrew Potter's daughter Susannah Potter.

[§] Abi Stockwell was the widow of Ebenezer Stockwell, who was her second husband. When they were married, she was Mrs. Abi (Holbrook) Lee.

1836; Joseph B. CUTLER, 1839, '40; Luther K. **DRURY**, 1838; William SKEELS, 1841; Luther MEIGS, 1843; L. K. **DRURY**, 1845; Luther MEIGS, 1846; Daniel WATSON, 1847; 1848 and '52, no choice; Jesse CUTLER, 1849; A. P. **HERRICK**, 1850; Jacob CORMAN, 1851, '56; Calvin **DRURY**, 1853, '54; Asa WILSON, 1855; Henry BAXTER, 1857; Warren ROBINSON, '59, '60, '64, '65; Amos SKEELS, 1861; O. S. RIXFORD, 1862, '63, '68; Melvin CHURCH, 1866; J. B. SMITH, 1867.

SELECTMEN

Peter **SAXE**, 1806, '07. '11; Amass HOWE, 1806, '07; Levi HUNGERFORD, 1806; Elkana **ALBEE**, 1810, '20, '28-'35; Abel **DRURY**, 1810, '12, '14; Warren TOWNSEND, 1807, '11; John **BARR**, 1812-'14, '31, '32, '38; Uri HILL, 1812, '13; John AVERILL, 1820-'26, '33, Thomas BEST, 1826-'28; Conrad **SAXE**, 1821; Ebenezer **STOCKWELL**, 1821; Joseph B. CUTTER, 1822-'26, '32, '33, '39; Abraham BLAKE, 1822, '23; Edward C. HASKINS, 1823, '24; William SKEELS, 1824, '25, '40-'42; Sanford SANDERSON, 1825-'28; John B. RHODES, 1830, '31; C. H. JENISON, 1829, '30, `37, '38, '41; Luther MEIGS, 1828-'30, '54-'56 ; Abraham HOLLENBECK, 1828; Luther K. **DRURY**, 1825, '26, '45; Eliphalet **ALBEE**, 1832; Israel S. JENISON, 1834-'37; Benjamin F. HOLLENBECK, 1835'37; Samuel GATES, 1838; Noah BEST, 1839, '47, '49, '63, '65, '66 ; Cornelius PALMER, 1839; Jacob CARMAN, 1840, '50; Nelson NYE, 1841 ; Clark **ALBEE**, 1842-'45; Samuel GATES, 1842; E. D. **HYDE**, 1844, '45; Allen **BARR**,* 1846; I. S. Jenison, 1846, '48, '51,'52, '53, '56, '58, '60, '61, '62, '64; Daniel WATSON, 1846-'50, '54; C. P. PIERCE, 1847; Henry STINEHOUR, 1848; M. R. AVERILL, 1849; W. C. STEVENS, '50, 53, '61, '62; Smith FARRAND, 1851-'53; Warren ROBINSON, 1854, '55, '65-'67; Harry SMITH, 1855, '57; E. R. FROST, 1856, '57; F. TARBLE, 1857, '58; D. H. FARRINGTON, '58, '59 ; J. R. SMITH, 1859, '60; William TEACHOUT, 1859, '60; Calvin **DRURY**, 1861-'64; S. W. JENISON, 1863,-'66; Burton DIMON, 1867; John A. FITCH. 1867, '68; David SUNDERLIN, 1868; A. H. SPEAR. 1868.†

TOWN CLERKS

Jonathan BUTTERFIELD, 1791-'97; Thomas BEST, 1798; Matthew **SAXE**, 1799, 1800, '05, '06; Silvanus COBB, 1803, '04; John **BARR**, 1814-'24; Peter **SAXE**, 1810, '11 '28, '29; Oramel CUMINS, 1822, '23; William FARRAR, 1820-'22; Loring CARPENTER, 1825; Abel **DRURY**, jr., 1826, '27; Jesse CARPENTER, 1830 -'37; O. F. ROBINSON, 1839-'41; Benjamin PEAKE, 1842-'44; B. PEAKS, 1845, '46, Wm.

---

* Allen Barr was surely a son of either John Barr or Conrad Barr, Jr., and therefore a second cousin, several removes, from Jessie Stockwell.
† As noted above, Ebenezer Stockwell was a great-grandfather of Jessie Stockwell. The other selectmen whose surnames are shown in bold type are relatives or in-laws of Jessie Stockwell, although the exact relationship of all of them to Jessie has not been computed.

ROBINSON, 1847, '48; A. P. **HERRICK**, '49, '50, '60-'68; Calvin **DRURY**, 1851-'54; Lucius GREEN, 1855; L. K. **DRURY**, 1856; William MARTIN, 1857-'58.

FIRST CONSTABLES

Isaac ASSELTINE, 1791; John WAGONER, 1792, '93: George WILSON, 1794; John CRAY, 1795, '96; Timothy **WINTER**, 1797, '98; Hercules LENT, 1804, '09, '10; ____ Proper, 1806; Newcomb LAMBKINS, 1811; Edward C. HASKINS, 1812, '20; Luther K. **DRURY**, 1821, '22, '34; Daniel FILLEMORE, 1810; '23, '26, '28; B. F. HOLLENBECK, 1827; Clark **ALBEE**, 1830-'33; Jerhmell CUMINS, 1835-'39, '42-'44; Urial D. FILLEMORE, 1840, '41; Philo **DRURY**, 1845, '46; O. F. ROBINSON, 1847-'50; C. P. PIERCE, 1852-'57; J. P. PLACE, 1858-'68.

MILITIA

To attain to a commission in the militia, was for many years looked upon as an important mark of honorable distinction. But as "June trainings" have been rendered famous for all time to come by a more prolific pen, and the general account of militia officers in one town will probably be its history in most others, the writer feels justified in passing over that portion of our annals briefly. Highgate companies of militia at regimental musters, for many years, however, would outflank most other companies on parade, and apparently were a strong, athletic race of men, and remarkably adapted, physically, for military life.

The only names of men in town who were promoted to a captaincy, which I have obtained, are:

Capts. -- Timothy **WINTER**, Jacob CROY, Conrad **SAXE**, Luther MEIGS, Lumas MEIGS, Franklin HOLLENBECK, William HILLIKER, Jerahmill CUMINS, Jacob MCGOWEN, Elisha **BARR**, J. S. JENISON, Hannibal SHELTUS,

Vol. Rifle Uniformed. -- Capts. Conrad **BARR**, Harvey **HYDE**. Lorenzo G. POMEROY, brigadier-general.

The uniformed companies took great pride in appearing well upon parade, and performed their evolutions promptly. The militia companies usually took more interest in their rations than in their evolution, and were generally reckless as to their appearance.

WAR OF 1812

Highgate, in the war with England, as in the great Rebellion, was ready to furnish its men. It appears from the record, that the soldiers to guard the lines, and that were stationed at Swanton Falls, were detached by order of the President. Conrad **SAXE** was captain of the 2d Company of the 1st Regiment and 1st Brigade of detached Militia. This 2d Company was raised from the towns of Highgate, Swanton, St. Albans, Georgia, Milton and Westford. The number from Highgate was 11, viz: Chester MILLER, David STICKNEY, Samuel HUBBELL, Moses MARTINDALE, David **HERRICK**,[*] Nathaniel JOHNSON, John CORMAN, Henry CHAPPELL, David MOORE, David SAGAR, Peter BREWER. This company were detached for 6 or 9 months and served out their time at Swanton Falls in 1812. The commissioned officers in this company were Capt. Conrad **SAXE**, Lieut. Heman HOYT, Ensign Heman BLANCHARD.

Highgate being a border town, it is not strange that such a portion of its inhabitants as those whose loyalty was overpowered by avarice, should enlist in the smuggling enterprise. To such, gold is always tempting, and it is doubtful if gold was ever so plenty since the organization of our government as at that period. British gold and silver somehow found its way into the States, and every substantial farmer had his old blue stocking-leg filled with it. The writer well remembers seeing heaps of it passing front hand to hand among the farmers. Every boy carried more or less of the real pewter jingling in his pockets, and of course there was more or less smuggling and occasionally the smugglers got sore heads, but what of that, as they were getting prompt pay for the risk.

Captain Conrad **SAXE**, at the time of the battle of Plattsburgh, raised a company of volunteers, principally from Highgate, and started for the battle ground, and succeeded in reaching Grand Isle, but failed to get passage in season to participate in that memorable and well fought battle. Frequent rumors of approaching squads of Indians were circulated among the inhabitants, and families were congregated together, every moment expecting the tomahawk and scalping-knife. On these occasions the older members of the families would relate the anecdotes of Indian massacres during the Revolutionary war that would raise the hair upon the beads of us urchins, as the quills of a porcupine. However the Indians never came during the war. The victory on Lake Champlain and the skedadling of the British land forces back to Canada, gave the frontier settlers quiet again. I am not aware that, during this war, there was any serious depredation committed on either side, along the border. Those engaged in smuggling were not so much enemies to their country as friends of gain. When two countries are at war, there is more or less of this illicit traffic carried on. Human nature is nearly the same in all countries, hence the necessity of embargoes and stringent prohibition. The cannonading in the naval engagement on Lake Champlain was distinctly heard in Highgate and Swanton. Although but 8 years old, the writer has not forgotten the solemnity of the occasion, nor the anxiety depicted upon the countenances of old men who remained at home, as it was believed on the result of the battle depended our future peace. Not only that, but nearly every family had sent some of its members with such weapons as could be procured, either guns or pitchforks, to the scene of action. Life or death hung in the balance, hence the anxiety.

---

[*] David Herrick is surely a son of either A. P. or Daniel Herrick, and therefore he may be a distant cousin of Jessie Stockwell. However, his ancestry is unknown at this time.

PART TWO

RADICAL REBELLION

As Highgate is a border town, any trouble over the line is sooner felt than in towns more remote. The people of the town are peaceably disposed and have no disposition to interfere with the government of the adjacent Province; but when there is difficulty in Canada more or less of the disaffected citizens will leave for the States. It was so in the Radical Rebellion. Canadian refugees in considerable large numbers might be found at the public and private houses, who put their own version upon affairs in Canada, and it is the most natural thing in the world that they should enlist the sympathies of the people on this side of the line, and this rebellion made quite a commotion in Highgate for a short period, but I am not aware that more than two or three participated in any invasion across the lines. The writer was teaching school at the time in the west part of the town, the school-house being on the direct road from Missisquoi bay to Swanton Falls. Just before 9 o'clock A. M., a small body of unarmed men and boys (perhaps 20 in number) from the Canada side, halted in front of the school-house, when Capt. GAYNON walked up to the door, upon which was posted a proclamation of some leading radical (I believe, Dr. NELSON), and turning to his men explained to his Company the purport of it in French, when his men gave three lusty cheers for PAPINENU and resumed their march again. Just as school closed, at. 4 P.M., a company of men and boys, numbering perhaps 150 or 200, again halted in front of the school-house, on their way back with arms in their hands. I took the liberty to pass around the company in review, to see what kind of material the invading army was composed of. I found them mostly French boys, who might have done good service in the garden or a potato-patch, but not quite the right material to conquer old England, or face a well-trained soldiery. I doubt whether there were 10 good guns in the company. They had along with them their artillery, two small cast-iron cannon, ouch as our boys use on the 4th of July, tied or withed on to the axle-tree of an old one-horse-cart, drawn by a horse that would have paid but a very small crow-tax. There were but two or three Americans in the company, only one I believe, with a sword dangling by his side. Such as they were, they soon started on their march again. At Moore's Corners they met an opposing force in ambush, which fired upon them from behind houses, barns, rocks and fences. Of course the boys were put to flight. One poor fellow, whose name I have forgotten, was fatally wounded, and Capt. GAYNON slightly in the knee. The United States government ordered out two companies of militia to guard the lines in Highgate, who were out from 8 to 14 days, for which service most of them received their land warrants. One or two barns were burned on each side of the line; but by whom, I believe, it was never ascertained. Gen. John E. WOOL was finally sent to the frontier, and in a few days took two leading radicals (one Dr. NELSON) in charge, and the armed rebellion soon came to an end. There were two volunteer companies raised in Highgate and Franklin, but failed to get organized before the finale. …

THE GREAT REBELLION,

Right well do our noble boys, who served in the Union army, during the war of the great Rebellion, deserve a place in history. The name of every true soldier merits an enduring record. The honor of a victory should be divided between the officers and men, and instead of saying that such a general has gained a victory, it should be said that the army under the command of such a general has gained it. Our Highgate boys have cheerfully responded to every call, and by their patriotism and heroic bravery confrere a lasting honor upon their native town. The descendants of our faithful soldiers will glory in saying, "My father, or grandfather was a soldier in that war, or that he shed his blood in defense of the Union." … … Of the names of the soldiers, from Highgate, who served in this war, as far as they are available, I have furnished a, list for another portion of this work-the military county chapter where the respective towns of this county appear so many brave platoons side by side …

THE REBEL RAID IN '64.

The quiet of Highgate was again disturbed by the raiders who so unceremoniously made their appearance in the town of St. Albans and gobbled up quite a bundle of greenbacks from the banks there. For some reason, however, they rather slighted Highgate and took another route on their return to the land of rebel sympathizers. There was no force placed upon the line to keep raiders out of Highgate, but a small guard was enrolled to guard the two bridges across the Missisquoi River at Highgate Falls and East Highgate, leaving the frontier town without protection. However, a small company of cavalry was raised at the Centre of the town which might have done good service had there been anything to do. But as the raid was begun and ended in a day, the company had no opportunity to show their mettle. …

FORM OF THE TOWNSHIP, SOIL, GEOLOGY, ETC.

… It is probable there is no town in the county, if there is in the State, that has such a varied soil and surface. Near the Missisquoi and Rock Rivers, there are several interval farms, which, having been cropped for nearly 100 years continue to yield an abundant harvest of either hay or grain. The Missisquoi River enters the town from the S. E., making a detour towards the centre of the town; thence to the W. thence S. W., leaving it again upon the S. line within about 1 mile of Swanton Falls; thence turning to the N. W. It washes the western shore of an extensive marsh, and empties its waters into Missisquoi Bay. Rock River (a small river) enters the town from the east, running west, thence N. W., thence north, crossing Canada line into the Queen's dominions, but not finding its position congenial, returns again into Highgate and empties into Missisquoi Bay near Walter C. STEVEN's, in the west part of the town. Some portions have an alluvial soil. There is quite a tract of pine-plane land, north and east of Highgate Falls principally, with light, sandy soil, which with thorough manuring yields fair crops. Other portions of the township have a clay bottom, soil, a clay loam, with the portion of clay in the mixture to make the soil rich and strong, and, when well tilled, as productive as any in the County.

There is one singular feature with regard to the soil in Highgate, its sudden change from clay to sand. In some cases, on one side of a shallow ravine, not 2 rods wide, may be found a bottomless bed of clay and on the other side, sand extending downward to the slate rock, and in some cases to an unknown depth. In the west part of the township is found swampy land with a rich black, muck soil, perhaps the best meadow land in town, and some portions near Highgate gore are a gravelly loam, with low, swampy meadowlands in connection. The eastern part of the township is quite hilly and a large portion between the hills is nearly covered with boulders of all imaginable sizes, insomuch that to a careless observer it would seem that the farmer would have to sharpen his sheep's noses, to enable them to get at the grass which grows between the stones most luxuriantly. It is believed, however, that an acre of those hilly portions produces more feed than an acre of any other land devoid of stone. In short, our hilly pastures are the most valuable grazing land for the dairy or for sheep.

Water is abundant in every part of the town, living springs and streams, in so much that its inhabitants seldom suffer for the want of it. It is probable there is not another town in the state, that will stand drought better, or where the husbandman gets more amply paid for his labor.

The lime-rock makes its appearance in the west part of the township, and farther east we have a slate formation, tilted up edge-wise, which, some portion of the way, forms the bed of the Missisquoi River. ... . The rock is hard -- not flinty -- and breaks like marble-rock, in any direction, and would make a valuable stone for buildings or abutments.

The surface of the township is decidedly uneven. Near the river it is considerably cut up by ravines, and the north half of the town abounds in low hills, swamps and valleys. The rock, which crops out of these hills quite plentifully, is different from any other rock in town, mongrel in composition, very much broken up, but not round, making good wall-stone, bordering a trifle upon the sand-rock. So romantic is this section of the town, that it is not strange that it has sent out its poet, but rather that its inhabitants are not all poets.

M. E. CHURCH AT HIGHGATE CENTER.

During the past season the Methodist Episcopal society have erected at this place a substantial brick church at a cost of $8,500, which is nearly completed. The dedication will take place about the middle of February next. The house is in the north village, and is, perhaps, the best meeting-house in town, and its internal arrangements are admirable for comfort and convenience.

January, 1869.

METHODIST STATISTICS.
FROM REV. JAMES ROBINSON.

Rev. Elijah HEDDING (afterwards Bishop) is supposed to have preached the first Methodist sermon in town, in 1799. Rev. Thomas BEST was the first settled minister; Church organized 1822; First members -- E. P. HASKINS and wife, Daniel **HERRICK** and wife, Luke HITCHCOCK and wife, Daniel FILMORE and wife, Amasa JOCELYNE and wife, Thos. BEST and wife, with other names unknown-old records lost; present number of members, 95. Preachers entered services as follows; Revs. Samuel WEAVER 1829, Dillon STEVENS, '30-'33, I. LEONARD, '33-'35, Wm. RICHARDS '35, John GRAVES, '36, C. CHAMBERLIN,'37, B. A. LYON, '38, O. E. SPICER, '39-'41, A. DIXON, '41--'43, John SEAGA, '43-'45, Chas. LEONARD '45-'47, J. D. WHITE '47-49, J. H. BROWN '49-'51, Oren GREG '51-'54, S. H. CLEMENS '54-'56, W. R. PUFFER, '56, J. E. KIMBALL, '57-'59, C. R. HAWLEY '59, H. C. ROBINSON '60, J. S. MOTT '61-'63, B. COX, '63, R. CHRISTIE (local) '64, J. M. PUFFER '65-'67, James ROBINSON '67-'68. Meeting-house built 1823; parsonage built, 1826; 1st organization S. School, cannot tell; books in S. School Library, 765.

THE CONGREGATIONAL CHURCH.
BY REV. E. J. COMINGS

The first Congregational Church of Highgate was organized in a school-house in the N. W. part of the town, Oct. 28, 1811, Rev. Benjamin WOOSTER officiating. The names of the 15 original members were, as follows: Conrad **BARR**, Hezekiah HARNDEN, John JOHNSON, John STINEMATS (STINETS in modern times), John **BARR**, Henry LOUK, Eunice TICHOUT, Anna **SAXE**,[*] Martha **BARR**,[†] Catherine STINEHOUR, Rachael JOHNSON, Sarah **DRURY**, Sarah WILLIAMS, Hannah STINEMATS, and Rachel HARNDEN. … …

---

[*] This Anna Saxe may be the widow of Godfrey Saxe, and the mother of Godfrey's daughter Anna Saxe, who married Joseph H. Stockwell. Joseph and Anna (Saxe) Stockwell were grandparents of Jessie Fidelia Stockwell. The given name of Joseph Stockwell's mother-in-law is unknown, but I propose – based on the information in this paragraph – that she may have been this Anna Saxe. I cannot find any single or widowed woman named Anna Saxe in the Saxe genealogy who was alive and of age at this time, so I suggest that this Anna Saxe was Godfrey's widow. Godfrey died in 1807. His daughter Anna Saxe, who was born in 1804, would not have been old enough to have been a founding member of the Congregational Church in 1811, but his widow would presumably have been comfortable there with her in-laws, the Drurys and the Barrs.

[†] Martha Barr was a daughter of Conrad and Elizabeth (Weaver) Barr and a sister of Conrad (Jr.) and John Barr. She was 19 years old and single in 1811; she married Jared Long in 1814 and had at least one child by him – Clark Levi Long (b. 1831) – and perhaps more, since she had been married 17 years when Clark was born.

ST. JOHN'S EPISCOPAL CHURCH, HIGHGATE.

The material from which to make a history of this parish is very limited. The record of several years of its early existence, if one was kept, has been lost. What is here written respecting it prior to 1837, has mostly been gathered from individuals in private conversation.

The house of worship in this parish was built about the year 1831. It is a substantial brick building, and is large enough to seat 250 persons. It was consecrated May 1, 1833. In 1835 the original building was much improved by the addition of a chancel and vestry-room and by painting the whole. This desirable change was effected through the liberality of Messrs. S. W. and S. S. KEYES. In 1837, the Hon. Heman **ALLEN** gave a bell, a font, of Italian marble; a massive silver communion service, and books for the altar, desk and pulpit. About the same time, mainly by the three gentlemen above named, an organ, of excellent quality and tone, was procured and placed in the church. …

PAPERS FROM MRS. M. E. W. SKEELS.

There is a story related of two of ROGERS' men, disbanded after his expedition to Canada, the name of one was COBB, the other unknown. They undertook to make their way to the south part of the State; they had been suffering for food and had been so reduced as to be obliged to eat human-flesh, as it was said, also that they had burned an Indian village. When they reached the north part of this town, near **Saxe**'s mill, they found several Indians fishing; who forthwith took them prisoners, and marched them to the north-west part of the town; where the Indians claimed possession of their knapsacks, and in the knapsack of one of the men whose name is unknown, was found a portion of pappoose flesh, which sealed his fate; he was burned at the stake. COBB expected to share the same fate, but was however only retained prisoner, and soon gained the confidence of the Indians so that he was allowed to go on a hunting excursion with them, and watching his opportunity escaped, crossed the river and, followed the Hungerford brook, a part of the time creeping on his hands and knees or wading up the rapids, till at last he succeeded in crossing the mountains, reaching the habitation of men. He afterwards came to see his brother, Squire COBB, and related the story here written. …

Conrad **BARR** was born in New York, and removed, with his family, to Missisquoi Bay, thence to Highgate in March, 1787. He dug a spot in the deep snow and erected a cabin, but soon after built a saw pit, sawed boards and erected comfortable dwellings; reared a family in town, and lived many years honored and respected. Two sons still live in town, **John** and **Conrad**, and have held town offices. John **BARR**, now, one of the oldest residents in the place, still recollects many of the incidents connected with their early settlement. ...

JOHN **SAXE**, a German, born in Rhinebeck, Duchess Co., N.Y., removed to Highgate; A.D. 1787, with a family of 8 sons and 1 daughter -- namely **John, George, William, Matthew, Godfrey, Peter, Jacob, Conrad and Hannah**.* Mr. **SAXE** was a man of ability and perseverance, every way calculated to endure the hardships of a first settlement; he had, with his family, many difficulties to encounter, many trials to endure; they were harassed by Indians and wild beasts, Mr. **SAXE** was at one time obliged to swim the river, breaking the ice with his hands. He had much to do with the settlement and organizing of the town. **John**, the eldest son, died at the age of 22; **George** was a hunter and drover, **William** a surveyor, **Matthew** a millwright, and subsequently a merchant; he was the first town clerk, several times represented the town, and held many other town offices. **Godfrey** died at the age of 28. **Peter** remained on the old homestead, a farmer and merchant, a man of business: he several times represented the town; the poorer class always voted for him, for, said they, we all owe Peter. He is the father of the famous **John G. SAXE**, the poet. **Jacob** SAXE, a merchant and furnace man, has done extensive business in town.

Conrad SAXE, a blacksmith and farmer, is still living; he has long been an esteemed member of the M. E. church, and for near 40 years a class-leader. He is now aged and infirm, waiting quietly on the banks of the dark river for the last summons "Come this side."

ANDREW POTTER, one of the earliest settlers, removed from Clarendon to St. Albans Bay, thence to Keyes' Falls, which were then named, after him, **Potter**'s Falls, and for a long time bore that name; he built the first mill in town; his daughter, 13 years of age, was the first female in that section, she afterwards married **Elkena ALBEE**.

REV. PHINEAS KLINGSLEY, first pastor of the Congregational church, a faithful and honored minister who labored for the conversion of his people and the building up of the church, a man respected and beloved by all who knew him and especially the people of his charge, has been very recently called to his eternal reward. He was to have furnished a sketch of his life and labors in Highgate, for this work, but his labors are ended, and there are many other persons whose names should stand conspicuous in the history of the town, whose biography must remain unwritten, as there were none to record it, and they have passed away; their names alone must for a time recall them to remembrance. Among these are COBB, HOWE, PHELPS, STINETS, RECKORD, and, later, **DRURY**, HASKINS, TILMON, CUTLER, KEYES, HUNGERFORD and SKEELS,

---

* John Saxe was a great-great grandfather of Jessie Stockwell. His eight sons and one daughter are named here, and a bit is written about each of the sons including Jessie's great-grandfather Godfrey Saxe: John, George, William, Matthew, Godfrey, Peter, Jacob, Conrad and Hannah.

MRS. SUSANNAH ALBEE, wife of Elkanah ALBEE, died in Highgate, aged 63. Mrs. A. was born in Clarendon, from which place her parents removed with her at the age of 3 years, and settled at St. Albans Bay, then a dense forest. After a residence here of 10 years, she was carried to "Keyes'* Falls," in Highgate, up the Missisquoi in a batteau, there being no land roads. She was the first female carried to that point for settlement. After some years she married, and settled, where she lived to raise a large family and see the wilderness retire before the hand of cultivation. In meeting the trials and toils peculiar to the settlement of a new country, Mrs. A. was remarkable for courage and fortitude and for patience to endure them. Benevolence to the needy was a prominent trait in her character. She had been long a much beloved member of the Congregational church, and her death was calm and peaceful.

THE POET OF HIGHGATE
BY MRS. M. R. W. SKEELS.

For I've captured once your saucy muse.

---

* A rather plain, but natural illustration withal, of the estimate of the more ignorant people found in every community -- perhaps more in the rural district-of any unlucky child, or youth, who has the mystery in his face of undeveloped talent -- a genius they can neither read nor comprehend. -- Ed.

JOHN GODFREY SAXE.

John Godfrey SAXE was born at Highgate, Franklin Co., Vt., on the 2d day of June, 1816. From 9 to 17 he worked on his father's farm and went to school. Then he entered the Grammar-School of St. Albans, and after the usual preparatory studies the college at Middletown, Ct., where he graduated Bachelor of Arts, in the summer of 1839. "While at college he had no reputation as a speaker or writer; but he was considered a fine scholar, especially in the languages, a very pleasant fellow, and the best talker in the place. It is rather odd, though, considering the immemorial custom of all collegians and the literary aspirations of most young men, he wrote nothing at college, nor until several years after he had graduated, when he was in apparently unpropitious circumstances, viz. in the holy bonds of matrimony and the tedious study of the law. "For several years after, he practiced in the courts, writing verses occasionally, and attending to the interests of his party in that part of the world -- for SAXE is something of a politician. He edited the Burlington Sentinel for a short time, running for the office of district-attorney, which he was talented and popular enough to gain, and writing and delivering college and anniversary poems, and lectures. He has certainly won applause by his lectures, very generally. ...

I'm a perfect Colossus of roads !"

---

* Rowena Keith Saxe (1839-1915), daughter of Jacob, who was the son of John, the Loyalist, married Emerson Willard Keyes, who is presumably of the Keyes family of Highgate.

He resided at Burlington a number of years, but for some over six years now has lived in the city of Albany, and gives himself quite to his profession as the humorous poet of his age and country. Mr. **SAXE** published the first edition of his poems in 1849, and the last by Ticknor & Fields, Boston, in 1868, 12 me. 465 pp. The earliest edition has run -- the last publishers, in their late edition of his complete poetical works, say -- through some 23 editions. ...

A GROUP FROM SAXE
Poems and Extracts ...

WHEN I MEAN TO MARRY ...

NEVER TOO LATE TO MEND ...

SLEEP ...

Appendix F
Documents Related to Anna (Saxe) Stockwell

A page that shows Stockwell births, deaths, and marriages, written in longhand, was found in the Hill Family Bible in Clarion, Wright County, Iowa, where it was photographed by George J. Hill in 1962. The page of Stockwell births that is laid into the Hill Family Bible shows "Joseph H. Stockwell was born May 5th, 1802," "Anna M. Saxe was born February 10th, 1804," and "Joseph Stockwell was married to Anna M. Saxe July 8th, 1823." The births of eleven children are then given, ending with Samuel S., and two additional lines which appear to be deaths of children. Although the entry for Anna Saxe is very faint, it does appear to be February 10th, 1804. That Bible is now in the possession of Myron Hill, Jr., of Clarion. A photograph taken in 1962 of the page of Stockwells appears below, laid onto the cover of the Hill Family Bible.

A letter of 12/21/05 from Addie L. Shields, Historian, Clinton County, N.Y., to George J. Hill enclosed eight pages of double-sided copies of typed pages with hand-drawn illustrations from "McLellan Cemetery Records of Clinton County with Index" including "Old Mooers Cemetery - Town of Mooers - Clinton County - New York" on which in alphabetical order (unpaginated) appears "WOODLEY Stockwell " [drawing of WOODLEY monument] "(front) WOODLEY / (on base) --- (side) Wilbur M / 1872-19 / Jennie L. / His Wife / 1872-1939 / (side) Anna M. / Saxe Wife of Jos. Stockwell / Died / Feb. 4, 1890, AE. 86 Ys. / hs. Wilbur / Jennie"

Baptismal Record of Benajah Flavel Stockwell
Son of Joseph H. and Anna Maria Stockwell
Born 14 August 1836.
Baptized 16 November 1856, Clarenceville, Quebec
1856 Methodist Church Register – Clarenceville, Quebec – Baptism – Stockwell, B.F. "Benajah Flavel, son of Joseph Stock- / well, farmer of the Siegnory of Foucault / and of Anna Maria his wife was born on / the fourteenth day of August in the year of / Our Lord Eighteen hundred and thirty six; / and was baptized in the sixteenth day of / November in the year Eighteen hundred and fifty six / By me / John Tompkins / Wesleyan Minister / Witnesses / L. Sinfora [?] / John H. Gomland [?]" This record of his baptism was found on 24 June 2009 on Ancestry.com. The original page was photocopied and printed. It is said to be from "Quebec Vital and Church Records (Drouin Collection), 1621-1967. … "Most of the records in this collection include baptisms, marriages, and burials. However, several other types of church records are also included. These records may be confirmations, dispensations, censuses, statements of readmission to the church, etc."

Mabel Kennedy Stockwell, *The Stockwell Genealogy* show Joseph H. Stockwell and his wife Anna and their children, and their son Benajah Stockwell's family:
P. 463: Joseph Stockwell married July 8, 1823/25, Anna M. Saxe (Sachs). Children: (#7): 174137, Benajah F., born Aug. 14, 1836 at Stanbridge, Can.
P. 468. Benajah Flavel Stockwell married Oct. 5, 1861 at Highgate, Vt., Emily F. Hyde. … Children (#1): Jessie Fidelia, born Sept. 7, 1863 at Peoria, Ill. Married Sept. 7, 1882, George J. Hill, and had at least four children.

Parentage, birth, and marriage of Emily L. Hyde
Her husband, Benajah F. Stockwell
Six children

From: Charles E. Tuttle, *Hyde Family: A Partial Record of One Branch. Descendants of Samuel, Who Came from London to Boston in 1639 and Jonathan, Who Came to America in 1647* (Rutland, Vermont: The Tuttle Company, 1931). Reprint from Rufus S. Warner, Ludlow, Vt., N.D.

Page 25

"*Children of Harvey, Luther, Henry, and Fidelia G. (Potter) Hyde* ...

IV. Emily L. b. Nov. 27, 1840; m. Oct. 5, 1861, Benajah F. Stockwell; live in Fryeburgh, Ia. Meth. E. Their children are:

1. Jessie F. Stockwel, b. Sept. 7, 1863.
2. Eugene S. Stockwell, b. May 10, 1865.
3. Ruby Stockwell, b. , 1868.
4. Emma C. Stockwell, b. , 1871.
5. Herbert Stockwell, b. 1874.
6. Grace L. Stockwell, b. April 7, 1877."

Appendix G

John Saxe to Jessie Fidelia Stockwell

Summary of Proofs for Generations 1, 2, 3, 4, and 5

Generation 1
John Saxe, the Loyalist, and his wife, Catherine Weaver

John Saxe was born in Langensalza, Kingdom of Hanover (now Bad Lanensalzaa, Thuringia, Saxony, Germany), 10 November 1732. He died at Saxe's Mills, Highgate, Franklin County, Vermont, on 12 March 1808 and was buried in the town cemetery in Philipsburg, Missisquoi County, Quebec, Canada. John Saxe was a Loyalist who moved with his family and other Loyalists from Dutchess County, N.Y., to Missisquoi Bay, Canada, after the Revolutionary War. He married, in Rhinebeck, Dutchess County, N.Y., 18 November 1771, Catherine Weaver, born at Philadelphia, Pennsylvania, on 10 January 1744; died at Highgate, Franklin Co., Vermont, 10 January 1791. She was buried in the town cemetery in Philipsburg, Quebec. **John and Catherine (Weaver) Saxe had nine children, of whom the fifth was a son, Godfrey Saxe**.

Bunnell, *The New Loyalist Index*: "John Sax / b. 10 Nov 1732 d. 12 Mar 1808 m. NY Cath. Weaver b. 10 Jan 1744 Phila Pa. Fr. Langensaltza, Germany, Rhinebeck, NY Stl: Philipsburg, Quebec, Canada" [secondary source]

J.G.S.[John Godfrey Saxe II], *Genealogy of the Saxe Family*: "Saxe was born in 1732 at Langensaltza, in the Kingdom of Hanover, Germany." "On November 18, 1771, at Rhinebeck . . . he married Catherine Weaver. . . . She was born in Philadelphia, in 1744." "According to a manuscript written by his son William in Quebec in 1824, he had assisted a Major Cautine of the British Army to penetrate through the lines of the American troops. In June, 1786, John moved with his family to Missisquoi Bay." "his death on March 13, 1808. Catherine . . . died on January 10, 1791" "1. JOHN SAXE. B. 1732 at Langensalza, Germany, D. March 12, 1808, Highgate, Saxe's Mills, M. Catherine Weaver Nov. 18, 1771, Rhinebeck, N. Y., B. 1744, Philadelphia, Pa. D. Jan. 10, 1791." [secondary source]

From Nancy Kelley, Kinship: "Roberts, *New York in the Revolution as Colony and State*. Vol. 2. (n.d.), p. 230-1 - Tories and Suspected Persons, various dates 1776-1785. SAX, John - suspected person" [primary source]

John Saxe, Loyalist

From Nancy Kelly, Kinship: Marriages Prior to 1784: SAX, John, married WEAVER, Catherine on 11.18.1771 Found in Marriage Bonds, vol 17, p258 [primary source]

C. Thomas, *Contributions to the History of the Eastern Townships* (1866), 15: "Philipsburg ... The first party of white men . . . came in the fall of 1784 . . . John Sax" [secondary source]

Letter 19 August 2005 to George J. Hill from Jean Darrah McCaw re John Saxe:: "When the Revolution broke out he swore allegiance to the King and was put in prison from which he escaped and served in Yager's' Loyalst Corps. . . . In 1783, when the settlements in western Quebec (Upper Canada) were prepared for settlement there were several settlers who wished to settle in the Missisquoi Bay area west of Lake Champlain. John Saxe is listed on a petition dated 1783 and another in 1786. He bought land in the Seigniory of St. Armand from Thomas Dunn, south of the Peter Miller, in a place that became known as Saxe's Mills. When the boundary line was drawn this became part of Vermont." [secondary source]

Warren Robinson (ed.), and Amos Skeels (d. ca. 1861), *History of Highgate* (ed. and published by Miss Abby, Maria Hemenway (1871): "First settlers …. In 1785-6 ... John Saxe" "1791, Catherine, wife of John SAXE, died; supposed to be the first death in town." "JOHN SAXE, a German, born in Rhinebeck, Duchess Co., N.Y., removed to Highgate; A.D. 1787, with a family of 8 sons and 1 daughter -- namely John, George, William, Matthew, Godfrey, Peter, Jacob, Conrad and Hannah" [secondary source]

Aldrich, Lewis Cass. "History of the Town of Highgate" (Chapter 31), in *History of Franklin and Grand Isle Counties Vermont* (Syracuse, N.Y.: D. Mason & Co., 1891), 593-611. Cass accepts and confirms the information in Robinson and Skeels *History of Highgate* [secondary source]

Generation 2
Godfrey Saxe and a woman, whose name is unknown

Godfrey Saxe, son of John and Catherine (Weaver) Saxe, was born in Rhinebeck, Dutchess County, N.Y., 28 January 1778. He died on 16 August 1807, probably in Philipsburg, Missisquoi County, Quebec, or in Highgate, Vermont, and was perhaps buried in the town cemetery in Philipsburg. **Godfrey Saxe and an unnamed woman, who may not have been his wife, had a daughter Anna Maria Saxe.**

J.G.S.[John Godfrey Saxe II], *Genealogy of the Saxe Family*: "son . . . Godfrey died at the age of twenty-eight." [N.b., by dates given elsewhere in this book, Godfrey actually d. at age 29]. "Matthew, Godfrey and Peter Saxe kept the first store." The fifth child and fifth son "50. Godfrey Saxe, B. Jan. 28, 1778, D. Aug. 16, 1807;" "family of 8 sons and 1 daughter ... Godfrey died at the age of 28" "50. GODFREY SAXE. [daughter] 501. Anne Saxe, M. Joseph Stockville" [sic: apparently a mis-reading of Stockwell in script] [secondary source]

Letter 19 August 2005 to George J. Hill from Jean Darrah McCaw re John Saxe:
CHILDREN
JOHN   1772-1793
GEORGE   1773-1853
WILLIAM   1774-1840
MATTHEW   1776-1836
GODFREY   1778-1807 ..." [secondary source]

Warren Robinson (ed.), and Amos Skeels, *History of Highgate* (ed. and published by Miss Abby, Maria Hemenway (1871): "1801, Matthew, Godfrey and Peter SAXE kept the first store and tavern" "SELECTMEN ... Ebenezer STOCKWELL, 1821" [secondary source]

Reynolds, Cuyler (ed). *Genealogical and Family History of Southern New York and the Hudson River Valley: A Record of the Achievements of Her People in the Making of a Commonwealth and the Building of a Nation.* Vol 3. New York: Lewis Historical Publishing Company, 1914, 1094-1098. "Godfrey Saxe ... generation 2 ... a son of John and Catherine (Weaver) Saxe, who died 'at twenty-eight'." [secondary source]

Allen L. Stratton, *History of the South Heroe Island Being the Towns of South Hero and Grand Isle, Vermont ... in Two Volumes.* Vol. 1 (North Hero, Vt., n.d.), p. 151, the Petition of Elisha Reynolds & Christopher Pickle for a Ferry (1804) in Highgate, Vt., 12 August 1804, is signed by 37 Subscribers, including Matthew Sax, Conrad Barr, and Godfrey Sax. The petition was "Passed by the General Assembly, 1 Nov 1804 (Ms. Vt. State Papers, Vol. 44, pg. 150.) (Laws of Vt., 1804, pg. 56.)" [primary source]

An undocumented item regarding this Godfrey Saxe on Ancestry.com states that he died at Philipsburg, Quebec, and was buried in the Philipsburg town cemetery. There is no reason either to refute or accept this information, so I have listed it as being possible.

Generation 3
Joseph H. Stockwell and his wife, Anna Maria Saxe

Anna Maria Saxe, daughter of Godfrey Saxe and a woman whose name is unknown, was born on 10 February 1804, probably in Highgate, Franklin County, Vermont. She died in Mooers, Clinton County, N.Y., on 4 February 1890 and was buried in the Old Mooers Village Cemetery in Mooers, N.Y. She married, on 8 July 1823 (or possibly 1825), Joseph H. Stockwell, son of Ebenezer and Abi (Holbrook) Stockwell, who was born in Burlington, Vermont, 5 May 1802, and died in Burlington, 22 September 1870; he was buried in Burlington, Vt.. The site of the marriage is unknown, but it was probably in

Highgate, Vermont. **Joseph H. and Anna Maria (Saxe) Stockwell had eleven or twelve children, of whom the seventh was Benajah Flavel Stockwell.**

"50. GODFREY SAXE. [daughter] 501. Anne Saxe, M. Joseph Stockville" [sic: apparently a mis-reading of Stockwell in script]   [secondary source]

Warren Robinson (ed.), and Amos Skeels, *History of Highgate* (ed. and published by Miss Abby, Maria Hemenway (1871): "Andrew POTTER. . . built the first house and barn-in the limits of the village, in about 1795 . . . Ebenezer STOCKWELL came into town in 1809, moved into the POTTER house, and was the principal agent, or foreman, for Mr. ALLEN until 1819." "Abi STOCKWELL [died] 1846   82 years" "The first Congregational Church of Highgate was organized in a school-house in the N. W. part of the town, Oct. 28, 1811. . . The names of the 15 original members were, as follows: Conrad BARR, , , , John BARR, . . . Anna SAXE" [secondary source]

Page of Stockwell births that is laid into the Hill Family Bible shows "Joseph H. Stockwell was born May 5th, 1802," "Anna M. Saxe was born February 10th, 1804," and "Joseph Stockwell was married to Anna M. Saxe July 8th, 1823." [primary source]

A letter of 12/21/05 from Addie L. Shields, Historian, Clinton County, N.Y., to George J. Hill: "McLellan Cemetery Records of Clinton County with Index" including "Old Mooers Cemetery - Town of Mooers - Clinton County - New York" . . . Anna M. / Saxe Wife of Jos. Stockwell / Died / Feb. 4, 1890, AE. 86 Ys." [primary source]

Drouin Collection of Quebec Vital and Church Records, 1621-1967: "1856 Methodist Church Register – Clarenceville, Quebec – Baptism – Stockwell, B.F. Benajah Flavel, son of Joseph Stock- / well, farmer of the Siegnory of Foucault / and of Anna Maria his wife was born on / the fourteenth day of August in the year of / Our Lord Eighteen hundred and thirty six; / and was baptized in the sixteenth day of / November in the year Eighteen hundred and fifty six" [primary source]

Mabel Kennedy Stockwell, *The Stockwell Genealogy*: P. 463 "Joseph Stockwell married July 8, 1823/25, Anna M. Saxe (Sachs). ...Children: (#7): 174137, Benajah F., born Aug. 14, 1836 at Stanbridge, Can." [secondary source]

Gemeration 4
Benajah Flavel Stockwell and his wife, Emily Lodiweska Hyde

Benajah Flavel Stockwell, son of Joseph H. and Anna Maria (Saxe) Stockwell, was born at Stanbridge, Missisquoi County, Quebec, Canada, on 14 August 1836. He was baptized at the Methodist Church, Clarenceville, Mississquoi County, Quebec, on 16 November 1856. He died at Oklahoma City, Oklahoma, on 28 March 1919 and was buried at Graceland Cemetery, Rowan, Wright County, Iowa. He was married 8 April 1861 in

Highgate, Vermont, to Emily Lodiweska Hyde, daughter of Harvey and Fidelia Gadcourt (Potter) Hyde, who was born 27 November 1840 in Highgate, Vermont, and died in Wright County, Iowa, 28 May 1879. She is buried in the Graceland Cemetery, in Rowan, Iowa. **Benajah and Emily (Hyde) Stockwell had six children, of whom the eldest was Jessie Fidelia Stockwell.**

Drouin Collection of Quebec Vital and Church Records, 1621-1967: "1856 Methodist Church Register – Clarenceville, Quebec – Baptism – Stockwell, B.F. Benajah Flavel, son of Joseph Stock- / well, farmer of the Siegnory of Foucault / and of Anna Maria his wife was born on / the fourteenth day of August in the year of / Our Lord Eighteen hundred and thirty six; / and was baptized in the sixteenth day of / November in the year Eighteen hundred and fifty six" [primary source]

Mabel Kennedy Stockwell, *The Stockwell Genealogy*: P. 463: "Joseph Stockwell married July 8, 1823/25, Anna M. Saxe (Sachs). ...Children: (#7): 174137, Benajah F., born Aug. 14, 1836 at Stanbridge, Can." [secondary source]

Charles E. Tuttle, *Hyde Family: A Partial Record of One Branch. Descendants of Samuel, Who Came from London to Boston in 1639 and Jonathan, Who Came to America in 1647* (Rutland, Vermont: The Tuttle Company, 1931). Reprint from Rufus S. Warner, Ludlow, Vt., N.D. Page 25. "*Children of Harvey, Luther, Henry, and Fidelia G. (Potter) Hyde* ...IV. Emily L. b. Nov. 27, 1840; m. Oct. 5, 1861, Benajah F. Stockwell; live in Fryeburgh, Ia. Meth. E. Their children are: 1. Jessie F. Stockwell, b. Sept. 7, 1863." [secondary source]

Benajah Flavel Stockwell death certificate, Oklahoma City, OK, says burial was at Rowan, Iowa [primary source]

Benajah Flavel Stockwell Obituary, bound with Funeral of Dr. [E. S.] Stockwell, 11 pp., with covers, n.d., ca. 1921 [secondary source]

Marriage of Benajah Stockwell and Emily Hyde was located by the Town Clerk of Highgate, Vt., in February 2003: Highgate Clerk (Cora A. Baker) "4-8-1861 / Marriage Emily Hyde A6 B. F. Stockwell" (Undated handwritten note from Baker to George Hill in response to his letter of 17 January 2003)" [primary source]

George J. Hill found the following graves in Rowan, Iowa, on July 17, 2006: Graceland Cemetery, Rowan, Iowa, on the east bank of the Iowa River - "STOCKWELL monument, 50 ft SW of Hill family group. Ranging to the N from the STOCKWELL monument are stones with the following inscriptions: Lucy J   Oct 18, 1833 Mar 30, 1914 [Her death date shows she was Mrs. Lucy (Hannings) Stockwell, 2nd wife of Benajah Stockwell]. Father   Aug 14, 1836 Mar 28, 1919 [This is Benajah Stockwell]. Mother Nov 27, 1840 May 28, 1879" [This is Emily (Hyde) Stockwell] [primary source]

Generation 5
Jessie Fidelia Stockwell and her husband, George J. Hill

Jessie Fidelia Stockwell, eldest child of Benajah Flavel and Emily Lodiweska (Hyde) Stockwell, was born at Peoria, Peoria County, Illinois, 7 September 1863. She died at Clarion, Wright County, Iowa, 12 September 1940, and was buried at the Graceland Cemetery, Rowan, Wright County, Iowa. She married, at Fryeburg, Wright County, Iowa, 7 September 1882, George J. Hill, son of Charles W. and Adelia Catharine (Riley) Hill, who was born at Caton, Steuben County, New York, 5 January 1857. He died at Clarion, Iowa, 2 June 1952, and was buried at the Graceland Cemetery in Rowan, Iowa. **George J. and Jessie Fidelia (Stockwell) Hill had nine children, of whom the fifth son and ninth child was Gerald Leslie Hill.**

Mabel Kennedy Stockwell, *The Stockwell Genealogy* show Joseph H. Stockwell and his wife Anna and their children, and their son Benajah Stockwell's family:
P. 463: Joseph Stockwell married July 8, 1823/25, Anna M. Saxe (Sachs). Children: (#7): 174137, Benajah F., born Aug. 14, 1836 at Stanbridge, Can.
P. 468. Benajah Flavel Stockwell married Oct. 5, 1861 at Highgate, Vt., Emily F. Hyde. ... Children (#1): Jessie Fidelia, born Sept. 7, 1863 at Peoria, Ill. Married Sept. 7, 1882, George J. Hill, and had at least four children. [secondary source]

From: Charles E. Tuttle, *Hyde Family: A Partial Record of One Branch. Descendants of Samuel, Who Came from London to Boston in 1639 and Jonathan, Who Came to America in 1647* (Rutland, Vermont: The Tuttle Company, 1931). Reprint from Rufus S. Warner, Ludlow, Vt., n.d.
Page 25 "*Children of Harvey, Luther, Henry, and Fidelia G. (Potter) Hyde* ...
IV. Emily L. b. Nov. 27, 1840; m. Oct. 5, 1861, Benajah F. Stockwell; live in Fryeburgh, Ia. Meth. E. Their children are: 1. Jessie F. Stockwel, b. Sept. 7, 1863". [secondary source]

.The record of Jessie (Stockwell) Hill's death was provided by the Wright County Registrar of Vital Records on 9 December 2002, stating: "STATE OF IOWA County Record Certificate of Death Certificate No.   Bk 2 #49
DECEDENT'S NAME Jessie Fidelia Hill DATE OF DEATH November 12, 1940 PLACE OF DEATH Wright County   Grant Township SEX Female   AGE 77 yrs. 0 mos. 5 days RACE   White MARITAL STATUS   Married   SURVIVING SPOUSE Geo. Hill PLACE OF DISPOSITION   Cemetery X   Rowan IMMEDIATE CAUSE OF DEATH   Myocardial Failure DUE TO   X
DATE RECEIVED BY REGISTRAR   X [not shown on record]
NOTATIONS   X Issued 12-9-02 By Dwight N. Reiland   Wright County C1498880" [primary source]

Jessie Fidelia Stockwell appears in *Genealogy of the Hill Family in America*, page 8, sheet #7, married to person 68, George J. Hill [secondary source]

References for George J. Hill, who is person #68 in *Genealogy of the Hill Family in America* [secondary source]

The record of George J. Hill's death was provided by the Wright County Registrar of Vital Records on 9 December 2002, stating: "STATE OF IOWA County Record Certificate of Death Certificate No.   Bk 4 Pg 210 DECEDENT'S NAME George J. Hill DATE OF DEATH June 2, 1952 PLACE OF DEATH Wright County   Clarion SEX Male AGE 95 years RACE   White MARITAL STATUS   Widowed SURVIVING SPOUSE   X PLACE OF DISPOSITION Graceland Cemetery   Rowan IMMEDIATE CAUSE OF DEATH   Cerebral thrombosis DUE TO   malnutrition and arteriosclerosis DATE RECEIVED BY REGISTRAR   June 11, 1952 NOTATIONS   X Issued 12-9-02 By Dwight N. Reiland   Wright County C1498881" [primary source]

"George J. Hill" Obituary; and "George Hill, 95, County Pioneer, Succumbs Monday" (from Wright County *Monitor*) [secondary source]

George J. Hill is married to Jessie Fidelia Stockwell 1741372 in *The Stockwell Genealogy* [secondary source]

Hill Family Bible shows marriage of George J. Hill and Jessie Fidelia Stockwell, 7 September 1882 [primary source]

General Index
Chapters 1-5
(Excluding the Appendices and Notes)

1st Michigan Regiment, 62
90th Division, U.S. Army, 72
A.E.F. (American Expeditionary
    Forces), 19, 65, 72
Abbott, Caroline.
    See Keyes, Caroline Abbott
Abolitionist Party, 34
Act of Union, 1841, 8
Act, Proclamation, of 1792, 8
Aguire, Alice. *See* Saxe, Alice Aguire
Alarm of June 29, 1777, 33
Albany, Albany Co., N.Y., 13, 42, 57, 59
Albany Co., N.Y., 13
Albany Law School, 56
Allbert, Prince, 34
Albert Lea, Minn., 52
Alburgh, N.Y., 17, 19, 21
Allen, Clarence E., M.D.
    (m. Minerva Saxe), 62
Allen, Clarence Keith (300), 62, 71
Allen, Dorcas Irene (301), 62, 71
Allen, Ella K.
    See McCollum, Ella K. Allen
Allen, Ethan, 11
Allen, Heman, 11
Allen, Horace Eugene (299), 62, 71
Allen, Ira, 11
Allen, Minerva Saxe
    (m. Clarence E.), 48, 62
Alton, Ill., 47
America(n), 2, 3, 7
Amherst College, 71
Amsterdam, the Netherlands, 2
Ansbach Jaegers, 7
Antwerp, Belgium, 34, 72
Argonne, 72
Arizona, 47
Atanurbi, Ekeba.
    See Jewett, Ekeba Atanurbi

Atwell, Jodelphia Amelia.
    See Saxe, Jodelphia Atwell
Ayckland, 17
Bad Langensalza, Germany, 1-2
Bahr, Conrad. *See* Barr, Conrad
Bailargeon, C. F., Bishop, 37
Baker, Susan Maria.
    See Saxe, Susan Maria Baker
Baldwin, Martha. *See* McCollum,
    Martha Baldwin Flannery
Baltimore, Md., 56
Barford, 17
Barnston, 17
Barr family, 23, 24
Barr, Anna.
    See Saxe, Godfrey
Barr, Conrad, 4, 7, 10, 11, 19, 21-3, 29
Barr, Elizabeth (dau. of John), 23
Barr, Elizabeth Weaver
    (m. Conrad), 4, 10, 22-3, 29
Barr, John, 22-3
Barr, Martha, 22-3
Bartlett's Familiar Quotations, 13, 42
Bascom, Elizabeth Wead Saxe
    (m. Henry), 44, 59
Bascom, Henry
    (m. Elizabeth Wead Saxe), 59
Bascome, Sophia.
    See Sollace, Sophia Bascome
Bascome, Susannah Stetson, 43
Battle Creek, Mich., 43
Battle of Baldwin Field, 62
Battle of James Island, 62
Bay, Missisquoi. *See* Missisquoi Bay
Beatrice, Neb., 53
Beekman family, 6
Beekman, Margaret. *See* Livingston,
    Margaret Beekman
Beekman, William, 6
Belgium, 72
Bellows, Col. Benjamin (Regiment), 33

Benedict, M. L.
    (m. Ruby Ellen Stockwell), 69
Benedict, Ruby Ellen Stockwell
    (m. M. L. Benedict), 53-5, 69
Bennington, Vt., 13, 24, 38-40, 55
Berry, Elizabeth.
    See Stockwell, Elizabeth Berry
Bersen, Calif., 62
Bible, 2, 11, 40
Bickford family, 41
Bickford, Grace Merwin.
    See Keyes, Grace Bickford
Bickford, Harriet S. Stockwell
    (m. ___ Bickford), 41, 52
Bloxham, Myra.
    See Stockwell, Myra Bloxham
Boston, Mass., 47, 56, 72
Bosworth, Frances Pumpelly
    (m. Joseph Sollace), 43, 57
Bosworth, Hepsibeth Sollace
    (m. Nathaniel), 43
Bosworth, Joseph Sollace, Justice
    (m. Frances Pumpelly), 43, 57
Bosworth, Mary A.
    See Saxe, Mary A. Bosworth
Bosworth, Nathaniel
    (m. Hepsibeth Sollace), 43
Bourett, Edmond A.
    (m. Sarah C. Drury), 62
Bourett, Edmond Calvin (297), 62, 71
Bourett, Frederick Drury (298), 62, 71
Bourett, Hannah Lucile (295), 62, 71
Bourett, Hortense V. S. (296), 62, 71
Bourett, Sarah C. Drury
    (m. Edmond A.), 62
Brawley, Calif., 63-4
Britain (and British), 6, 7, 28, 32, 42
Brooke, Lorraine.
    See Saxe, Lorraine Brooke
Brookline, Mass., 56-7, 69
Brooklyn, N.Y., 42, 57
Brown, Charlotte Saxe (m. John), 35, 51
Brown, John (m. Charlotte Saxe), 51
Bryce, Catharine.
    See Hogaboom, Catharine Bryce
Buffalo, N.Y., 49

Bunnell, Addie.
    See Stockwell, Addie Bunnell
Bunnell, Benjamin
    (m. Louise Schoonmaker), 68
Bunnell, Louise Schoonmaker
    (m. Benjamin), 68
Burlington, Vt., 10, 13, 65-6
Burma, 53, 69
Burroughs, Eliza J.
    See Saxe, Eliza J. Burroughs
Burroughs, Sarah.
    See Saxe, Sarah E. Burroughs
Burtis, Sara F. *See* Saxe, Sara F. Burtis
California, 45, 47
Cambria, Niagara Co., N.Y.,
    24, 33-4, 48-9, 64
Cambria Centre Cemetery,
    Niagara Co., N.Y., 12, 24, 33
Cambridge, Lamoille Co., Vt., 24, 26, 60
Campbell, Nancy Valina.
    See Scovell, Nancy Campbell
Canada (also *See* Quebec and various
    towns), 1, 6-16, 22, 27, 30, 32-3,
    37, 44, 63, 65
Canisius College, 72
Carter, Anna. *See* Saxe, Anna Carter
Carter, Charlotte Saxe (m. Ira), 16, 35
Carter, Ira (m. Charlotte Saxe), 35
Carveth, Hector Russell
    (m. Josephine McCollum), 72
Carveth, Josephine McCollum
    (m. Hector Russell), 63, 72
Catholic. *See* Roman Catholic
Catholic University of America, 72
Caton, Steuben Co., N.Y., 67
Cautine, Major (British Army), 7
Cemetery. *See* cemeteries, by name
Census, U.S., 19, 21, 28-30, 40, 52, 55
Cerro Gordo Co., Ia., 66
Chamberlin, Edgar J.
    (m. Sarah Griffin Place), 61
Chamberlin, Sarah Griffin Place
    (m. Edgar J.), 47, 61
Chambly, 17
Champlain, Lake. *See* Lake Champlain

Chase, Elizabeth.
    See Saxe, Elizabeth Chase
Chazy Landing, N.Y., 28
Chazy, Clinton Co., N.Y.,
    18, 19, 28, 37, 51
Chicago, Ill., 71-2
Chicago University, 72
Chittenden Co., Vt., 21, 28
Church (*See* churches, by name)
Civil War, 45, 52, 62
Clarenceville, Quebec, 53
Clarion, Wright Co., Iowa, 40, 66-7
Cleveland, Ohio, 56
Cliffton, 17
Clinton Co., N.Y., 13, 18, 37-9
Collender, Mary.
    See Sands, Mary Collender
Colt, Hetzel (m. Juliette Scovell), 48
Colt, Josiah Boardman Scovell (189;
    m. Mary Lydia Hewitt), 48, 63
Colt, Julia Maria (92).
    See Lovell, Julia Maria Colt
Colt, Juliette Scovell (m. Hetzel), 34, 48
Colt, Leander (m. Mary Helen Saxe), 38
Colt, Mary Elizabeth Scovell (316),
    63, 71
Colt, Mary Helen Saxe (m. Leander),
    20, 38
Colt, Mary Lydia Hewitt
    (m. Josiah Scovell), 63
Compton, 17
Concise Dictionary of American
    Biography (Scribner) 13, 42
Congregational Church, 21-2, 23, 33
Conneautville, Penna., 62
Connecticut, 7, 42
Connecticut Agricultural School, 57
Connecticut River, 17
Connor, Ida May.
    See Saxe, Ida May Connor
Corinth, Miss. (Battle of Shiloh), 45
Cornell University, 64, 71-2
Coutermanche, Emma. *See* Stockwell,
    Emma Coutermanche
Cox, Amelia Virginia. *See* Jewett,
    Amelia Virginia Cox

Coyle, Gertrude.
    See Saxe, Gertrude Coye
Crump, Louise Wheaton.
    See Saxe, Louise Crump
Cyclopedia of American Literature
    (Duyckinck), 42
D.A.R. (Daughters of the American
    Revolution), 45
Daniels, Flora Jane.
    See Saxe, Flora Jane Daniels
Danville, N.Y., 59
Davies, Mary Hawley.
    See Jewett, Mary Hawley Davies
De Veau Neck, 62
Dedham, Mass., 40
d'Emirs, Abbe, 36-7
Dill family, 41
Dill, Adelia Sophia. *See*, Stockwell,
    Adelia Sophia Dill
Dominican Convent, Vienna, Austria, 72
Douglass, Elizabeth.
    See Saxe, Elizabeth Douglass
Drew University, 69
Drew, Abagail. *See* Saxe, Abagail Drew
Drury, Abel, 43, 48
Drury, Grace B.
    See Saxe, Grace B. Drury
Drury, Hannah Saxe (54; m. Zephaniah
    Keith), 32-3, 47-8, 62
Drury, Horace S. (181), 48, 62
Drury, Minerva Saxe (183). *See* Allen,
    Minerva Saxe
Drury, Sarah C. (182).
    See Bourett, Sarah C. Drury
Drury, Sarah Keith
    (m. Abel Drury), 22, 43, 48
Drury, Sarah Keith.
    See Saxe, Sarah Keith Drury
Drury, Zephaniah Keith
    (m. Hannah Saxe), 32, 47-8
Dubuque, Iowa, 67
Dunham family, 41
Dunham, Lucy Ann Stockwell
    (m. Martin Dunham), 41, 55
Dunham, Martin (m. Lucy Ann
    Stockwell), 41, 55

Dunning family, 13
Dunning, Clarissa.
    See Saxe, Clarissa Dunning
Durant, Alice Rowena Hyde
    (m. Fayette), 46, 60
Durant, Caroline Maria (268), 60, 70
Durant, Ellen Hannah (267), 60, 70
Durant, Fayette
    (m. Alice Rowena Hyde), 60
Durant, Homer Eaton (270), 60, 70
Durant, Julia Ella (269), 60, 70
Dutch, 6
Dutchess Co., N.Y., 3-5, 12, 15, 16, 18,
    20, 27, 29
Duyckinck, Evert A., and George, 42
Eastern Townships of Lower Canada, 8
Eaton, 17
Ecole Notre Dame, Namur, Belgium, 72
Edward, Prince, 18
Edwards, Nancy Helen. *See* Smith,
    Nancy Helen Edwards
El Paso, Texas, 64
Elting, Janet. S*ee* Hotaling, Janet Elting
Emporia, Kan., 62
English/England, 3, 33, 37, 72
Erfurt, Hanover, Germany, 1
Erie Canal, 47
Esopus, N.Y., 5-7
Esopus Indians, 6
Estey & Saxe, New York City, 45
Europe, 2, 56
Fairbanks, Sarah Electa Saxe
    (m. Warren S.), 51, 65
Fairbanks, Warren S.
    (m. Sarah Electa Saxe), 65
Fairhaven, Vt., 45
Family History Center, 23
Fellows, George, 4
Ferguson, Andrew, M.D. (m. Elizabeth
    Catherine Saxe), 38
Ferguson, Elizabeth Catherine Saxe,
    20, 38
First Methodist Church,
    Madison, N.J., 45
Fisher, Evelyn Foster. *See* Saxe, Evelyn
    Foster Fisher

Flannery, Mrs. Martha Baldwin. *See*
    McCollum, Martha Flannery
Fort Collins, Colo., 69
Fort Edward, N.Y., 7, 20
Fort Ticonderoga, N.Y., 33
Foster, Maryette. *See* Stockwell,
    Maryette Foster
Foster, Simeon, 10
France (and French), 19, 36-7, 65
Franklin Co., N.Y., 21
Franklin Co., Vt., 1, 12, 21, 24, 26-9, 33
Franklin, La., 63
Franklin, N.H., 65
French and Indian War, 2
Fresno, Calif., 38
Fryeburg(h) (now Rowan), Wright Co.,
    Iowa, 53-4, 66-7, 69
"Furnace Lot," Highgate, Vt., 18, 28
Gallagher, Donald Joseph, Capt. (327),
    64, 72
Gallagher, Francis Waters, M.D. (m.
    Mary Elizabeth McCollum), 64
Gallagher, Hiram, M.D., Lieut. (325),
    64, 74
Gallagher, Leo, Lieut., LL.B, Ph.D.
    (326), 64, 72
Gallagher, Mary Elizabeth McCollum
    (m. Francis), 48, 64
Gallagher, Paul. Lieut., M.D.
    (324), 64, 72
Geary, Camille Scovell McCollum
    (m. John Richard), 63, 72
Geary, John Richard
    (m. Camille McCollum), 72
Genealogy of the Saxe Family (Saxe), 1,
    6, 10, 18, 19, 21, 23-5, 30, 32-3,
    37, 41-2, 47, 64, 69
General Assembly of Vermont, 21
General Electric Co., 72
General Motors Acceptance
    Corporation, 71
General Motors Continental (Europe),
    72
Geneva, Switzerland, 71
George III, King of England, 2, 6
George Washington University, 71

Georgetown University, 72
German(y), 1-5, 12, 22, 33-4, 56, 70
Germany, East (D.D.R.), 2
Gibbs, Anna Saxe (m. John), 16, 36
Gibbs, Caroline (90), 36, 51
Gibbs, John (m. Anna Saxe), 36
Glens Falls, N.Y., 7
Godfrey, Rhoda Ann.
    See Scovell, Rhoda Ann Godfrey
Goldman, Sachs, 69
Google, 42
Graceland Cemetery, Rowan, Iowa, 53-5
Grand Isle, Vermont, 31, 37
Grand Trunk Railroad, 61
Grant Township, Wright Co., Ia., 67
Graves family, 13
Graves, Betty. *See* Saxe, Betty Graves
Green Mountain Boys, 11
Greenfield, Saratoga Co., N.Y., 29
Griggs, Ellen. *See* Saxe, Ellen Griggs
Griggs, grandfather of James Saxe, 56
Griggs, Lucy Saxe (m. William), 35, 51
Griggs, William N., 51
Hadley, Delia. *See* Saxe, Delia Hadley
Hainich National Park, Thuringia, 2
Hakey, Martha Aralla. *See* Stockwell,
    Martha Aralla Hakey
Hall, Hiram, 37
Hall, Lotta. *See* Place, Lotta Hall
Hall, Louisa J.; *See* Saxe, Louisa J. Hall
Hall, Susan, 37
Hancock, Lucy.
    See Stockwell, Lucy Hancock
Hannibal, N.Y., 52
Hannings, David A., 54, 66
Hannings, Edith, 54
Hannings, Lucy, Mrs. *See* Stockwell,
    Mrs. Lucy Hannings (m. Benajah)
Hanover, 1, 2
Harper, Frances M.
    See Saxe, Frances M. Harper
Harvard College, 56-7
Harvard Law School, 56, 72
Harvey Community Congregational
    Church, 66-7
Harvey, H. E., Rev., 66

Heflon, Emily. *See* Place, Emily Heflon
Henry IV, Emperor, 2
Hereford, 17
Hessian, 7
Hewitt, Mary Lydia. *See* Colt, Mary
    Lydia Hewitt
Hicks, Anne Longton. *See* Scovell,
    Anne Longton Hicks
Highgate, Vermont, 1, 9-16, 19-33, 40-3,
    47, 52-4, 65-6
Highgate Falls, Vermont, 8, 11, 24, 40
Hill, Adelia Catharine Riley
    (m. Charles W.), 67
Hill, Adelia Emma, 68
Hill, Charles W.
    (m. Adelia Catharine Riley), 67
Hill, George J. (m. Jessie Stockwell),
    66-8
Hill, George James, M.D., 39
Hill, Gerald Leslie, 66, 68
Hill, Grace Lodawesca, 68
Hill, Harland Eugene, 67
Hill, Jessie Fidelia Stockwell
    (m. George J.), 38, 41, 53-5, 66-8
Hill, Leroy George, 68
Hill, Myron Emery, Sr., 67-8
Hill, Myron, Jr., 40
Hill, Nellie Leola, 68
Hill, Ruby Adella, 67-8
Hill, William Benjamin, 67
Hilliard, Cecile Saxe (m. David S.),
    36, 51
Hilliard, David S. (m. Cecile Saxe), 51
History of Highgate (Robinson), 15, 21,
    23, 25-6
"Hog Island," Highgate, Vt., 21
Hogaboom family, 41
Hogaboom, Catharine Bryce
    (m. Samuel), 52
Hogaboom, Cordelia. *See* Stockwell,
    Cordelia Hogaboom
Hogaboom, Eliza Ann. *See* Stockwell,
    Eliza Ann Hogaboom
Hogaboom, Samuel
    (m. Catharine Bryce), 52

Holbrook, Abi.
    See Stockwell, Abi Holbrook Lee
Holmes, John B.
    (m. Elizabeth Lillian Saxe), 58
Holt family, 13
Holt, Charlotte. *See* Saxe, Charlotte Holt
Hone Hill, 62
Honey Hill, 62
Hoosick Falls, N.Y., 65
Hotaling, Janet Elting (m. Philip), 16
Hotaling, Philip, 16
Houston, Texas, 63, 72
Hudson Valley (& River),
    5-8, 20, 27, 30
Hungerford, Lucy.
    See Jewett, Lucy Hungerford
Hyde family, 41
Hyde, Alice Rowena (157).
    See Durant, Alice Rowena Hyde
Hyde, Emily (Emma) Lodiweska.
    See Stockwell, Emily L. (m. Benajah)
Hyde, Fidelia Gadcourt Potter
    (m. Harvey), 54
Hyde, George Byron
    (m. Maria Saxe), 46
Hyde, Harvey (m. Fidelia Potter), 54
Hyde, Maria Saxe (m. George Byron Hyde), 22, 29, 46
Illinois, 47, 68
Indian(s), 10, 17, 25, 32
Indian Stream, 17
Ingraham, Elizabeth M. Stockwell
    (m. Lucian S.), 55, 69
Ingraham, Lucian S.
    (m. Elizabeth M. Stockwell), 69
Innsbruck Philosophical Institute,
    Austria, 72
Iowa, 40, 53, 67
Iowa River, 54, 66-7
Ireland, 52
*Isle La Mott*e (Stratton), 37
Isle La Motte, Vt., 19, 37
Isle of Pines, Cuba, 57
Isle-aux-noix, 17
J. G. S. *See* Saxe, John Godfrey [II]

Jaegers, Ansbach. *See* Ansbach Jaegers
Jameson, Joanna.
    See Scovell, Jonanna Jameson
Japan, 72
Jennison, Clark Saxe (274), 60, 70
Jennison, Mary Wead Saxe
    (m. Nahum Edward), 46, 60
Jennison, Nahum Edward
    (m. Mary Wead Saxe), 60
Jennison, Ralph Drury (275), 60, 70
Jennison, Robert Farrar (276), 60, 70
Jewett family, 13, 27
Jewett, Ada Anna (186).
    See Jones, Ada Anna Jewett
Jewett, Amelia Virginia Cox
    (m. Erwin), 62
Jewett, Carrie A. Underwood
    (m. Thomas Scovell), 71
Jewett, Charles, Hon. (m. Charlotte Scovell), 27, 34, 48
Jewett, Charles, Jr. (187), 48, 63
Jewett, Charles II (188), 48, 63
Jewett, Charles Cox (302; m. Rose Platt; m. Ekeba Ataurbi), 62, 71
Jewett, Charles Dean (307), 62, 71
Jewett, Charlotte Catherine Scovell
    (m. Charles), 27, 34, 48
Jewett, Edward Dickinson (308), 62, 71
Jewett, Edward Saxe, Maj. (185; m. Sarah Louise Kirsh; m. Mary Hawley Davies), 48, 62
Jewett, Ekeba Atanurbi
    (m. Charles Cox), 71
Jewett, Elizabeth Cox, 71
Jewett, Elizabeth.
    See Saxe, Elizabeth Jewett
Jewett, Elizabeth.
    See Scovell, Elizabeth Jewett
Jewett, Erwin Scovell, Capt. (184; m. Amelia Virginia Cox), 48, 62
Jewett, Gid Henry Chipman (309), 62, 71
Jewett, Harry Erwin (304), 62, 71
Jewett, Katherine (306), 62, 71
Jewett, Lucy Hungerford
    (m. Samuel), 27

Jewett, Mabel Platte (310), 62, 71
Jewett, Mary Hawley Davies
    (m. Edward Saxe), 62
Jewett, May (305), 62, 71
Jewett, Rose Platt (m. Charles Cox), 71
Jewett, Samuel, 27
Jewett, Sarah Louise Kirsh
    (m. Edward Saxe), 62
Jewett, Thomas Scovell [Jr.], 71
Jewett, Thomas Scovell, Rear Adm.
    (303; m. Carrie Underwood), 62, 71
Johns Hopkins University School of
    Medicine, 72
Johnson, Emma Maria.
    See Saxe, Emma Marie Johnson
Jones, Ada Anna Jewett (186; m.
    William Edward), 48, 63
Jones, Allan Saxe (311), 63, 71
Jones, George Bayard (313), 63, 71
Jones, Katherine Scovell (312). See
    Rew, Katherine Scovell Jones
Jones, Roland Jewett, Capt. (314), 63, 71
Jones, Walter Boardman, Lieut. (315),
    63, 71
Jones, William Edward
    (m. Ada Anna Jewett), 63
Judson, Mary E.;
    See Saxe, Mary E. Judson
Kaatsban Reformed Church,
    Dutchess Co., N.Y., 15
Kansas City, Mo., 62, 71
Keenan, Margaret. See McCollum,
    Margaret Keenan
Keith family, 13
Keith, Rowena. See Saxe, Rowena Keith
Keith, Sarah. See Drury, Sarah Keith
Keyes, Arthur (171), 47, 61
Keyes, Caroline Abbott
    (m. Homer Eaton), 61
Keyes, Conrad Saxe (172; m. Grace
    Merwin Bickford), 47, 61
Keyes, Emerson Willard
    (m. Rowena Saxe), 47
Keyes, Grace Merwin Bickford
    (m. Conrad Saxe Keyes), 61

Keyes, Homer Eaton
    (173; m. Caroline Abbott), 47, 61
Keyes, Katherine Keith (285), 61, 70
Keyes, Rowena Keith (174), 47, 61
Keyes, Rowena Keith Saxe
    (m. Emerson Willard), 29, 47
Keyes' N.Y. Court of Appeals Reports
    (Keys), 47
Kingston, N.Y., 5, 16, 18
Kingston Reformed Church, 16, 18
Kip family, 6
Kirsh, Sarah Louise.
    See Jewett, Sarah Louise Kirsh
Kraft, John, 25
Laachl Lake, 17
Lacadie, Quebec, 36
Ladd, Cora. See Saxe, Cora Ladd
LaFayette, Ind., 64
LaGrange, Ill., 60
Lake (*See* lakes, by name)
Lake Champlain, 7, 8, 11, 12, 18-20,
    22, 27, 30, 31, 40, 53
Lake George, 7, 20
Lake Memphramagog, 17
Lamoille Co., Vt., 24, 26
Lamprich, 37
Langensalza, First Battle of, 2
Langensalza, Kingdom of Hanover, 1, 2
Langensalza, Second Battle of, 2
Latitude 45, 17
Latter Day Saints, 23
Laws of Vermont, 21
Lee, Abi Holbrook (m. Joseph Lee;
    m. Ebenezer Stockwell), *q.v.*
Lee, Joseph (m. Abi Holbrook), 40
Lempster, 33
Leroy family, 13
Leroy, Rachel. See Saxe, Rachel Leroy
Lewiston, N.Y., 48, 49, 63-4, 71
Lewiston Academy, 33
Lincoln, Abraham, 54
"Little Jerry, the Miller" (Saxe), 35
Liverpool, England, 72
Livingston, Janet
    (m. Richard Montgomery), 6
Livingston, John, 6

Livingston, Robert G. (Rent Book)
    (m. Margaret Beekman), 4-7, 20
Lockport, N.Y., 38, 47, 63-4, 71-2
Lockwood family, 13
Lockwood, Maria.
    See Saxe, Maria Lockwood
London, England, 72
Los Angeles, Calif., 71-2
Lovell, Francis (m. Julia Colt), 51
Lovell, Julia Maria Colt
    (m. Francis), 38, 51
Lovell, Lawrence Colt, 1st. Lt. (212),
    19, 52, 65
Lower Canada (aka Canada East), 8
Lowry, Gertrude.
    See Saxe, Gertrude Lowry
Loyalist(s), 6-8, 20, 22, 27, 30
Lum, Emma Caroline Stockwell Price
    (m. ___ Lum), 69
Lutheran Church, 3, 4, 11, 33
Lynn, Mass., 42
Madison, N.J., 45, 69
Marquette, Pierre, 37
Massachusetts, 40
Massachusetts Bar, 56
Massachusetts Institute of Technology,
    71
Massachusetts Title Insurance Co., 57
McCollum, Anna Fidelia (192). See
    McGuire, Anna McCollum
McCollum, Camille Scovell (323).
    See Geary, Camille McCollum
McCollum, Ella (m. Silas Wright), 63
McCollum, Ella Kate (321).
    See Ralston, Ella McCollum
McCollum, Eugene Lawrence, Hon.
    (319), 63, 72
McCollum, Fidelia Scovell
    (m. Hiram), 33-4, 48
McCollum, Francis Xavier (318), 63, 71
McCollum, Hiram (320), 63, 72
McCollum, Hiram (m. Fidelia
    Scovell), 48
McCollum, Hiram Thomas (190; m.
    Margaret Keenan), 48, 63
McCollum, James Bernard (317), 63, 71

McCollum, John Timon (193; m. Mary
    Mulloy; m. Mrs. Martha
    Baldwin; m. Martha Jane
    Stewart), 48, 63-4
McCollum, Josephine (322). See
    Carveth, Josephine McCollum
McCollum, Margaret Keenan
    (m. Hiram Thomas), 63
McCollum, Martha Baldwin Flannery
    (m. John Timon), 63
McCollum, Martha Jane Stewart
    (m. John Timon), 63-4
McCollum, Mary Elizabeth (194).
    See Gallagher, Mary McCollum
McCollum, Mary Mulloy
    (m. John Timon), 63
McCollum, Silas Wright (191;
    m. Ella K. Allen), 48, 63
McGuire, Anna Fidelia McCollum
    (m. Dennis Charles), 48, 63
McGuire, Dennis Charles (m. Anna
    Fidelia McCollum), 48, 63
McKechnie, James Henry (m. Mabel
    Wead Saxe Jennison), 60
McKechnie, Mabel Wead Saxe Jennison
    (m. James Henry), 60
Medford, Mass., 60
Medicine Hat, Alberta, Canada, 65
Merkle, John, 4, 15 (m. Margaret
    Weaver)
Merkle, Margaret Weaver, 4, 15
Merwin, Huldah.
    See Saxe, Huldah Merwin
Methodist Church, 54, 66, 69
Methodist Church, Clarenceville,
    Quebec, 53
Methodist Church, Clarion, Ia., 66-7
Methodist Church, Fairhaven, Vt., 45
Methodist Episcopal (M.E.) Church,
    Highgate, Vt., 32
Michigan, 43, 48-9, 62, 71
Mickle, Andrew H., Mayor, 58
Mickle, Mary Reynolds.
    See Saxe, Mary Mickle
Middlebury College, 42, 48
Mid-Hudson Valley. See Hudson

Mill St., Rhinebeck, N.Y., 5
Milton, Vt., 19
Minnesota, 52
Missisquoi Bay, Canada, 7, 8, 13, 17, 20, 21, 27, 30
Missisquoi Co., Quebec, Canada, 1, 8, 9, 12, 40, 53
Missisquoi Historical Society and Museum , 9
Missisquoi River, 17
Mississippi, 45
Missouri Pacific R.R., 63
Mobile, Ala., 64
Montgomery, Maj. Gen. Richard (m. Janet Livingston), 6
Montreal, Canada, 13, 21, 25, 38, 43, 47, 58
Mooers, Clinton Co., N.Y., 13, 22, 38, 40, 53, 55, 69
Mulloy, Mary.
    See McCollum, Mary Mulloy
Munich, Germany, 37, 70
Murray, Clarke Co., Iowa, 53, 55
Muskogee, Okla., 53
Namur, Belgium, 72
Nashua, N.H., 39, 55
Nebraska, 44, 53
NEHGR. New England Historical and Genealogical Register, 42-3
New Hampshire, 38, 42
New York (state), 5, 6-8, 11, 12, 15-18, 20, 40, 41, 43, 52, 54, 69
New York Bar, 56
New York City, N.Y., 3, 6, 45, 47, 71-2
New York State Legislature / Assembly, 34, 41, 49, 69, 72
Newfane, N.Y., 63
Newport, 17, 33
Niagara Co., N.Y., 12, 24, 33-4
Niagara Falls, 72
Niagara University, 63
Nichols, Samuel, 1st Lt., 33
Niles, Mich., 48, 62-3, 71
Norman, Okla., 68
Northwestern University, 71
Norwich, Vt., 42

Nye, Charles, 9, 23
Oakwood Cemetery, Troy, N.Y., 57
Oberlin College, 34, 63-4
Officer, Ellen. See Saxe, Ellen Officer
Ohio, 62
Oklahoma, 53, 68
Oklahoma City, Okla., 52-4
Old Mooers Village Cemetery, Clinton Co., N.Y., 22, 38-9
Old Protestant Cemetery, Philipsburg, Quebec, 12, 20, 23
Omaha, Neb., 44
Onderdonk, Mary.
    See Scovell, Mary Onderdonk
Ontario, 35
Orwell, Vt., 28, 33-4, 48-9
Owen, Florence.
    See Saxe, Florence Owen
Parker, Caroline Miranda.
    See Scovell, Caroline Parker
Parvisse de St. Romauld, La, 36
Pennsylvania, 2, 3
Pensionat de la Ste. Maria, Namur, Belgium, 72
Peoria, Peoria Co., Ill., 53-4, 66-8
Philadelphia, Pennsylvania, 2, 3, 6, 12
Philipsburg (St. Armand West), Missisquoi Co., Quebec, Canada, 1, 7, 9, 12, 20, 21, 23, 40
Phillips, Emily. See Saxe, Emily Phillips
Piedmont, Calif., 59
Pittsburgh, Penna., 59, 63
Pittsford, Vt., 65
Place, Alice May Seward (m. James Conrad), 61-2
Place, Carl O. (293), 61, 71
Place, Charles Henry (180; m. Lotta Hall), 47, 62
Place, Clara L. (290), 61, 70
Place, Clarissa Eliza Saxe (m. James P.), 33, 47
Place, Emily Heflon (m. William Aubrey), 61
Place, Ethel G. (291), 61, 71
Place, Graham (294), 62, 71

Place, Harriet Saxe (176).
  See Smith, Harriet Saxe Place
Place, James Conrad (179; m. Alice May
  Seward), 47, 61
Place, James Fay (288), 61, 70
Place, James P. (m. Clarissa Saxe), 47
Place, Lizzie Landis (175), 47, 61
Place, Lotta Hall (m. Charles Henry), 62
Place, Olive F. (289), 61, 70
Place, Ruth Saxe (292), 61, 71
Place, Sarah Griffin (177). See
  Chamberlin, Sarah Griffin Pace
Place, William Aubrey
  (178; m. Emily Heflon), 47, 61
Platt, Rose. See Jewett, Rose Platt
Plattsburgh, N.Y., 45
Plattsburgh, Battle of, 28, 31
Pocolaligo, 62
Port Gilliland, N.Y., 28
Port Hope, Ontario, 35
Potter, Andrew, 11
Potter, Fidelia Gadcourt.
  See Hyde, Fidelia Potter
Potter, Freeborn, Capt., 11
Potter, General, 62
Potter, Noel, 11
Poughkeepsie, N.Y., 5
Poultney, Vt., 45
Presbyterian Church, 33
Prescott, Alice May.
  See Saxe, Alice May Prescott
Price, Emma Caroline Stockwell
  (m. Fred B.), 53-5, 69
Price, Fred B. (m. Emma Stockwell), 69
Prince Albert. See Albert, Prince
Proclamation Act of 1792, 8
Prohibition Party, 54
Protestant Church, 3, 33
Prussia(n), 2
Psi Upsilon, 56
Pumpelly, Frances.
  See Bosworth, Frances Pumpelly
Quebec Almanac, 8
Quebec City, 6, 16, 36
Quebec, Province, of Canada, 1, 8, 9,
  15-17, 20, 21, 27, 29, 37, 40, 47

Radcliffe College, 57
Ralston, Ella Kate McCollum
  (m. William Wallace), 63, 72
Ralston, William Wallace, M.D.
  (m. Kate McCollum), 72
Rankin, Augustin
  (m. Emma Rowena Saxe), 61
Rankin, Emma Rowena Saxe
  (m. Agustin), 46, 61
Red Hook, N.Y., 30
Reformed Church, 3-5
Revolutionary War, 6-8, 20, 32-3
Rew, Irwin
  (m. Katherine Scovell Jones), 71
Rew, Katherine Scovell Jones
  (m. Irwin), 63, 71
Rhine River, Germany, 5
Rhinebeck, Dutchess Co., N.Y., 3-7,
  12-20, 24, 27, 29, 30
Richardson, Edmund
  (m. Maria Ann Saxe), 38
Richardson, Maria Ann Saxe
  (m. Edmund), 19, 22, 38
Richelieu River, 16
Riley, Adelia Catharine.
  See Hill, Adelia Catharine Riley
Ring, George, 15
River Sorel, 16
Robinson, Hon. Warren, 15, 26
Rock Mill, 9
Rock River, Vermont, 9, 10, 26
Roessler & Hasslacher Chemical Co., 72
Roman Catholic Church, 18, 33, 36, 48
Rome, Italy, 37
Rowan, Wright Co., Iowa, 53-5, 66-7
Royal Canadian Academy, 58
Royal Montreal Golf Club, 58
Rush Medical College, 72
Russia, 72
Rutland, Vt., 65
Rycard, Katy.
  See Saxe, Katy Rycard
Sabbath, 34
Sachs, Eleanor Burtis
  (m. Howard), 57, 69
Sachs, Howard (m. Eleanor Saxe), 69

Safford family, 41
Safford, Abi R. Stockwell
 (m. ___ Safford), 41, 52
Saint-Armand (St. Armand), Quebec,
 Canada, 8, 9
Sainte Romauld, Quebec, Canada, 16, 37
Salmon River, N.Y., 28
Salzaha (now Bad Langensalza),
 Germany, 1
San Diego, Calif., 71
San Francisco, Calif., 43, 47, 72
Sands, Ferdinand
 (m. Mary Collender), 69
Sands, Mary Collender
 (m. Ferdinand), 69
Sands, Mary. See Saxe, Mary Sands
Santa Barbara, Calif., 57
Santa Clara, Calif., 45
Saranac Chapter, D.A.R., 45
Saratoga Co., N.Y., 29
Sartell, Cecile Saxe (m. Luther), 16, 36
Sartell, Luther (m. Cecile Saxe), 36
Sartell, William (89), 36, 51
Saxe & Robertson, New York City, 45
Saxe & Saxe, Boston, 57
Saxe (aka Sachs, Sachse, Sax), 1
Saxe, ___ (239a),
 daughter of James Alfred, 57
Saxe, ___ (of John Burtis [241]), 69
Saxe, Abagail [sic] Drew
 (m. 45 Jacob William), 46
Saxe, Agnes (70).
 See Woodward, Agnes Saxe
Saxe, Agnes Esther (254), 58, 70
Saxe, Alfred, Rev. (37 son of 8 Jacob;
 m. Elizabeth Chase), 29, 44
Saxe, Alfred (137), 44, 59
Saxe, Alfred Henry, Rev. (130;
 m. Phoebe Wisner), 44, 58
Saxe, Alfred Jacob, Rev. (249), 58, 70
Saxe, Alfred Jenkins (134), 44, 59
Saxe, Alfred Jenkins (144), 45, 59
Saxe, Alfred Keith (166; m. Emma
 Marie Johnson), 46, 61
Saxe, Alfred W. (168;
 m. Flrorence Owen), 46, 61

Saxe, Alice Aguire (m. John D.), 61
Saxe, Alice May Prescott
 (m. Ralph Jacob), 60
Saxe, Amelia Elizabeth (105), 41, 56
Saxe, Andrew, 7, 9
Saxe, Anna, 13, 21-4
Saxe, Anna (18 dau. of 3 George).
 See Gibbs, Anna Saxe
Saxe, Anna Carter (m. 12 Simon), 35
Saxe, Anna Maria (32 aka Anne, dau. of
 6 Godfrey). See Stockwell, Anna
 Maria Saxe
Saxe, Anna Wilson (m. 16 Peter), 36
Saxe, Arthur Griggs (236), 56, 69
Saxe, Arthur M. (151), 45, 59
Saxe, Arthur Wellesley, Dr. (40 son of
 8 Jacob; m. Mary Judson), 29, 45
Saxe, Arthur Wellesley (138;
 m. Mary Tillotson), 45, 59
Saxe, Arthur William (147), 45, 59
Saxe, Betty Graves
 (wife of 5 Matthew), 20
Saxe, Caroline (46 dau. of 8 Jacob),
 29, 46
Saxe, Carrie A. (152), 45, 59
Saxe, Catherine (11 dau. of 3 George).
 See See, Catherine Saxe; and
 Wight, Catherine Saxe See
Saxe, Catherine Officer (281), 61, 70
Saxe, Catherine Weaver (wife of 1 John,
 Loyalist), 3-5, 7, 10-20, 23-5,
 29-33
Saxe, Cecile (17 dau. of 3 George).
 See Sartell, Cecile Saxe
Saxe, Cecile (73), 35, 51
Saxe, Cecile (81), 36, 51
Saxe, Cecile (88).
 See Hilliard, Cecile Saxe
Saxe, Charles Edward (237), 56, 69
Saxe, Charles Gordon (115; m. Ellen
 Merwin Saxe 149), 43, 57, 59
Saxe, Charles Griggs (107), 41, 56
Saxe, Charles Hammon (106), 41, 56
Saxe, Charles Jewett, Hon. (33 son of 7
 Peter; m. Susan Baker; m. Ellen
 Griggs), 25, 27, 34, 41

Saxe, Charles Jewett (129), 44, 58
Saxe, Charles Merwin (245), 57, 59, 70
Saxe, Charles Philip (163;
    m. Ellen Officer), 46, 60-1
Saxe, Charles William (235), 56, 69
Saxe, Charlotte (13 dau. of 3 George).
    See Carter, Charlotte Saxe
Saxe, Charlotte (69).
    See Brown, Charlotte Saxe,
Saxe, Charlotte Holt
    (25 dau. of 5 Matthew), 19, 38
Saxe, Charlotte Holt
    (wife of 5 Matthew), 19
Saxe, Clarissa Dunning
    (wife of 9 Conrad), 32
Saxe, Clarissa Eliza (53 dau. of 9
    Conrad). *See* Place, Clarissa
    Eliza Saxe
Saxe, Conrad, Capt. (9 son of John,
    Loyalist), 7, 11-15, 29-32
Saxe, Cora Ladd (m. William Holt), 51
Saxe, DeForest Wead (139; m. Jimmie
    D. Stitt), 45, 59
Saxe, Delia Hadley (m. 15 Matthew), 36
Saxe, Edward, Capt. (39 son of 8 Jacob;
    m. Kate Vosburgh), 29, 45
Saxe, Edward C. (150), 45, 59
Saxe, Edward Jacob (143), 45, 59
Saxe, Edward Thomas (109;
    m. Louise Crump), 41, 56
Saxe, Edwin A.
    (52 son of 9 Conrad), 32-3, 47
Saxe, Eleanor Burtis (240).
    See Sachs, Eleanor Burtis
Saxe, Eliza J. Burroughs
    (m. 23 William Holt), 37
Saxe, Elizabeth Catherine (28).
    See Ferguson, Elizabeth Saxe
Saxe, Elizabeth Chase (m. 37 Alfred), 44
Saxe, Elizabeth D. (261), 60, 70
Saxe, Elizabeth Douglass
    (m. 27 Henry G.), 38
Saxe, Elizabeth Jewett (m. 7 Peter),
    25-7, 33, 42
Saxe, Elizabeth Lillian Sophia (123).
    See Saxe-Holmes, Elizabeth

Saxe, Elizabeth Scott
    (m. William F.), 58
Saxe, Elizabeth Wead (136).
    See Bascom, Elizabeth Wead Saxe
Saxe, Ellen B. (133), 44, 58
Saxe, Ellen Griggs
    (m. 33 Charles Jewett), 41
Saxe, Ellen Merwin (149).
    See Saxe, Ellen Merwin Saxe
Saxe, Ellen Merwin Saxe (149;
    m. Charles Gordon Saxe 115),
    45, 57, 59
Saxe, Ellen Mildred (248), 58-9, 70
Saxe, Ellen Officer
    (m. Charles Philip), 60-1
Saxe, Ellen Sollace (126), 44, 58
Saxe, Emily (83), 36, 51
Saxe, Emily Phillips (m. 14 John), 36
Saxe, Emma Marie Johnson
    (m. Alfred Keith), 61
Saxe, Emma Rowena (169). *See* Rankin,
    Emma Rowena Saxe
Saxe, Emmerson Ladd (211), 51, 65
Saxe, Eugene Crump (238), 56, 69
Saxe, Evelyn Foster Fisher
    (m. Herbert Kimball), 59-60
Saxe, Fanny Maria (127), 44, 58
Saxe, Flora Jane Daniels
    (m. 48 Heman Allen), 46
Saxe, Florence Owen (m. Alfred W.), 61
Saxe, Frances Caroline (158). *See*
    Stevens, Frances Caroline Saxe
Saxe, Frances Drury (280), 61, 70
Saxe, Frances M. Harper
    (m. George G.), 59
Saxe, Frances Maria (135), 44, 59
Saxe, Frank K. (148), 45, 59
Saxe, Franklin James (124; m. Mary
    Mickle Reynolds), 44, 58
Saxe, Frederic (42 son of 8 Jacob),
    29, 46
Saxe, Frederick Judson (145), 45, 59
Saxe, George (3 son of John, Loyalist),
    4, 5, 11-15, 22, 28-9
Saxe, George (22, of 4 William), 18, 37
Saxe, George (72), 35, 51

Saxe, George (86), 36, 51
Saxe, George Brown (114), 43, 57
Saxe, George G. (153; m. Frances M.
    Harper), 46, 59
Saxe, George Godfrey, Rev. (41 son of 8
    Jacob; m. Huldah Merwin), 29,
    45, 57
Saxe, George J. (19 son of 3 George),
    16, 36
Saxe, George W. (26 son of 5 Matthew),
    20, 38
Saxe, Gertrude Coyle
    (m. William Jenkins), 61
Saxe, Gertrude Lowry
    (m. William Arthur), 56
Saxe, Godfrey (father of 1 John,
    Loyalist), 1, 40
Saxe, Godfrey (6 son of John, Loyalist),
    6, 10, 12-15, 19-25, 29, 38, 40
Saxe, Grace B. Drury
    (m. 45 Jacob William), 46
Saxe, Grace Elizabeth (258), 59, 70
Saxe, Grace Maria (162).
    See Seavey, Grace Maria Saxe
Saxe, Hannah (10 dau. of John,
    Loyalist). *See* Scovell, Hannah
    Saxe
Saxe, Hannah (47, of 8 Jacob), 29, 46
Saxe, Hannah (54 dau. of 9 Conrad).
    See Drury, Hannah Saxe
Saxe, Harriet Jane (78), 35, 51
Saxe, Harriet Sollace (117), 43, 58
Saxe, Harriet T. (55 dau. of 9 Conrad),
    33, 48
Saxe, Helen (87), 36, 51
Saxe, Helen Douglas (255), 58, 70
Saxe, Heman Allen (48 son of 8 Jacob;
    m. Flora Daniels), 29, 46
Saxe, Henry G. (27 son of 5 Matthew;
    m. Elizabeth Douglass), 20, 38
Saxe, Henry Wisner (250), 58, 70
Saxe, Herbert Kimball (154; m. Evelyn
    Foster Fisher), 46, 59-60
Saxe, Homer Polk (121), 43, 58
Saxe, Horace Jacob (51 son of 9
    Conrad), 32-3, 47

Saxe, Howard Martin (122), 43, 58
Saxe, Huldah K. Merwin
    (m. 41 George Godfrey), 45, 57
Saxe, Ida May Connor
    (m. William Arthur), 56
Saxe, Ira Charles (77), 35, 51
Saxe, Jacob (8 son of John, Loyalist; m.
    Rowena Keith), 7, 11-15, 18, 27-
    9, 45
Saxe, Jacob William (45 son of 8 Jacob;
    m. Grace Drury; m. Abagail
    Drew), 29, 46
Saxe, James (36 son of 7 Peter; m. Sarah
    Sollace), 27, 43-4
Saxe, James (239c), 57
Saxe, James Alfred (110; m. Mary
    Alfred Wick), 41, 56-7
Saxe, James Burtis (242), 57, 69
Saxe, Jane (79), 36, 51
Saxe, Jessie Ellen (247), 58-9, 70
Saxe, Jimmie D. Stitt (m. DeForest
    Wead), 59
Saxe, Jodelphia Atwell (m. Rollin Peter),
    58
Saxe, John (1 aka Johan, Johann,
    Johannes), Loyalist, 1-33, 45
    birth and ancestry, 1
    to America, 2
    courtship and marriage, 3
    children's baptisms, 4
    miller, Rhinebeck, N.Y., 5
    Loyalist, 6-7
    settlement in Canada, 8
    settlement in Vermont, 9
    businesses in Vermont, 10-11
    death and burial, 12
    children, 13, 14
Saxe, John [Jr.] (2 son of John,
    Loyalist), 10, 13-15, 28-9
Saxe, John (14 son of 3 George; m. Katy
    Rycard; m. Emily Phillips), 11,
    16, 35-6
Saxe, John (82), 36, 51
Saxe, John (239b), 57
Saxe, John Brooke, 69

Saxe, John Burtis (241; m. Lorraine Brooke), 57, 69
Saxe, John D. (167; m. Alice Aguire), 46, 61
Saxe, John Drew (284), 61, 70
Saxe, John Godfrey (34 son of 7 Peter; m. Sophia Sollace), 13, 25-7, 34-5, 42-3, 59
Saxe, John Godfrey [II] (243; m. Mary Sands), 1, 32, 42-4, 47, 57, 69
Saxe, John Matthew (74), 35, 51
Saxe, John Theodore (113; m. Mary A. Bosworth), 43, 57
Saxe, John Walter (111; m. Sara F. Burtis), 42, 56-7
Saxe, Julia Frances (29 dau. of 5 Matthew). *See* Sharts, Julia
Saxe, Kate C. Vosburgh (m. 39 Edward), 45
Saxe, Katherine (165), 46, 61
Saxe, Katherine Louise (239), 56, 69
Saxe, Katy Rycard (m. 14 John), 35
Saxe, Laura Huldah (244), 57, 59, 69
Saxe, Laura Sophia (118), 43, 58
Saxe, Loan D. (50, of 9 Conrad), 33, 47
Saxe, Lorraine Brooke (m. John Burtis), 69
Saxe, Louisa J. Hall (m. 23 William Holt), 37
Saxe, Louise Maria (142), 45, 59
Saxe, Louise Wheaton Crump (m. Edward Thomas), 56
Saxe, Lucy (71). *See* Griggs, Lucy Saxe
Saxe, Luther Drury (160), 46, 60
Saxe, Mabel Wead (159). *See* Jennison, Mabel Wead Saxe; McKechnie, Mabel Jennison
Saxe, Marguerite (256), 59, 70
Saxe, Maria (44 dau. of 8 Jacob). *See* Hyde, Maria Saxe
Saxe, Maria Ann (24 dau. of 5 Matthew. *See* Richardson, Maria Saxe; and Scovell, Maria Saxe Richardson
Saxe, Maria Lockwood (m. 5 Matthew), 20

Saxe, Marion Freer (156). *See* Umry, Marion Freer Saxe
Saxe, Mary (76), 35, 51
Saxe, Mary (282), 61, 70
Saxe, Mary A. Bosworth (m. John Theodore), 43, 57
Saxe, Mary Alfred Wick (m. James Alfred), 57
Saxe, Mary E. Judson (m. 40 Arthur Wellesley), 45
Saxe, Mary Elizabeth (146), 45, 59
Saxe, Mary Ellen (112), 42, 57
Saxe, Mary Franklyn (259), 59, 70
Saxe, Mary G. (252), 58, 70
Saxe, Mary Helen (31 dau. of 5 Matthew). *See* Colt, Mary Saxe
Saxe, Mary Mickle Reynolds (m. Franklin James), 58
Saxe, Mary Montgomery Tillotson (m. Arthur Wellesley), 59
Saxe, Mary Osiette Trembly (m. 4 William), 18
Saxe, Mary R. (84), 36, 51
Saxe, Mary Sands (m. John Godfrey [II]), 69
Saxe, Mary Sollace "Mollie" (128), 13, 44, 58
Saxe, Matthew (5 son of John, Loyalist), 6, 11-15, 18-21, 25-9, 45
Saxe, Matthew (15 son of 3 George; m. Delia Hadley), 16, 36
Saxe, Matthew Conrad (30 son of 5 Matthew), 20, 38
Saxe, Maud Elizabeth (253), 58, 70
Saxe, Minerva Drury (120), 43, 58
Saxe, Nettie (85), 36, 51
Saxe, Olivia (80), 36, 51
Saxe, Peter, Hon. (7 aka Sax, son of John, Loyalist; m. Elizabeth Jewett), 7, 11-15, 19, 21-2, 24-9, 33, 45
Saxe, Peter (16 son of 3 George; m. Anna Wilson), 16, 36
Saxe, Peter, Col. (35 son of 7 Peter; m. Sarah Keith Drury), 22, 27, 43, 48

Saxe, Philip (283), 61, 70
Saxe, Phoebe Wisner (m. Alfred Henry), 58
Saxe, Pierre Telesphone, Fr.
    (21 son of 4 William), 18, 36-7
Saxe, Rachel Leroy (m. 3 George), 16
Saxe, Ralph Godfrey, Rev. (260), 59, 70
Saxe, Ralph Jacob (161; m. Alice May
    Prescott), 46, 60
Saxe, Rebecca Munson Wead
    (m. 38 Robert Jenkins), 44
Saxe, Robert Edward (170), 46, 61
Saxe, Robert Jenkins (38 son of 8 Jacob;
    m. Rebecca Wead), 29, 44
Saxe, Robert Jenkins, Jr. (140), 44-5, 59
Saxe, Rollin Peter (119; m. Jodelphia
    Atwell), 43, 58
Saxe, Rowena (43 dau. of 8 Jacob), 29, 46
Saxe, Rowena (141), 45, 59
Saxe, Rowena Keith (m. 3 Jacob), 29
Saxe, Rowena Keith (49 dau. of 8
    Jacob). See Keyes, Rowena Saxe
Saxe, Rowena Keith (251), 58, 70
Saxe, Sara F. Burtis (m. John Walter), 57
Saxe, Sarah E. Burroughs (m. 23
    William Holt), 37
Saxe, Sarah Electa (209). See Fairbanks,
    Sarah Electa Saxe
Saxe, Sarah Elizabeth (116), 43, 58
Saxe, Sarah Keith Drury
    (m. 35 Peter Saxe), 43, 48
Saxe, Sarah Storrs Sollace
    (m. 36 James), 43-4
Saxe, Simon (12 son of 3 George;
    m. Anna Carter), 16, 35
Saxe, Simon Peter (75), 35, 51
Saxe, Sophia Newell Sollace
    (m. John Godfrey), 43, 59
Saxe, Sophia Sollace (246), 58-9, 70
Saxe, Susan Maria Baker
    (m. 33 Charles Jewett), 41
Saxe, Theodore James (155), 46, 60
Saxe, Theodosia Wead (257), 59, 70
Saxe, Walter (131), 44, 58
Saxe, William (4 son of John, Loyalist)
    5, 7, 11-18, 22, 28-9
Saxe, William (20 son of 4 William), 18, 36
Saxe, William Arthur (108; m. Gertrude
    Lowry; m. Ida Connor), 41, 56
Saxe, William F. (132; m. Elizabeth
    Scott), 44, 58
Saxe, William H. (68), 35, 51
Saxe, William Henry (125), 44, 58
Saxe, William Holt (23 son of 5
    Matthew; m. Eliza Burroughs; m.
    Sarah Burroughs; m. Louisa
    Hall), 19, 37
Saxe, William Holt (91; m. Cora Ladd), 37, 51
Saxe, William Holt (210), 51, 65
Saxe, William Jenkins (164; m. Gertrude
    Coyle), 46, 61
Saxe's Brook, Highgate, Vt., 9, 10, 26
Saxe's Landing, 18
Saxe's Mill(s), 1, 9-11, 15, 23, 26-7, 30, 47
Saxe-Gothe, Hanover, 1, 34, 41
Saxe-Holmes, Elizabeth Lillian
    (m. John B. Holmes), 44, 58
Saxon(s)(y), 2, 11, 40
Schoonmaker, Louise. See Bunnell,
    Louise Schoonmaker
Schuyler family, 6
Scotia, N.Y., 55
Scott, Elizabeth. See Saxe, Elizabeth
    Scott
Scovell family, 13, 24
Scovell, Alice Louisa (198), 49, 64
Scovell, Anna Saxe (201), 49, 64
Scovell, Anne Longton Hicks
    (m. Robert Jameson), 72
Scovell, Augusta (196), 49, 64
Scovell, Caroline Miranda Parker
    (m. Stephen Decatur), 49
Scovell, Charlotte Catherine (56).
    See Jewett, Charlotte Scovell
Scovell, Elizabeth Eddy (203), 49, 64
Scovell, Elizabeth Eddy Shepard
    (m. Oliver Perry), 49

Scovell, Elizabeth Jewett
    (m. Oliver Perry), 27, 49
Scovell, Elizabeth Shepard (199),
    49, 64
Scovell, Ella Elizabeth (206), 49, 64
Scovell, Fidelia (59).
    See McCollum, Fidelia Scovell
Scovell, Frank Thomas (207), 49, 64
Scovell, Hannah Saxe (10 wife of Col.
    Josiah), 1, 11-15, 22-4, 27-9,
    33-4, 41, 47, 64
Scovell, Hezekiah Wilcox, 38
Scovell, Joanna Jameson
    (m. Josiah Thomas), 64
Scovell, Josiah Boardman, Col.,
    27, 33-4
Scovell, Josiah Boardman, LL.B (205;
    m. Rhoda Ann Godfrey),
    34, 49, 64
Scovell, Josiah Thomas, Prof. (195; m.
    Joanna Jameson), 64, 49
Scovell, Juliette (58).
    See Colt, Juliette Scovell
Scovell, Leonard Shepard (200), 49, 64
Scovell, Maria Ann Saxe Richardson
    (m. Hezekiah Wilcox), 38
Scovell, Mary Onderdonk
    (m. Thomas McDonough), 49
Scovell, Nancy Valina
    (m. Thomas Mcdonough), 49
Scovell, Oliver Perry, Hon. (61;
    m. Elizabeth Eddy Shepard; m.
    Elizabeth Jewett), 1, 27, 34, 49
Scovell, Oliver Perry (202), 49, 64
Scovell, Philo Jewett (204), 49, 64
Scovell, Rachel Boardman, 33-4
Scovell, Rhoda Ann Godfrey
    (m. Josiah Boardman), 64
Scovell, Robert Jameson, Capt.
    (328; m. Anne Longton Hicks),
    1fn, 34, 64, 72
Scovell, Rolf, 34
Scovell, Rowena (57), 34, 48
Scovell, Sammons Onderdonk (208),
    49, 64
Scovell, Stephen Decatur
    (60; m. Caroline Parker), 34, 49
Scovell, Thomas, Jr.
    (father of Col. Josiah), 33-4
Scovell, Thomas McDonough (62)
    (m. Mary Onderdonk; m. Nancy
    Valina Campbell), 33-4, 49
Scovell, William Parker (197), 49, 64
Seagel, Mary A. Stockwell
    (m. __ Seagel), 41, 52
Seattle, Wash., 69
Seavey, Charles Lewis
    (m. Grace Maria Saxe), 60
Seavey, Grace Maria Saxe
    (m. Charles Lewis), 46, 60
Seavey, Harold V. (278), 60, 70
Seavey, Helen Saxe (277), 60, 70
Seavey, Malcolm deForest (279), 60, 70
Sedgwick, Colo., 53
See, Caroline (67), 35, 51
See, Catherine Saxe (11; m. David), 16,
    22, 35
See, Charles (65), 35, 51
See, David (63; m. Catherine Saxe),
    22, 35, 51
See, Maria Ann Saxe (64), 22, 35, 51
See, William (66), 35, 51
Seminary of Our Lady of Angels, 63
Seven Years War.
    See French and Indian War)
Seward, Alice May.
    See Place, Alice May Seward
Sharts, Derwin (m. Julia Saxe), 38
Sharts, Julia Frances Saxe, 20, 38
Sheldon, Vt., 18, 27-8, 44-5, 65
Shepard, Elizabeth Eddy.
    See Scovell, Elizabeth Shepard
Shields, Addie L., 39
Shiloh, Battle of, 45
Siberia, Russia, 72
Sierra, 1fn, 35fn, 37fn
Skeels, Amos, 15, 25
Slafter, Eunice, 42
Slafter, Samuel, 42
Slaughter, John, 42
Smith, Catherine Wagner, 18

Smith, Clara Fannie (286), 61, 70
Smith, George (m. Harriet Saxe Place), 61
Smith, Harriet Saxe Place (m. George), 47, 61
Smith, Matthew (m. Catherine Wagner), 18
Smith, Moses, 65
Smith, Nancy Helen Edwards (m. Moses), 65
Smith, Nellie Sophia (286), 61, 70
Smith, Sarah Grace. *See* Stockwell, Sarah Grace Smith
Soldiers' Monument, Highgate, Vt., 31
Sollace family, 43
Sollace, Calvin, Judge, 43-4
Sollace, Hepsibeth. *See* Bosworth, Hepsibeth Sollace
Sollace, Sarah Storrs.
    See Saxe, Sarah Storrs Sollace
Sollace, Sophia Bascome (m. Calvin), 43-4
Sollace, Sophia Newell.
    See Saxe, Sophia Newell
South Carolina, 7
Spanish-American War, 72
St. Albans, Franklin Co., Vt., 13, 23-4, 26-7, 43, 52, 58, 65-6, 69
St. Albans Historical Museum, 23
St. Armand, Quebec. *See* Saint-Armand
St. Bridget's Asylum, Quebec, 36
St. Catherines, Ontario, Canada, 63
St. Francois, 17
St. John's, 17
St. Lawrence River, 36
St. Louis, Mo., 47, 63, 72
St. Mary's, Kansas, 64
St. Patrick's Cathedral, New York City, N.Y., 72
St. Paul's Lutheran Church, Red Hook, Dutchess Co., N.Y., 30
St. Paul's Lutheran Church, West Camp, N.Y., 24
St. Peter's Church ("Stone Church"), Rhinebeck, N.Y., 4, 15

Stanbridge, Quebec, Canada, 9, 15, 38, 40-1, 52-6
Stansledd, 17
State Papers of General Assembly of Vermont, 21
Stevens, Edwin Pitman, Rev. (m. Frances Caroline Saxe), 60
Stevens, Elizabeth Frances (272), 60, 70
Stevens, Frances Caroline Saxe (m. Edwin Pitman), 46, 60
Stevens, Franklin Rand (273), 60, 70
Stevens, Grace Drury (271), 60, 70
Stewart, Martha Jane. *See* McCollum, Martha Jane Stewart
Stitt, Jimmie D.
    See Saxe, Jimmie D. Stitt
Stockville, Joseph, 23.
    See Stockwell, Joseph H.
Stockwell family, 53, 66
The Stockwell Genealogy (Kennedy), 52f
Stockwell, ____ (child of Herbert and Lucy), 69
Stockwell, Abi Holbrook Lee (m. Ebenezer), 13, 14, 22, 38, 40
Stockwell, Abi R. (95).
    See Safford, Abi R. Stockwell
Stockwell, Addie Bunnell (m. Eugene), 68-9
Stockwell, Adelia Sophia Dill (m. Godfrey E.), 52
Stockwell, Albert (214), 52, 56, 65
Stockwell, Anna Maria Saxe (m. Joseph H.), 13, 14, 21-4, 38-41, 52-5
Stockwell, Annette V. "Nettie" (222).
    See Williams, Annette Stockwell
Stockwell, Benajah Flavel (99; m. Emily Hyde; m. Mrs. Lucy Hannings), 38-41, 53-5, 66-8
Stockwell, Benjamin Paul, 68
Stockwell, Beulah Vivian, 66
Stockwell, Bowman Foster, 68
Stockwell, Catherine H. (218). *See* Williams, Catherine Stockwell
Stockwell, Charles H. (215), 52, 65
Stockwell, Charlie G. (232), 55, 69

Stockwell, Cordelia Hogaboom
 (m. Joseph Matthew), 52
Stockwell, Daniel (219; m.
 Emma Coutermanche), 52, 65-6
Stockwell, David (96; m. Margaret Tye
 [Tighs]), 41, 52
Stockwell, David (221), 52, 66
Stockwell, Donald Willard, 65
Stockwell, Dorothy Elizabeth, 65
Stockwell, Ebenezer (m. Abi Holbrook
 Lee), 11, 13, 22, 24, 38, 40
Stockwell, Eliza Hogaboom (m. Joseph
 Matthew), 52
Stockwell, Elizabeth Berry
 (m. Samuel A.), 66
Stockwell, Elizabeth M. (230). *See*
 Ingraham, Elizabeth Stockwell
Stockwell, Emily Lodiweska Hyde
 (m. Benajah), 53-5, 66-8
Stockwell, Emma Caroline (228).
 See Price, Emma Caroline
 Stockwell; and Lum, Emma
 Caroline Stockwell Price
Stockwell, Emma Coutermanche
 (m. Daniel), 65-6
Stockwell, Emma Louise, 69
Stockwell, Eugene Earl, 68
Stockwell, Eugene Sanford (225; m.
 Myra Bloxham; m. Addie
 Bunnell), 53-5, 68-9
Stockwell, Foster Paul, 53-5, 65
Stockwell, Francis Olin, Rev.,
 54, 66, 68
Stockwell, George J. (or E.) (213; m.
 Sarah Grace Smith), 52, 65
Stockwell, Gertrude (234), 56, 69
Stockwell, Godfrey E. (94) (m. Adelia
 Sophia Dill), 40, 41, 52
Stockwell, Grace Lymna (229), 53-5, 69
Stockwell, Harold Samuel, 66
Stockwell, Harriet S. (97). *See*
 Bickford, Harriet S. Stockwell
Stockwell, Herbert Emery (Emory) (227;
 m. Lucy Hancock), 53-5, 69
Stockwell, Hermit (100; aka Kermit; aka
 Hennet), 41, 55

Stockwell, Ida (233), 56, 69
Stockwell, Jessie Fidelia (224). *See* Hill,
 Jessie F. Stockwell
Stockwell, Joseph A. (104), 41, 56
Stockwell, Joseph H. (m. Anna Maria
 Saxe), 13, 14, 22-4, 38-41, 52-5
Stockwell, Joseph Matthew (98)
 (m. Cordelia Hogaboom; m.
 Eliza Ann Hogaboom), 40-1, 52
Stockwell, L. Albert, 65
Stockwell, Lucy Ann (101). *See*
 Dunham, Lucy Ann Stockwell
Stockwell, Lucy Hancock (m. Herbert),
 69
Stockwell, Lucy Hannings, Mrs., 53-5,
 66
Stockwell, Malona Marcia.
 See Woodley, Malona Stockwell
Stockwell, Margaret (217), 52, 65
Stockwell, Margaret Tye (Tighs)
 (m. David), 52
Stockwell, Martha Aralla Hakey
 (m. Willard), 65
Stockwell, Mary A. (93).
 See Seagel, Mary A. Stockwell
Stockwell, Maryette Foster
 (m. Willard), 65
Stockwell, Merrow, 65
Stockwell, Millard Arthur (223), 52, 66
Stockwell, Myra Bloxham (m. Eugene),
 68
Stockwell, Ruby Ellen (226).
 See Benedict, Ruby Ellen
Stockwell, Samuel A. (220; m. Elizabeth
 Berry), 52, 66
Stockwell, Samuel S. (103) (m. Susan
 Woodley), 38-41, 55-6
Stockwell, Sarah Grace Smith, 65
Stockwell, Spencer Lewis, 69
Stockwell, Susan A. Woodley
 (m. Samuel S.), 38-40, 55-6
Stockwell, Ulysses S. (231), 55, 69
Stockwell, Willard (216; m. Maryette
 Foster; m. Martha Aralla Hakey),
 52, 65
"Stone Church" *See* St. Peter's Church

Stratton, Allen L., 37
Suspension Bridge, N.Y., 38, 63
Swanton, Vt., 19, 47-8, 60, 65, 71
Swanzey, Vt., 40
Switzerland, 56
Tampa, Fla., 60
Terre Haute, Ind., 64, 72
"The Blind Men and the Elephant" (Saxe), 42
The Cyclopedia of American Literature, 42
The Poetical Works of John Godfrey Saxe (Saxe), 42
Thirty Years War, 2
Three Centuries in Champlain Valley (Tuttle), 45
Thuringia, Germany, 1, 2
Tillotson, Mary Montgomery.
    See Saxe, Mary Tillotson
Tokyo, Japan, 72
Toronto, 47
Toronto University, 72
Tory/Tories. See Loyalist
Trembly family, 13
Trembly, Mary Osiette.
    See Saxe, Mary Osiette Trembly
Tremper, Catherine, 15
Troy Conference Academy, Poultney, Vt., 45
Troy, N.Y., 25, 41-3, 56-7, 75
Tuttle, Mrs. George Fuller, 45
Tye family, 41
Tye (Tighs), Margaret.
    See Stockwell, Margaret Tye
U.S. Army, 72
U.S. Army Medical Corps, 72
Ulster Co., N.Y., 5
Umry, Herbert (262), 60, 70
Umry, Keith Merwin (265), 60, 70
Umry, Marion Freer Saxe (m. Ralph Brainard), 46, 60
Umry, Marion Mabel (266), 60, 70
Umry, Ralph Brainard, Rev. (m. Marion Freer Saxe), 60
Umry, Ralph Brainard, Jr. (264), 60, 70
Umry, Thomas Van Orden (263), 60, 70

Underwood, Carrie A.
    See Jewett, Carrie A. Underwood
Union Act of 1841, 8
Union Pacific R. R. Co., 71
Unitarian, 31
University of Freiberg, 72
University of Michigan, 64
University of Texas, 72
Unstruct-Hainich Co., Thuringia, 2
Utica, N.Y., 65
Valley Forge, Pennsylvania, 3
Vermont Militia, War of 1812, 33-4
Vermont, 9-13, 18, 21, 22, 25, 27-8, 30, 33, 38, 40, 42, 53-4, 66 (and specific places)
Vermont Legislature, 25
Vermontville, Mich., 49, 64
Victoria University, 72
Vienna, Austria, 72
Virginia, 42
Vladivostok Siberia, Russia, 72
Vosburgh, Kate C.
    See Saxe, Kate C. Vosburgh
Wagner, Catherine.
    See Smith, Catherine Wagner
Walden, N.Y., 58
War (See wars, by name)
War Department, 72
War of 1812, 12, 28, 30-4
Washington (state), 69
Washington, D.C., 69
Washington University, 71
Waterloo, N.Y., 63
Watson, M. S. Z., surveyor, 16, 17
Wead, Rebecca Munson. See Saxe, Rebecca Munson Wead
Weaver, Catherine [?Katerina Weber];
    See Saxe, Catherine Weaver
Weaver, Elizabeth.
    See Barr, Elizabeth Weaver
Weaver, Margaret.
    See Merkle, Margaret Weaver
Weaver, William, 4, 5
Wellesley College, 71
Wesleyan University, 42, 44, 56
West Camp, N.Y., 24

West Chazy, N.Y., 28, 45
West Point Military Academy, 62
West Yarmouth, Mass., 56
Westmount, Quebec, Canada, 13, 58
Weybridge, Vt., 25, 27, 48
Wheaton, Ill., 60
Whig Party, 34
Wick, Mary Alfred.
    See Saxe Mary Alfred Wick
Wight, Catherine Saxe See, 35
Wight, John (m. Catherine Saxe See), 35
Williams, Albert (m. Catherine
    Stockwell; m. Anette Stockwell),
    65-6
Williams, Annette Stockwell,
    (m. Albert), 52, 65-6
Williams, Catherine H. Stockwell
    (m. Albert), 52, 65-6
Wilson, Anna. *See* Saxe, Anna Wilson
Wisner, Phoebe.
    See Saxe, Phoebe Wisner
Women's Society of Christian Service,
    66
Woodley family, 38-9, 40-1
Woodley, Jennie L. (m. Wilbur), 39
Woodley, Malona Marcia Stockwell
    (m. ___ Woodley), 41, 55
Woodley, Margaret (m. Samuel), 55
Woodley, Samuel (m. Margaret), 55
Woodley, Susan A. *See* Stockwell,
    Susan A. Woodley
Woodley, Wilbur K., 39
Woodstock, N.Y., 13, 24
Woodward, Agnes Saxe
    (m. J. Woodward), 35, 51
Worcester Country Club, 57
Worcester County Abstract Co., 57
Worcester, Mass., 57
World War I, 65, 72
World's Convention of Crippled
    Children's Organizations, 71
Wright Co., Iowa, 53-4, 66
Y.W.C.A., 71
Yale University Law School, 72
Yankee, 34
Yokohama, Japan, 72

ABOUT THE AUTHOR

GEORGE J. HILL, M.D., M.A., D.Litt., is Professor of Surgery Emeritus at the New Jersey Medical School, University of Medicine and Dentistry of New Jersey. He has been a Fellow in Molecular Biology at Princeton University and he was an Adjunct Professor of History at Kean University, Union, New Jersey.

A native of Iowa, Dr. Hill received his B.A. degree with honors from Yale University and the M.D. from Harvard. After retiring from the practice of surgery, he earned an M.A. in history at Rutgers-Newark and the D.Litt. in history from Drew University. Dr. Hill has written more than a dozen books on a wide range of topics, including prize-winning books on surgery, oncology, and leprosy. His master's thesis became a book on the environmental impact of Thomas Edison, and his doctoral thesis on a secret project of Church and State in the U.S. and Liberia was also published as a book. His most recent book is the story of his ancestor, John Saxe, who was a Loyalist in the American Revolution; it traces the history of the Saxe family for five generations.

Dr. Hill was a non-commissioned officer in the U.S. Marine Corps Reserve during the Korean War, and he was on active duty with the U.S. Public Health Service during the Cuban Missile Crisis. As a U.S. Navy Medical Officer, he served in Vietnam and he was recalled for duty as a surgeon during the First Gulf War. He was awarded the U.S. Meritorious Service Medal when he retired as a Captain in 1992. Dr. Hill is also an alpinist and an explorer, having hiked and climbed on all seven continents.

As a student of genealogy, Dr. Hill has proved his descent from many early Americans. He is a member of thirty-two lineage societies and he is a past or current national officer in six of these societies. His ancestors include James Feake, Sr., a goldsmith of London in 1615; Edward Fuller, who came on the *Mayflower* in 1620, and his son, Doctor Matthew Fuller; Luke Hill and Mary Hoyt, who were married in Windsor, Connecticut, in 1651; Jonathan Gillette, who died there in 1677; Henry Herrick, who became a freeman of Salem, Massachusetts, in 1630; Rebecca (Towne) Nurse, who was hanged there in 1692; Edward Howell, who became a freeman of Boston in 1638 and was a founder of the Hamptons on Long Island; Thomas Trowbridge, who was in New Haven, Connecticut, in 1638; Robert Long, who was a member of the Ancient and Honorable Artillery Company in 1639; the Rev. Obadiah Holmes, who was a founder of Rhode Island; James Prescott, of Hampton, New Hampshire, in 1665; William Rundle, a freeholder of Greenwich, Connecticut, in 1667; John Sharples, who came to Pennsylvania in 1682; John Manley, of Cecil County, Maryland, in 1712; and John Archibald, who died in Derry, New Hampshire, in 1651, and whose descendants were pioneer settlers of Truro, Nova Scotia.

www.ingramcontent.com/pod-product-compliance
Lightning Source LLC
Chambersburg PA
CBHW080432230426
43662CB00015B/2255